IMAGES
of America

SOUTHERN SCHUYLKILL COUNTY

I0806383

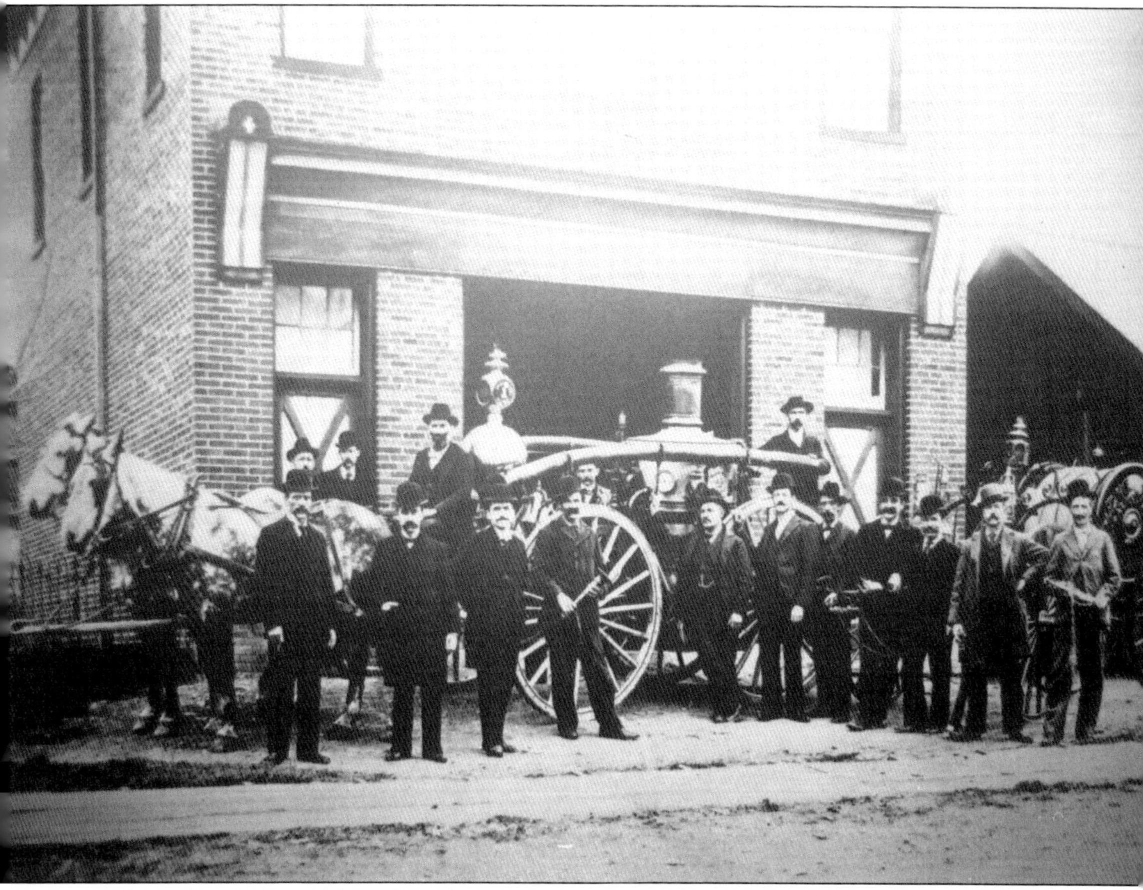

Orwigsburg's Friendship Hose Company No. 1. Built in 1891 on East Mifflin Street, this structure now serves as the home of the Orwigsburg Historical Society and Museum.

IMAGES
of America

SOUTHERN SCHUYLKILL COUNTY

Jennifer L. Bowen-Frantz

ARCADIA
PUBLISHING

ISBN 978-0-7385-9030-1

Published by Arcadia Publishing
Charleston, South Carolina

Printed in the United States of America

For all general information contact Arcadia Publishing at:
Telephone 843-853-2070
Fax 843-853-0044
E-mail sales@arcadiapublishing.com
For customer service and orders:
Toll-Free 1-888-313-2665

Visit us on the Internet at www.arcadiapublishing.com

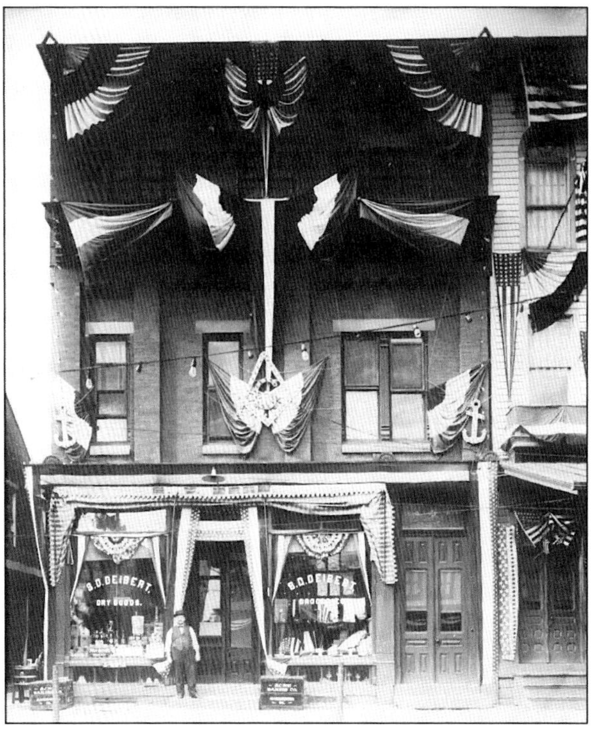

S.D. Deibert grocery and dry goods store, located on East Market Street in Orwigsburg, *c.* 1913.

Contents

Acknowledgments 6

Introduction 7

1. Scenes around Southern Schuylkill County 9

2. Institutions 25

3. Transportation 47

4. Business and Industry 65

5. Pathmakers and Times to Remember 95

Acknowledgments

This publication was made possible through the generous cooperation of Schuylkill County's historians. It is through their work and dedication to the preservation and documentation of southern Schuylkill County's history that this book became a reality.

The following people provided valuable information and photographs of the Auburn area: Charles Bohr, John Clauser, and Kermit Mengel. These gentlemen are devout historians of Auburn and its surrounding areas. Deep appreciation goes out to the Cressona Historical Society and its president, Bruce Kantner, for the images provided on Cressona. Many of the early canal photographs and pictures of Port Clinton were supplied by the Northern Berks-Southern Schuylkill Historical Society and members Luke and Anna Mae McLaughlin. Orwigsburg images were chosen from the vast collection of the Orwigsburg Historical Society and Mrs. Marie Deibert, a native resident of the borough. Several of the photographs relating to the history of Schuylkill Haven were collected by Jayne Sharadin.

I would also like to thank my husband, Glenn Frantz, and my parents, Evan and Philomena Bowen, who through their encouragement and support, helped me to persevere and see this project to the end.

Introduction

Schuylkill County was incorporated on March 11, 1811, and was created out of Northhampton and Berks Counties. Years later, portions of Columbia and Luzerne Counties were added. The actual territory, which makes up the southern portion of Schuylkill County, was established much earlier than 1811 by European settlers. While coal quickly became the focus in Schuylkill County's northern sector, agriculture and later manufacturing emerged as the backbone of southern Schuylkill's interests.

Although the actual mining process was conducted in northern Schuylkill County, towns located farther south, such as Schuylkill Haven, Landingville, and Port Clinton, played a significant role. Through the development of the Schuylkill Navigation System, both produce and coal were transported from Schuylkill County to Philadelphia. At its peak, the system carried close to 2 million tons of coal on mule-drawn canal boats.

Schuylkill Haven began as an agricultural community, but quickly found its place as an active canal town. Landingville, also a canal town, had the first tunnel ever built to carry a canal through a mountain. Orwigsburg, which was settled in the late 1700s, became Schuylkill County's first seat of government in 1815, due to the persistence and initiative of its early citizens. Eventually, manufacturing took hold, and Orwigsburg became a center for shoes and textiles. Rich farmland, dotted with the remnants of grist and lumber mills, abounds in the areas of New Ringgold and McKeansburg. Once a booming canal town, Port Clinton established its importance early on as a canal transport site.

In many ways the development of southern Schuylkill County mirrors the development of our nation. From its early European settlers searching for a better life to the introduction of transportation and industrialization, Schuylkill County has made its mark in Pennsylvania's history and has created a legacy for present and future generations.

One

Scenes around Southern Schuylkill County

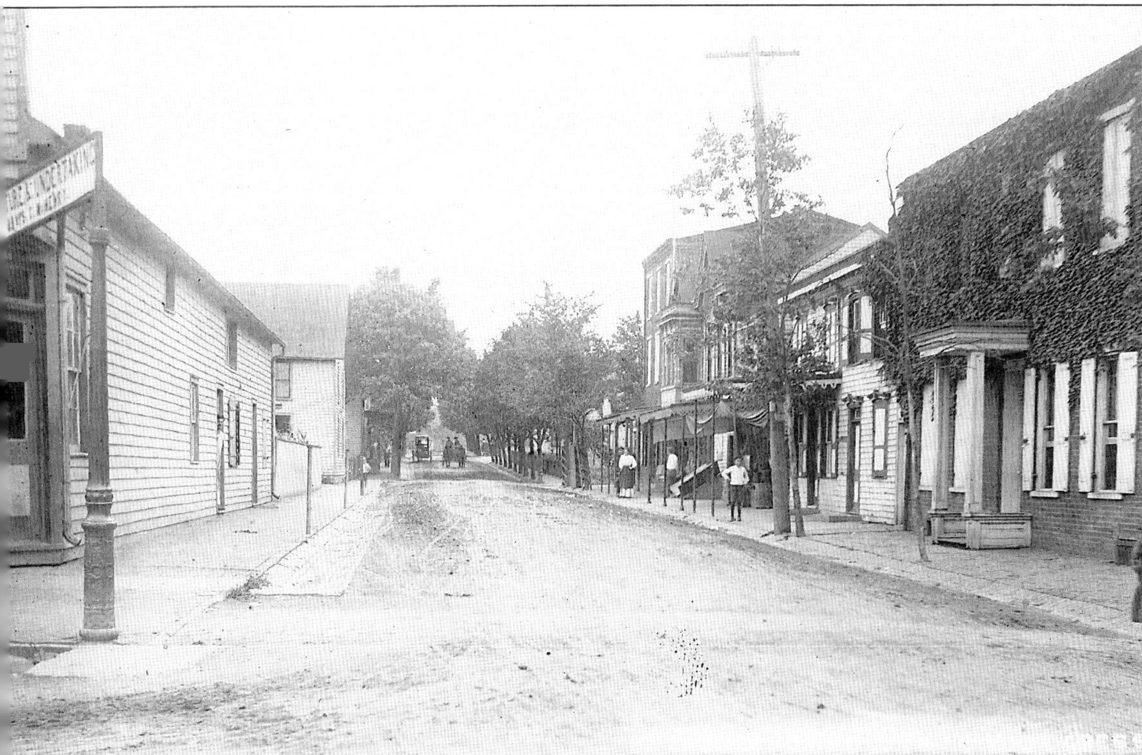

A view of Chestnut Street in Cressona, looking west, *c.* 1900. McHenry's Furniture and Undertaking business can be seen on the corner. It was quite common in the late 1800s and early 1900s for the local undertaker to also deal in furniture.

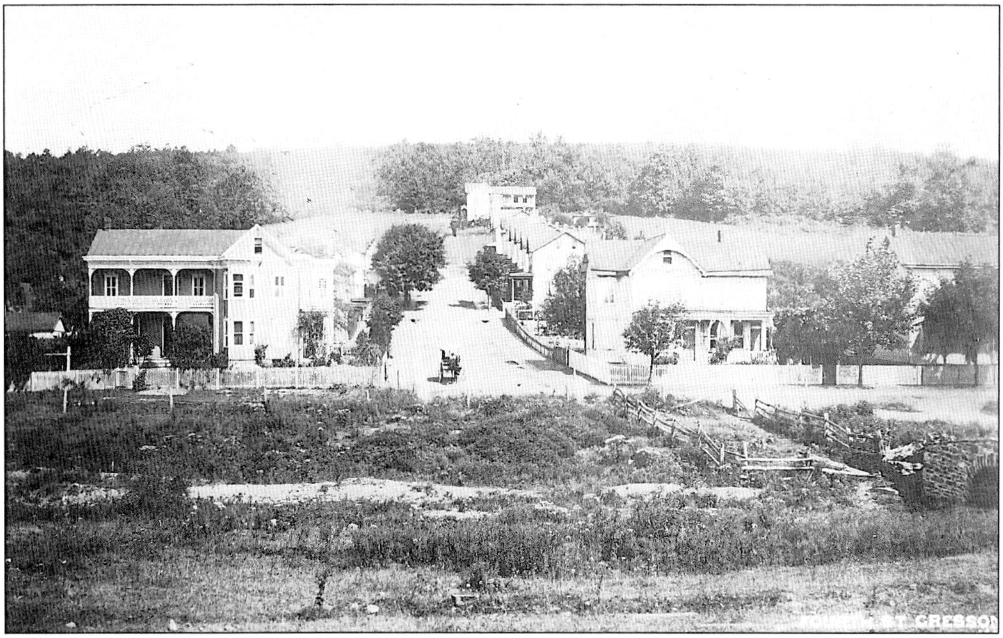

A view of Fourth Street in Cressona from Cemetery Hill, *c.* 1900.

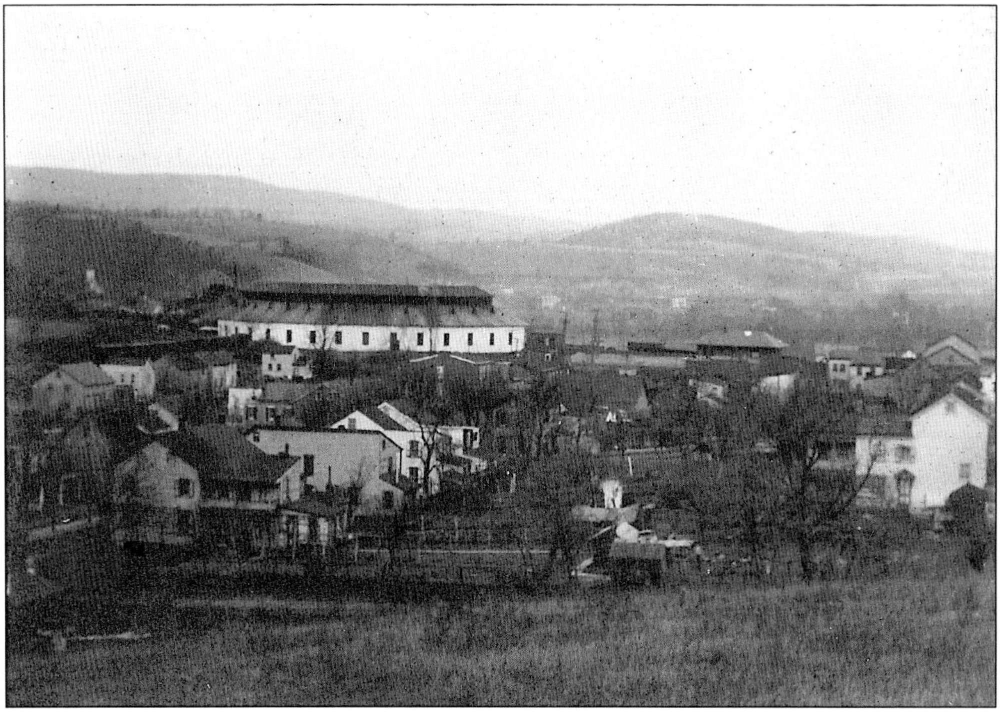

A view of Cressona taken from Cemetery Hill, *c.* 1900.

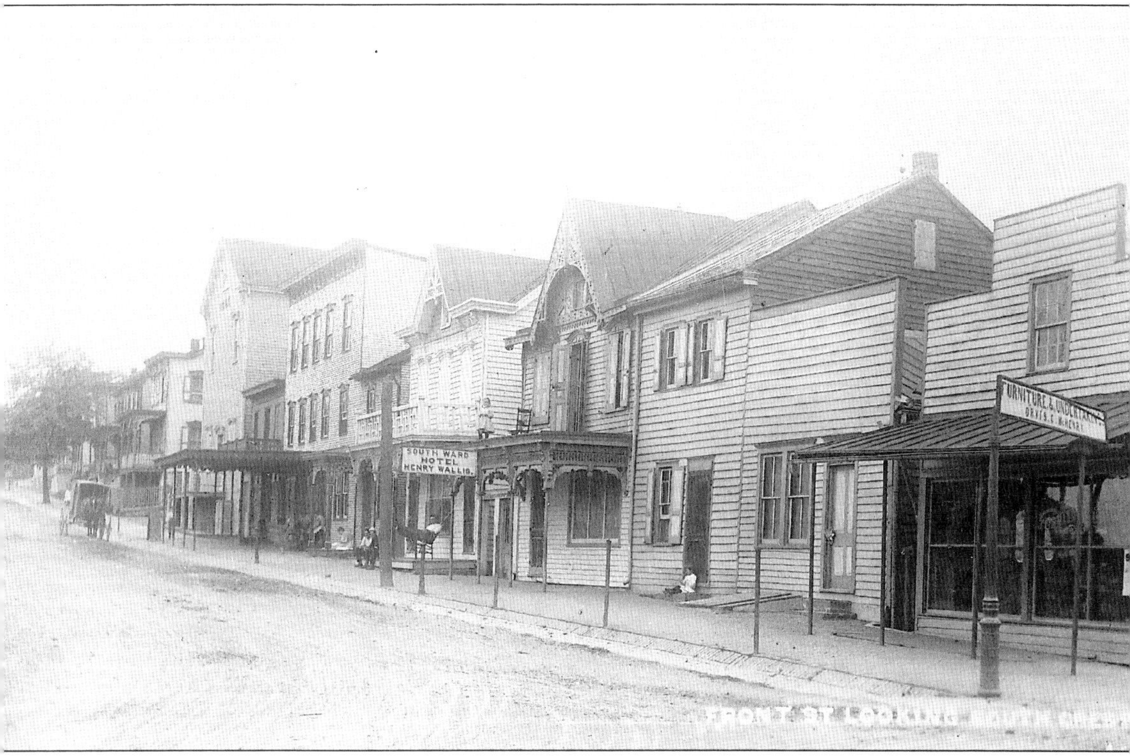

Front Street, looking south in Cressona, *c.* 1900. The South Ward Hotel can be seen in this photograph.

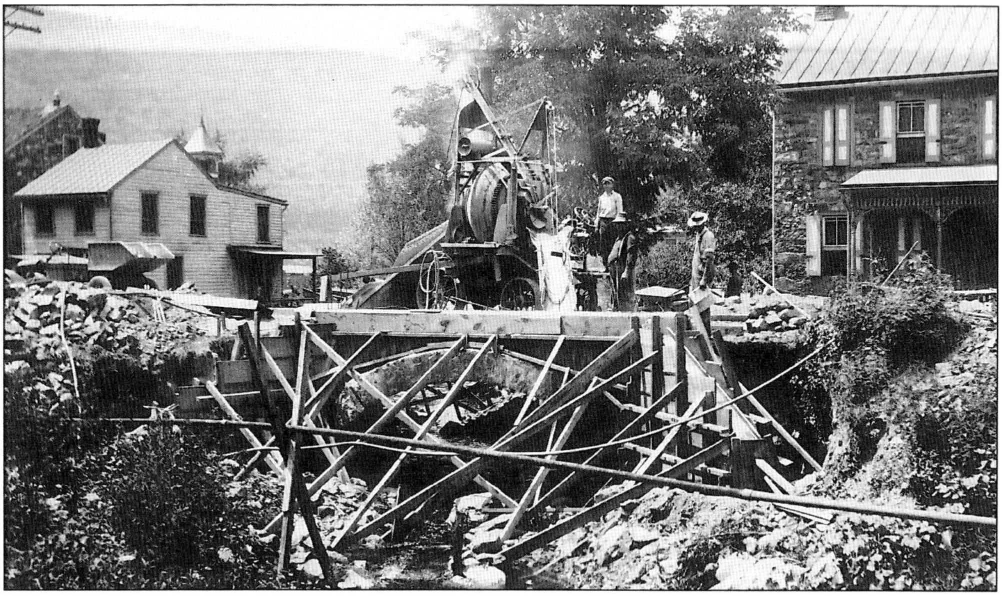

Building the bridge for the Centre Turnpike in Port Clinton. Begun in 1805, the Centre Turnpike was opened in 1808 and completed in 1812.

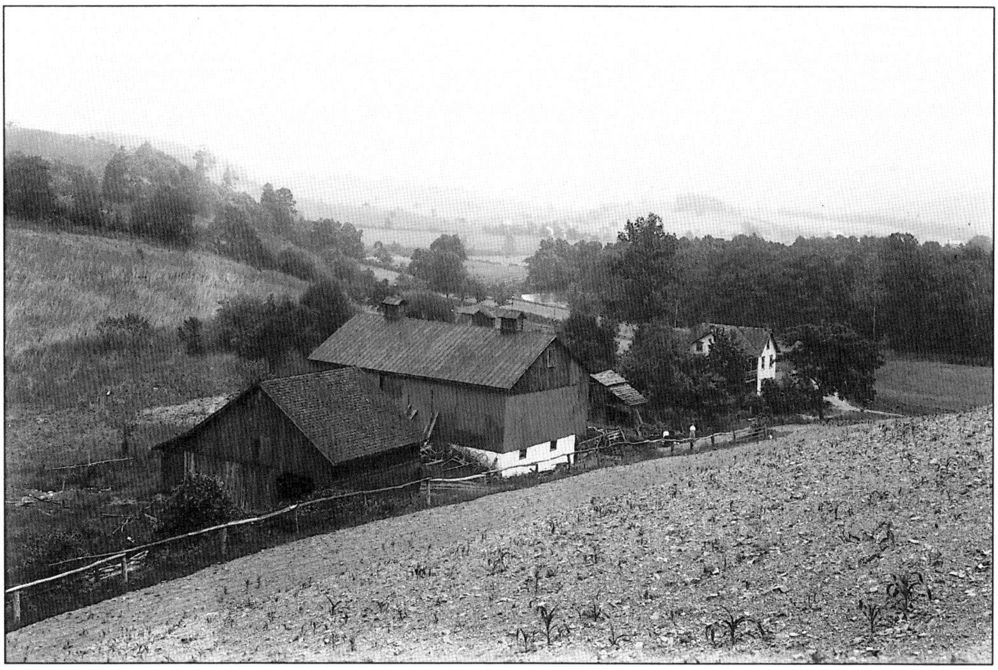

The farm of Samuel Mengle, looking northeast in Port Clinton.

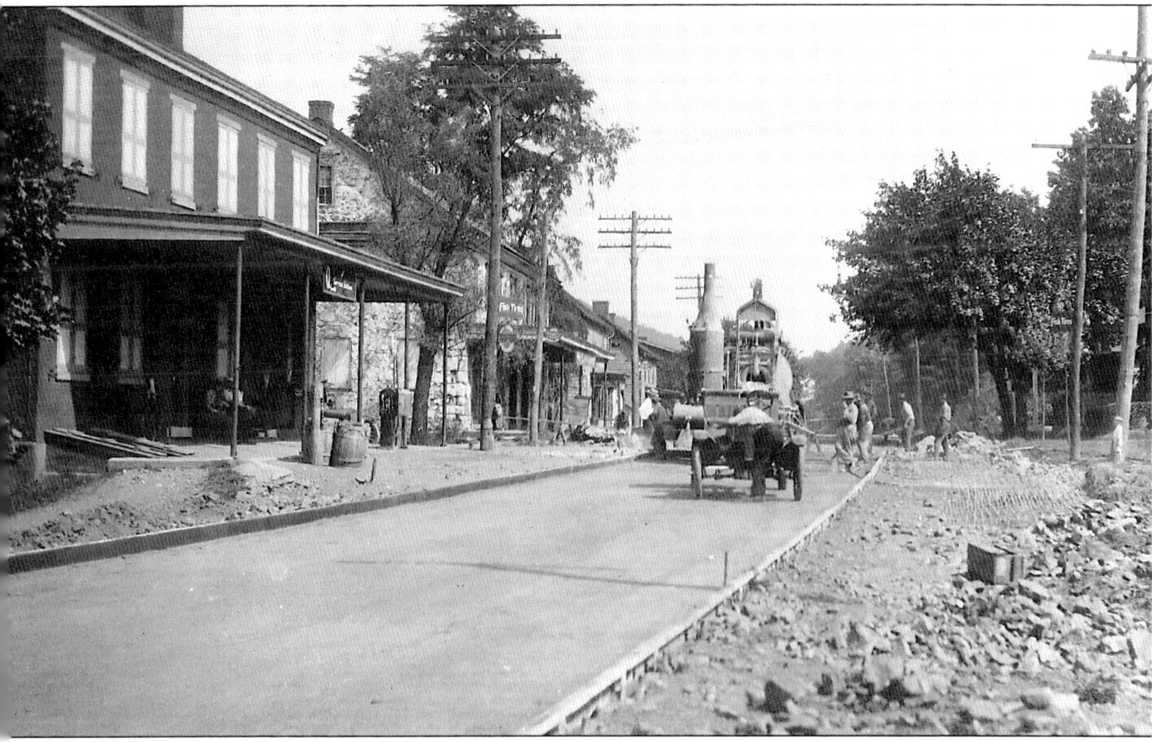

The building of the Centre Turnpike. This image, taken in Port Clinton, shows a section of the Centre Turnpike during construction. The Centre Turnpike was built between 1805 and 1812, but opened for travel in 1808. This early turnpike doubled as the "main street" for many of the towns it passed through, including Port Clinton.

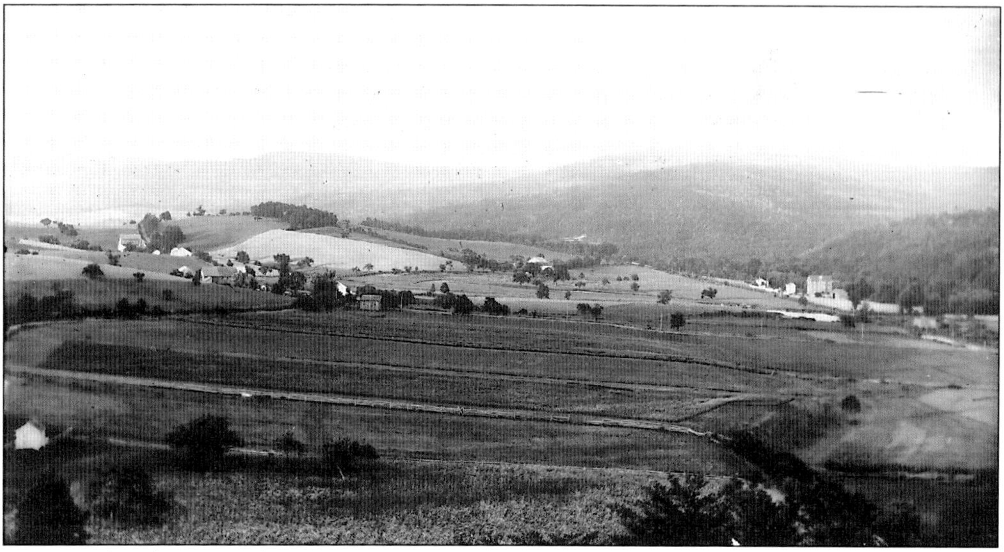

A view of Molino, Hawk Mountain, and Hartman's Hollow, near Port Clinton. The Centre Turnpike can also be seen in this image.

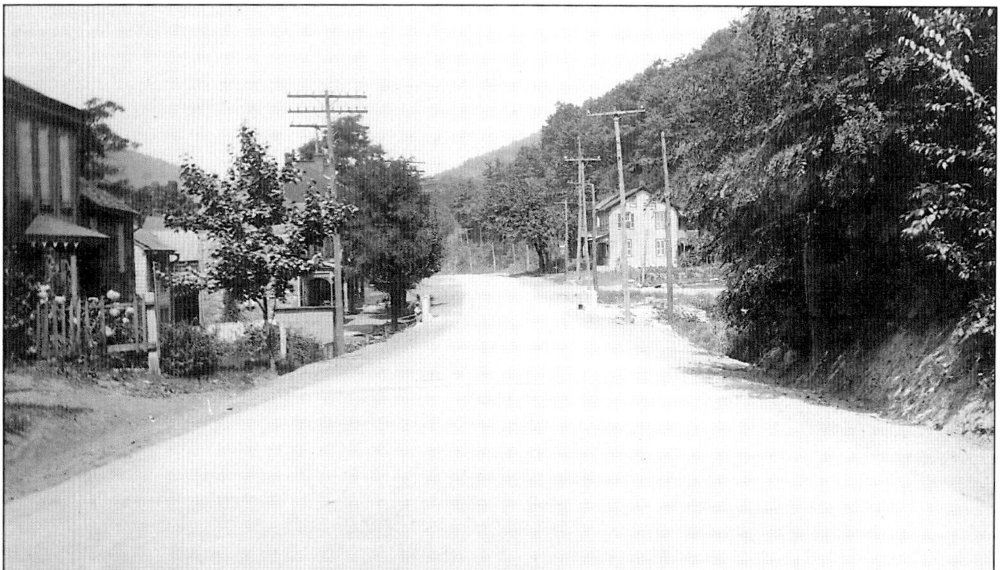

Another view of the completed Centre Turnpike in Port Clinton. In October 1808, a line of stagecoaches was instituted between Reading and Sunbury. The coal-mining industry necessitated travel, and by 1830 daily stagecoaches traveled to Reading, Philadelphia, and even New York.

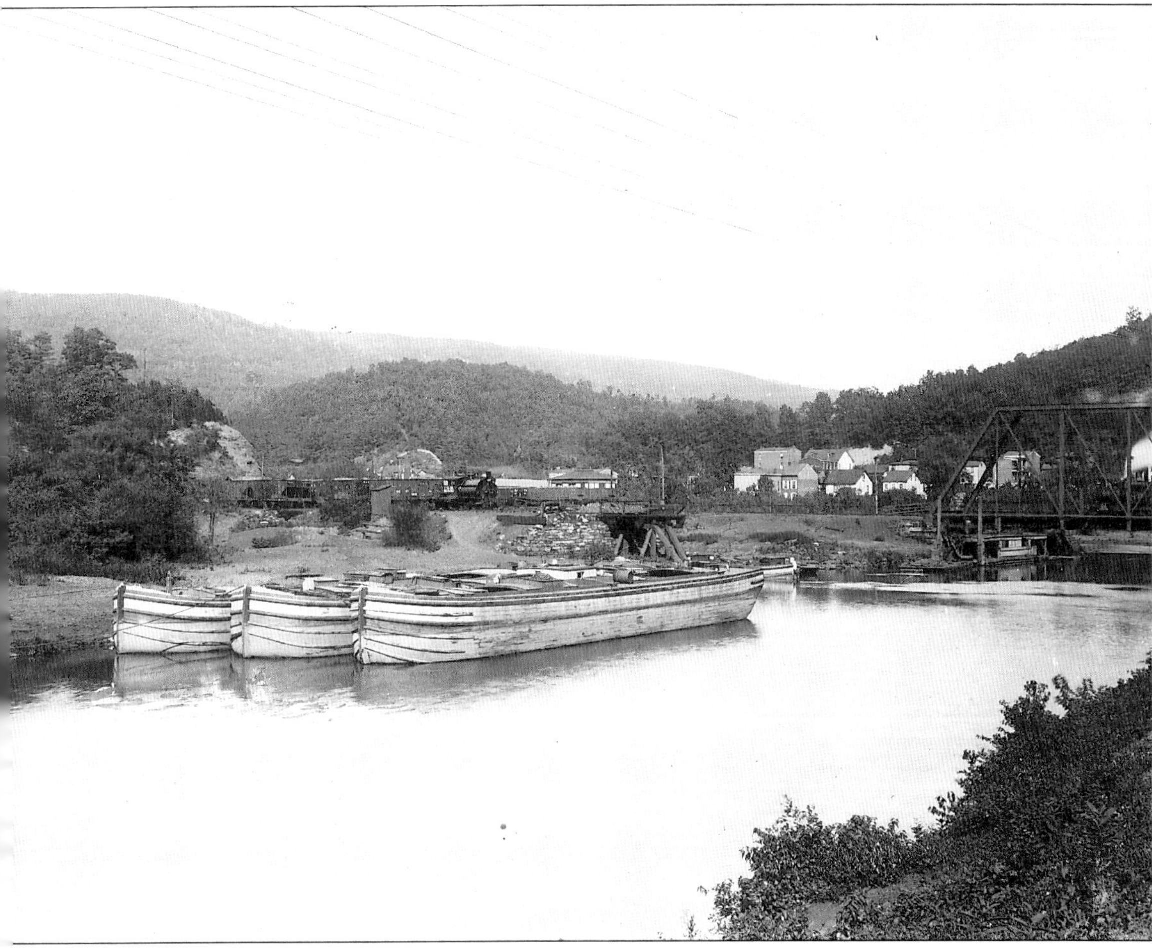

A view looking east in Port Clinton c. 1912. This photograph shows canal boats along the loading dock.

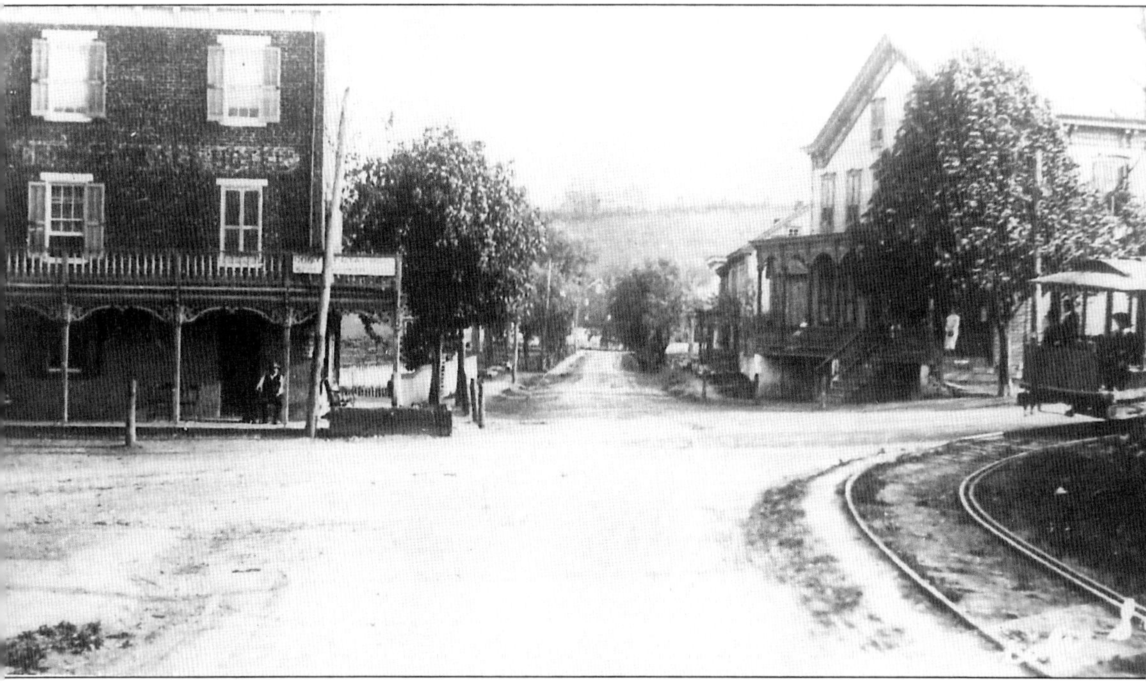

A trolley passing through the "crossroads" in Adamsdale around the early 1900s. The trolley line ran through the southern portion of Schuylkill County's coal region and between the towns of Schuylkill Haven, Adamsdale, and Orwigsburg. Adams Store, shown on the right side of this photograph, was one of the trolley stops.

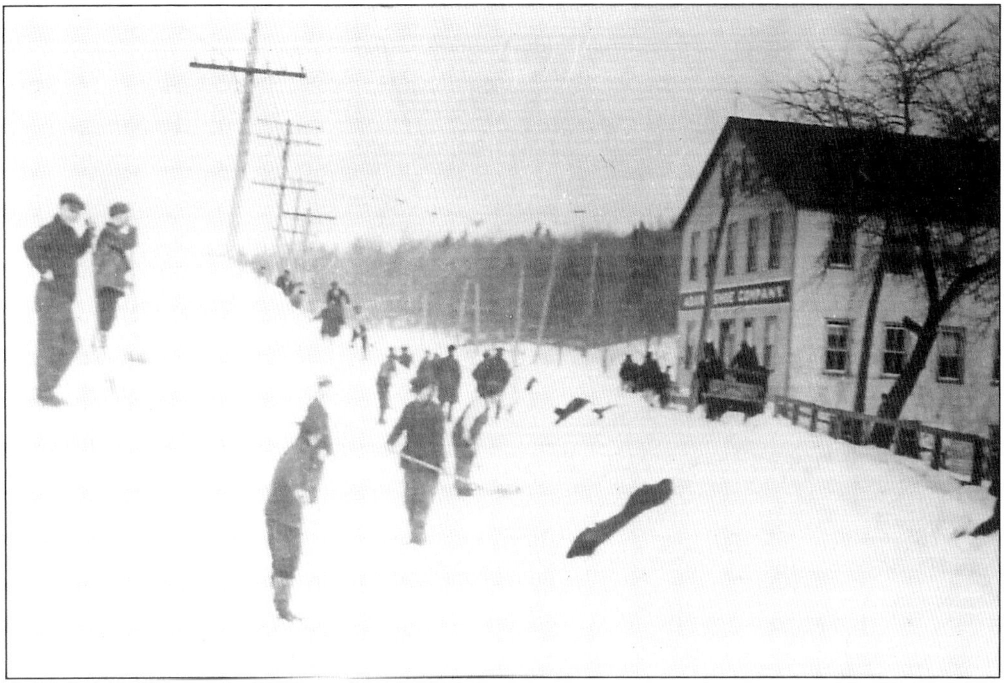

A wintry view taken in Adamsdale in the early 1920s. This image shows the Adams Shoe Factory.

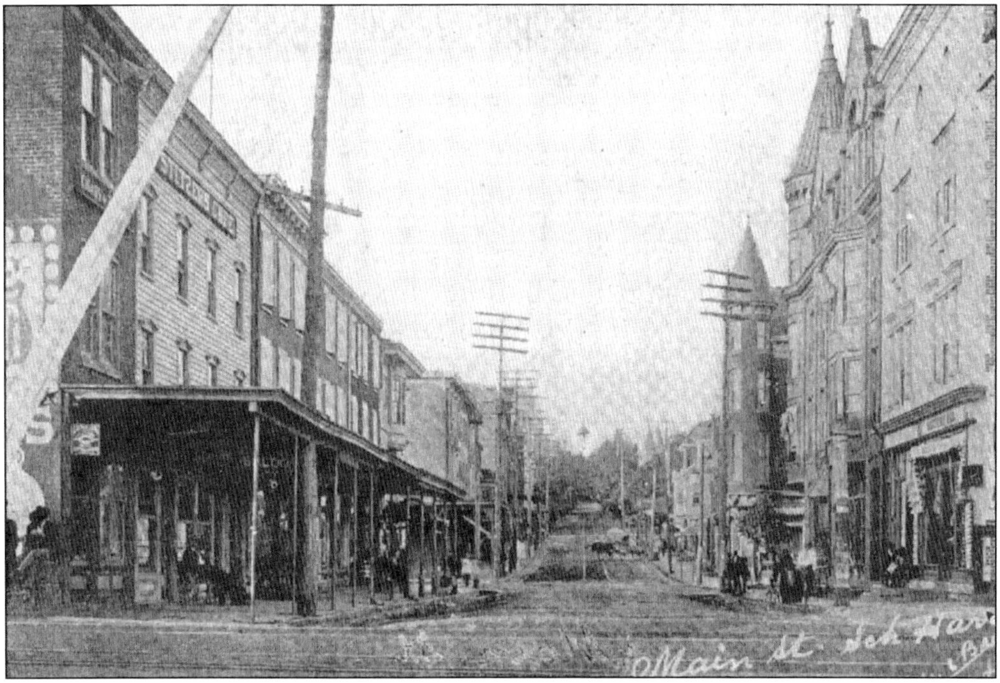

Schuylkill Haven's Main Street looking east. The original plot of the town was laid out by Jacob Dreibelbiss in 1811. Main Street was first known as Front Street.

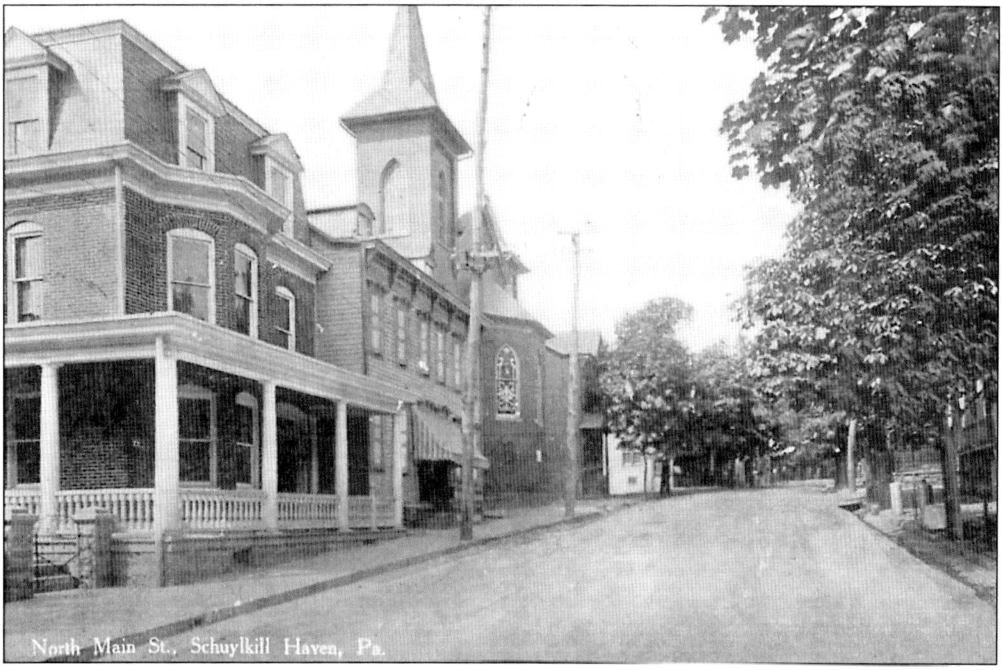

A view of North Main Street, Schuylkill Haven. Messiah United Brethren Church is visible in this photograph.

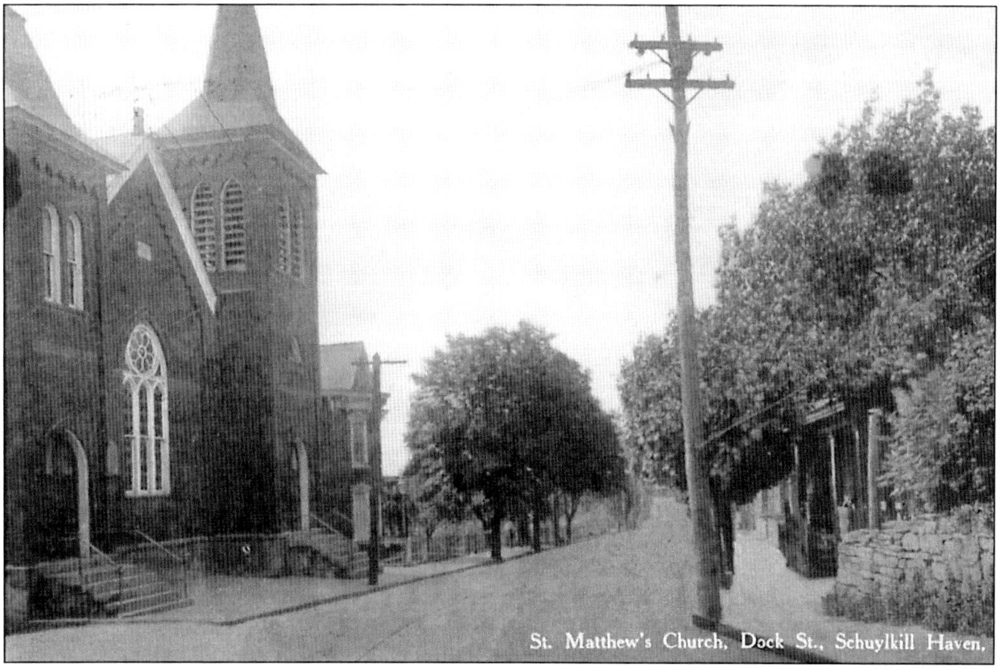

A view of Dock Street in Schuylkill Haven, *c.* 1911. St. Matthew's Evangelical Lutheran congregation built the church, shown in this image, in 1859.

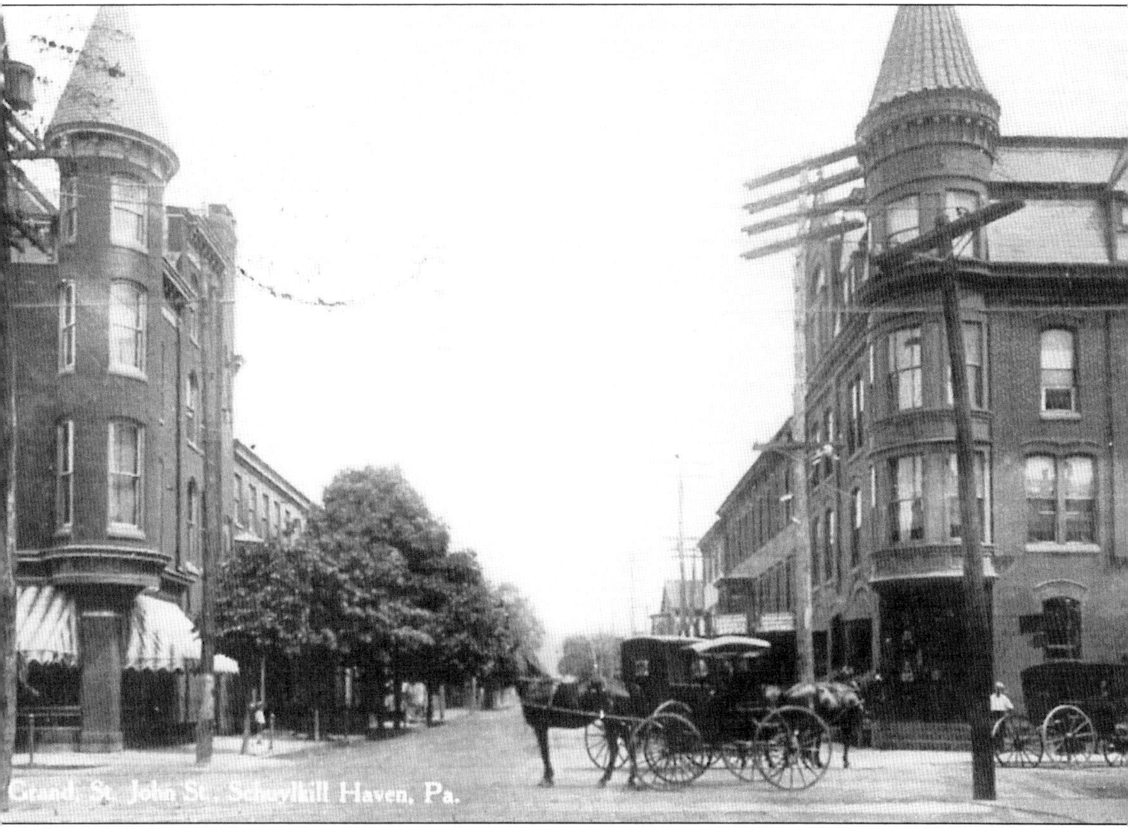

St. John Street in Schuylkill Haven, *c.* 1910. The Hotel Grand is in clear view on the right side of this image.

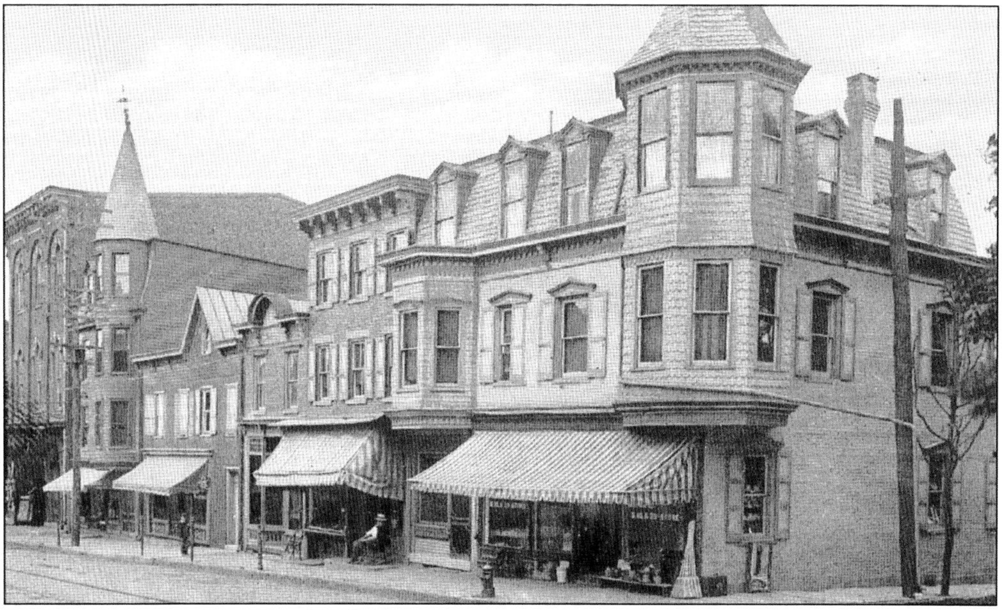

A view of Main Street in Schuylkill Haven. Note the old-fashioned "5 & 10 Cent Store" on the corner.

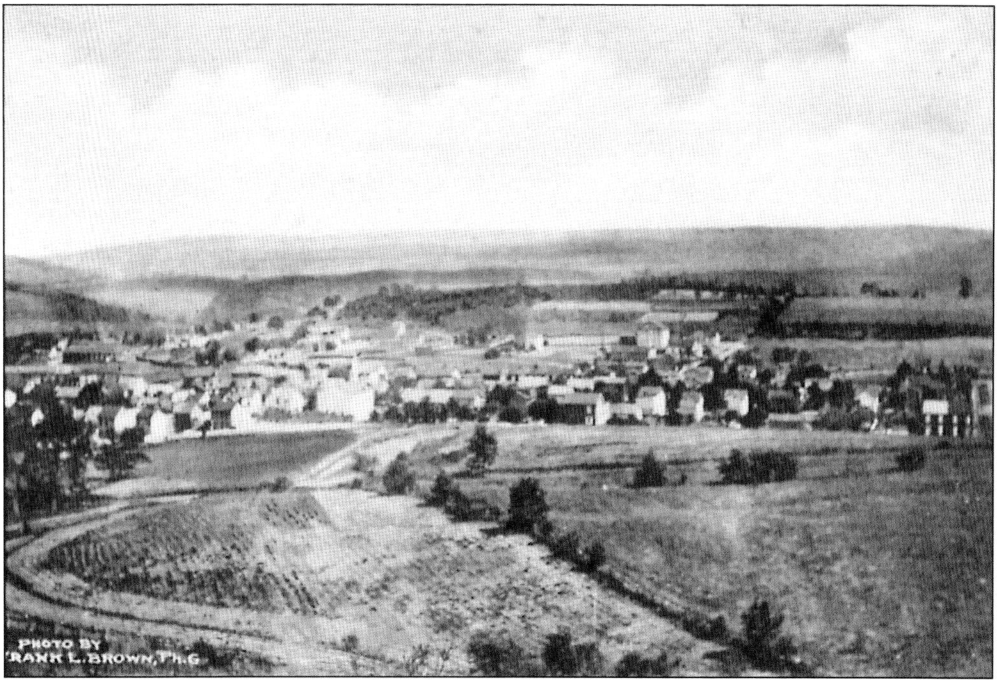

A view of Auburn from Bunker Hill, which serves as Auburn's northern boundary. Bunker Hill was leased by the Auburn Fish and Game Association and used as a hunting ground.

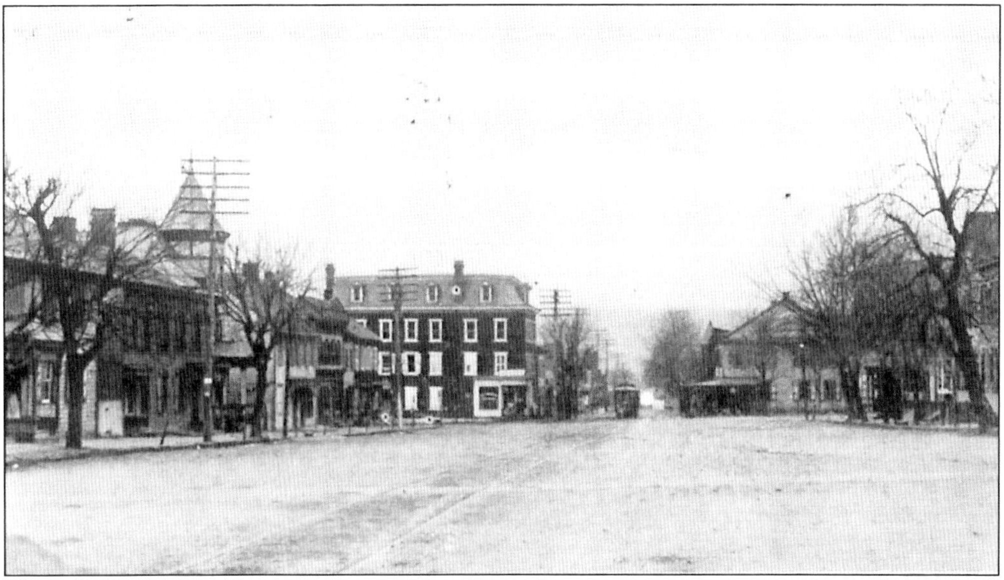

Orwigsburg's Centre Square, looking west, *c.* 1907. Note the trolley tracks running through the center of town. Trolley service to Orwigsburg began in 1898. On August 2, 1898, a trolley party was held to celebrate the opening. The decorated six-car party run toured the company's circuit with several hundred people aboard!

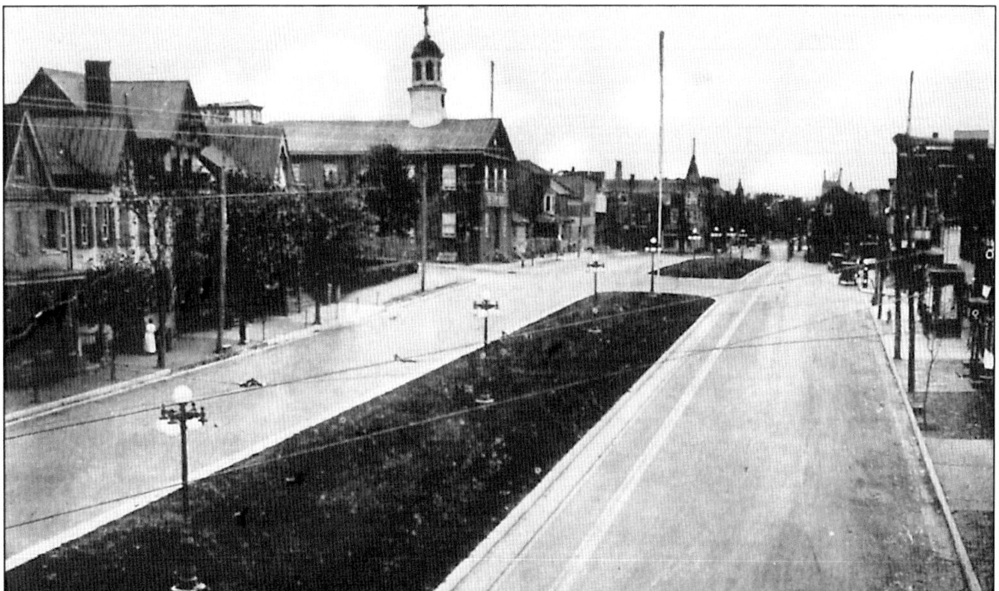

Centre Square, Orwigsburg, *c.* 1924. In 1921, the state constructed a concrete road running east to west. The grassy area shown in the center of this photograph was added by the borough. The lights were donated to the borough by Pottsville natives who were, at the time, living on West Market Street and wanted to honor the borough for serving as Schuylkill County's first seat of government.

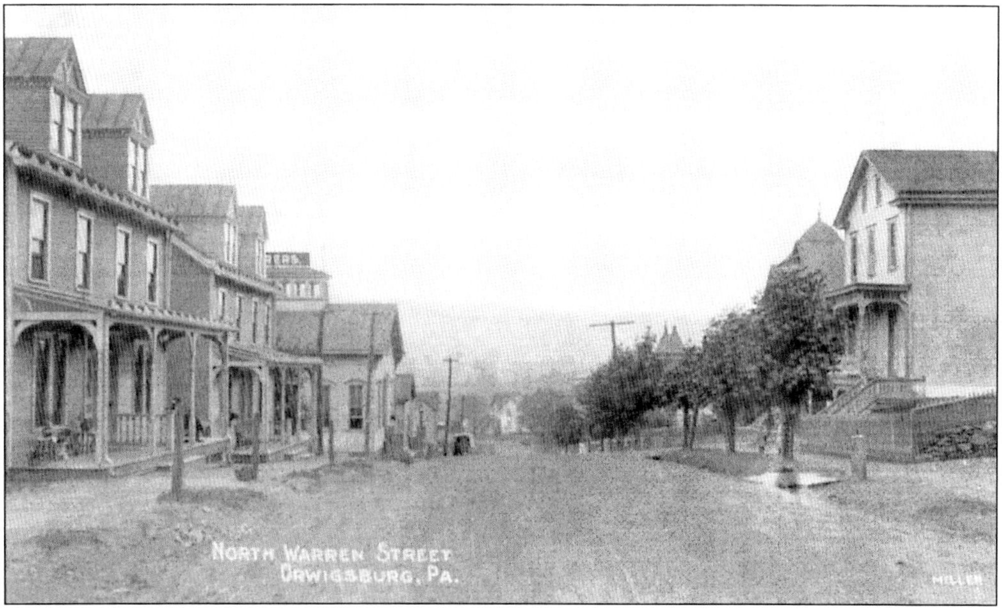

North Warren Street in Orwigsburg, c. 1907. Warren Street divided the town into east and west sections. The J.S. Zulick & Co., which was established in 1893 as a shoe manufacturing firm, can be seen in the background.

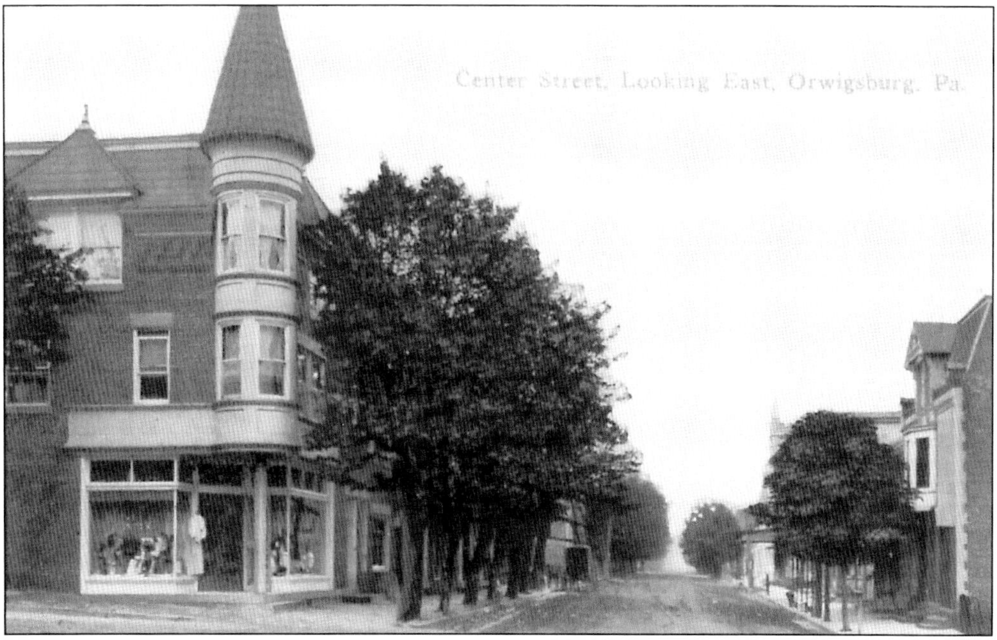

A view of Market Street looking east. This photograph also shows the business of George Werner, a store that specialized in women's clothing. It later became the Schultze Store.

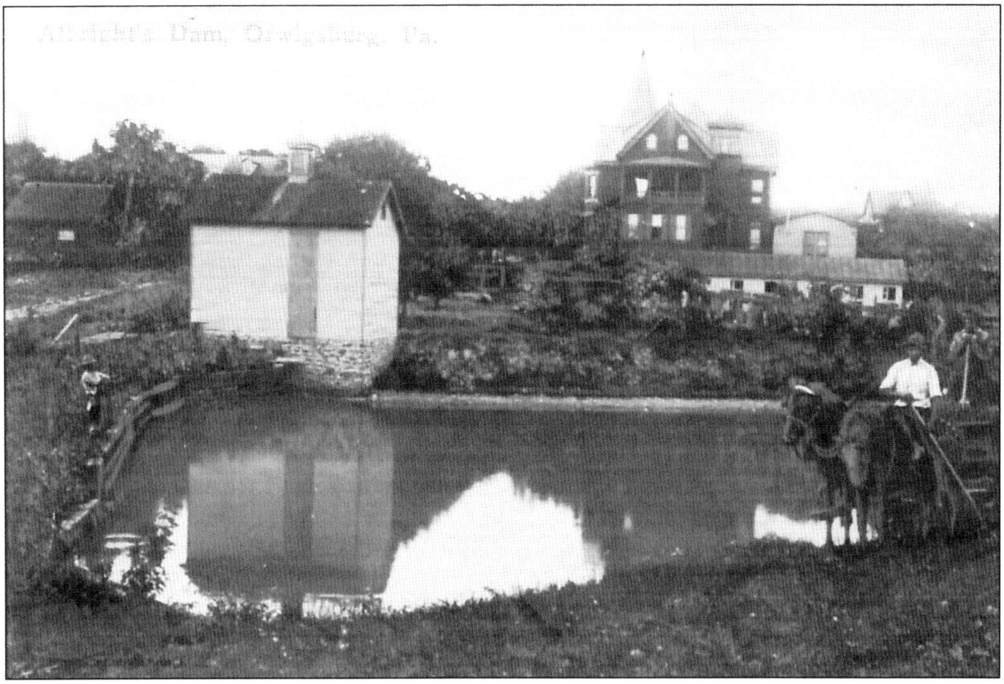

A section of Orwigsburg located along East Market Street. Both the home in the background and the dam belonged to H.S. Albright, the owner of one of Orwigsburg's most successful shoe companies.

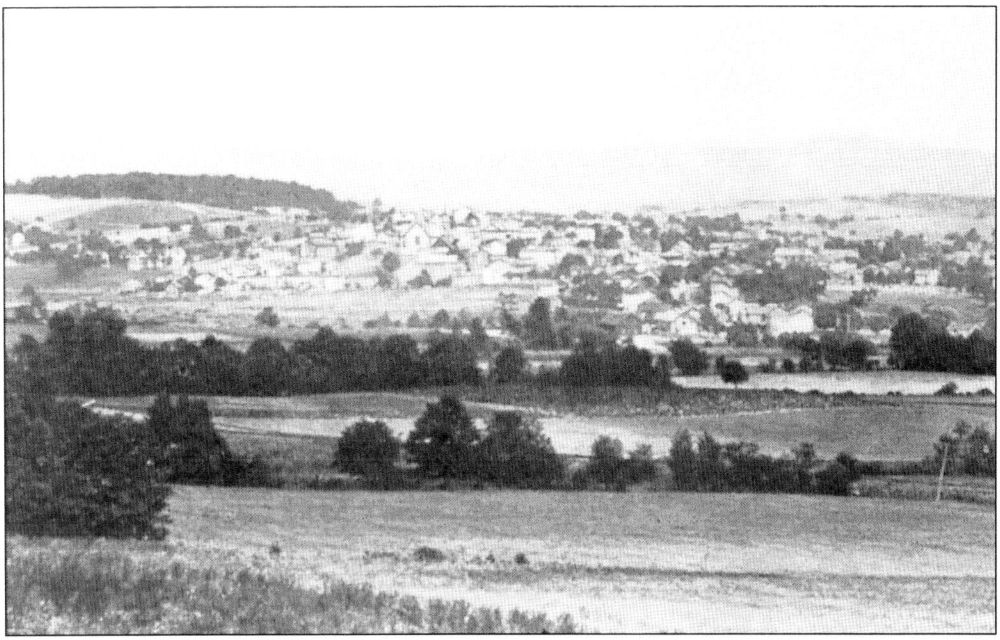

A scene looking southeast in Orwigsburg.

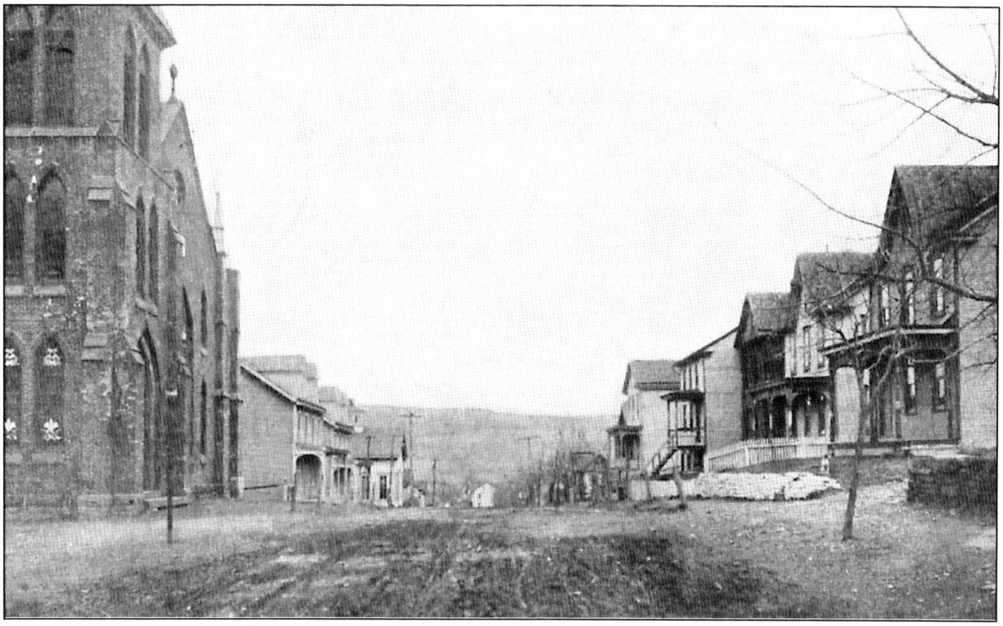

North Warren Street. This 1909 photograph of North Warren Street in Orwigsburg accentuates the early dirt roads that were common throughout the borough. St. Paul's Lutheran Church also appears in this image.

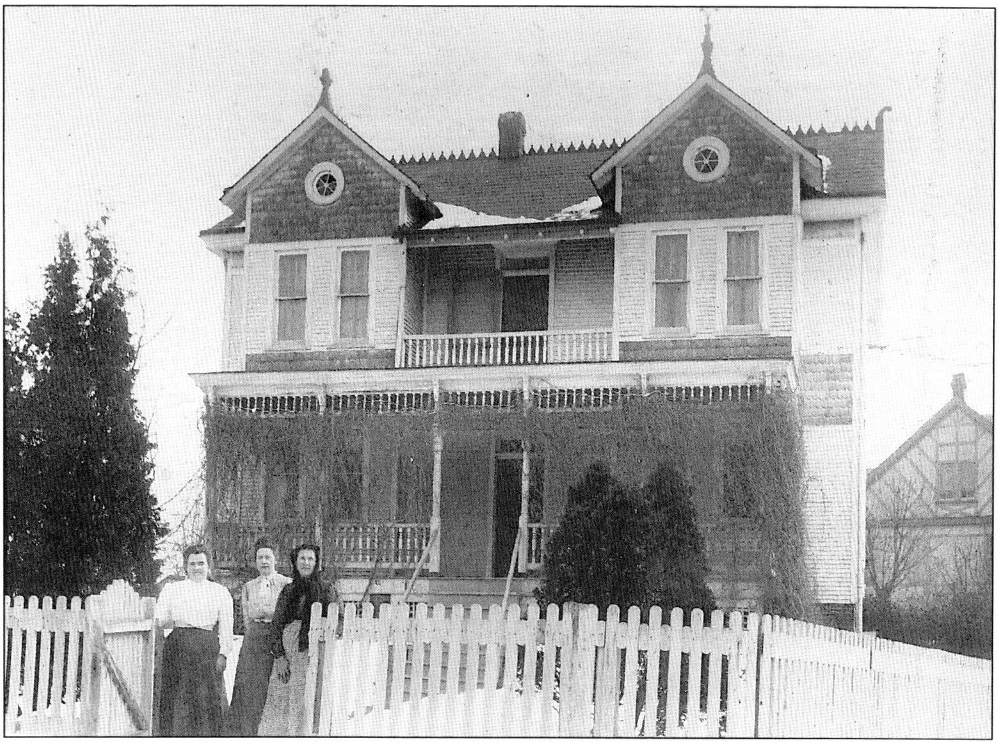

A house in Orwigsburg. This stately Victorian home is a good example of the types of homes that were built throughout the mid to late 1800s. The home, as it appears in this image taken around the 1890s, looks very much the same today.

Two

Institutions

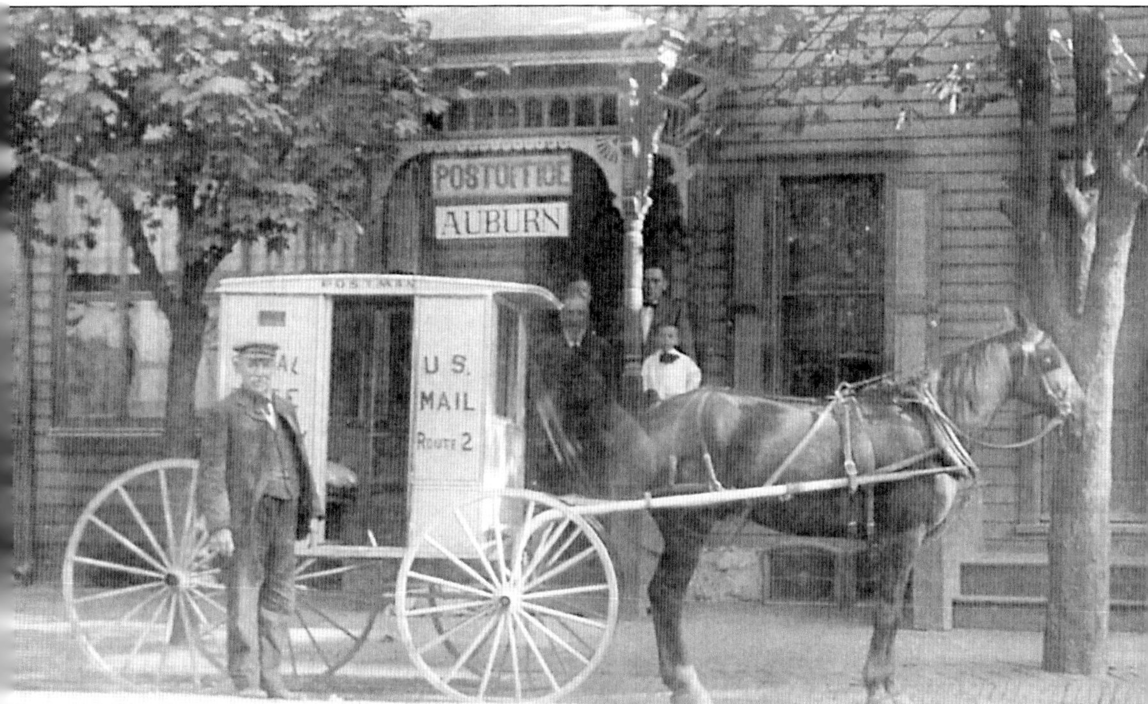

The Auburn Post Office. Located in a home on Market Street, the post office was in the front portion of the house, while a family lived in the rear and upstairs. Sam Borkey was the driver of the mail buggy at the time of this photograph.

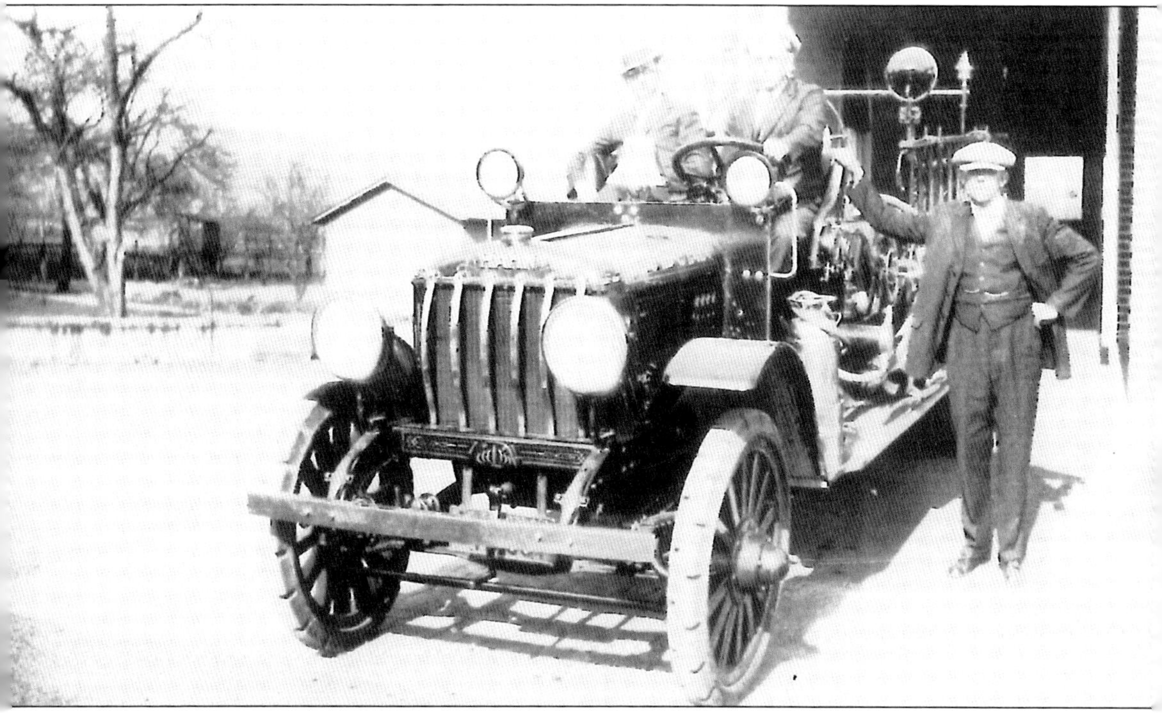

The Auburn Fire Company. George Levan organized the first fire company of Auburn in 1898. It was made up of volunteers known as the Vigilantes. In 1921, the brick building shown in this photograph was erected.

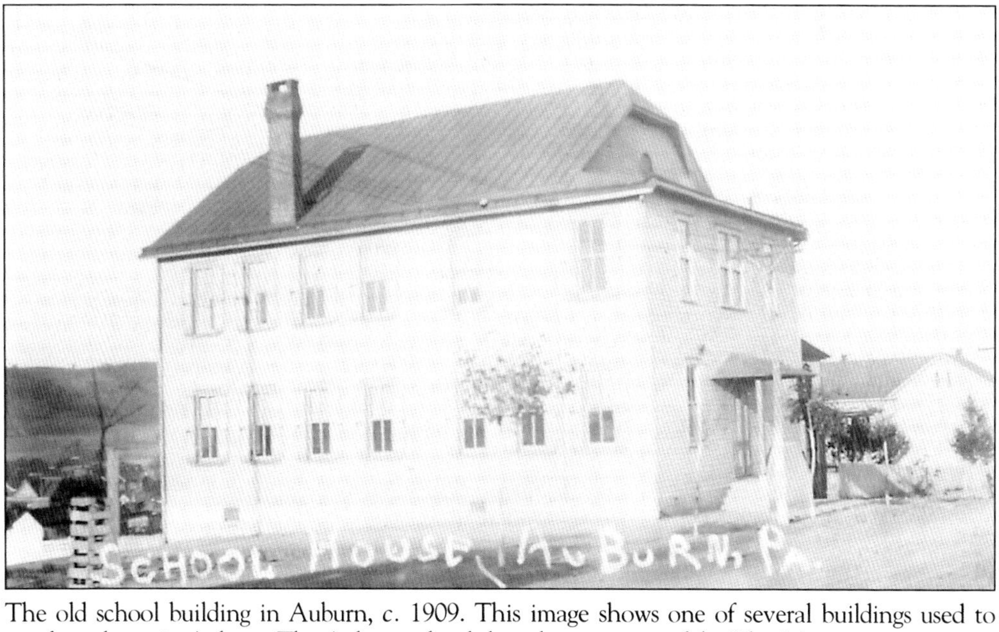

The old school building in Auburn, c. 1909. This image shows one of several buildings used to conduct classes in Auburn. The Auburn schools later became part of the Blue Mountain jointure.

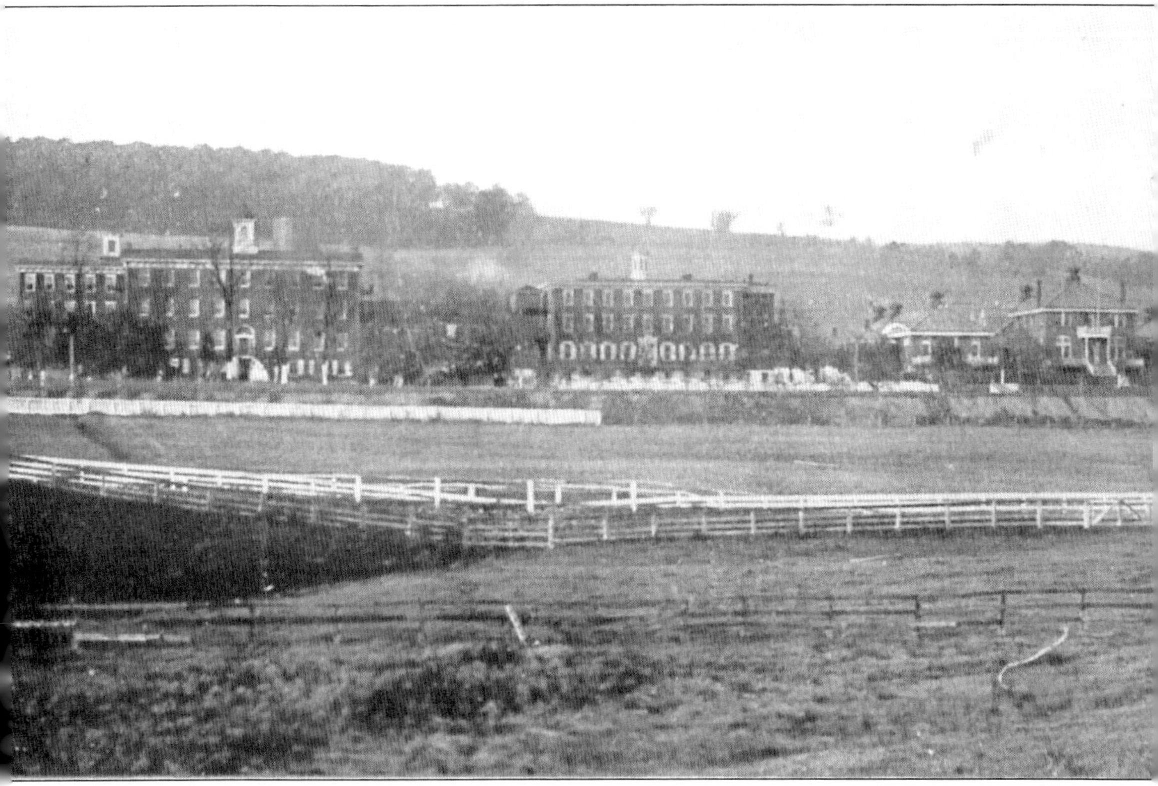

The Schuylkill County Alms House near Schuylkill Haven, *c.* 1910. A total of 283 acres of farmland was purchased and numerous structures were built, beginning in 1833, for the purpose of providing care for the insane, poor, and aged of Schuylkill County. The complex was intended to be self-sustaining and had a working farm, bakery, laundry, medical and surgical wards, rooms for lodging vagrants, and a school for poor children.

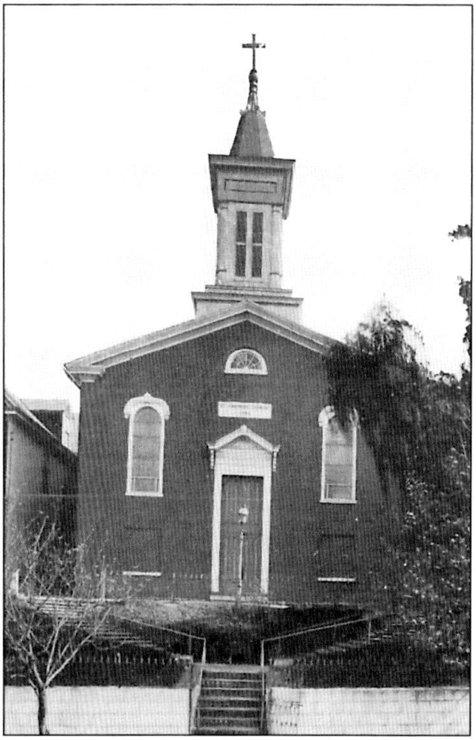

St. Ambrose Roman Catholic Church, formerly St. Paul's Lutheran Church, of Schuylkill Haven. Priests from Pottsville began to visit Schuylkill Haven regularly in 1847. For several years they held mass in a private house on Dock Street, until purchasing this building in 1863. Today the structure serves as an apartment building, and St. Ambrose has a new home located on the edge of town.

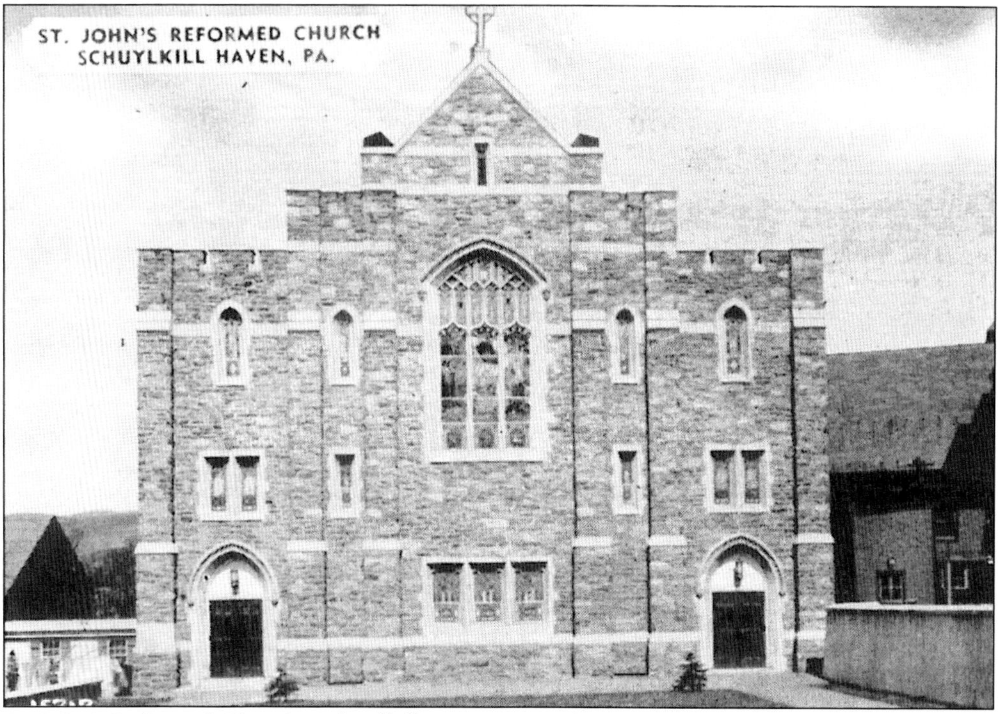

St. John's Reformed Church, Schuylkill Haven. St. John's Reformed Church was organized in 1862 with Reverend David Wolff serving as the first pastor. In 1875, the structure located on Main Street was built at a cost of $15,000.

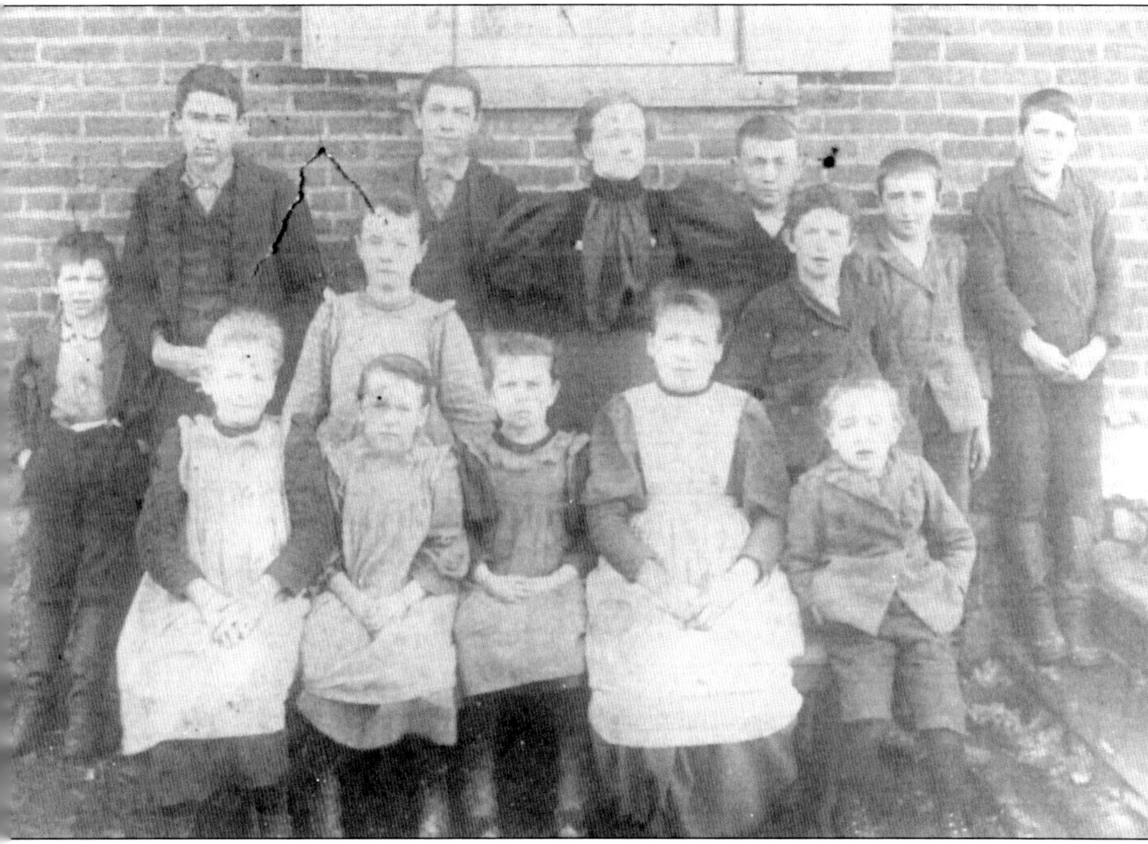

A c. 1900 class from the one-room schoolhouse located along Adamsdale Road near Schuylkill Haven. At the time this photograph was taken, the Schuylkill River flowed directly in front of the school. A few years later, the school became a private residence and has been owned by the family of Warren Bowen ever since.

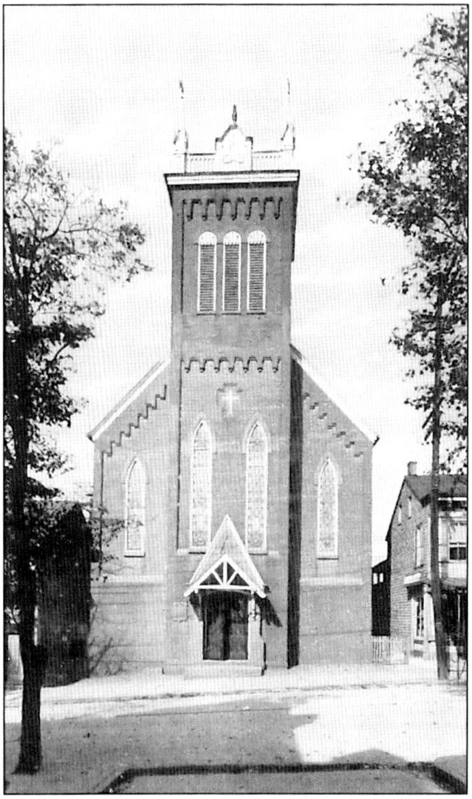

St. John's Reformed Church in Schuylkill Haven. The congregation of St. John's Church began holding services in a building on Main Street in 1862.

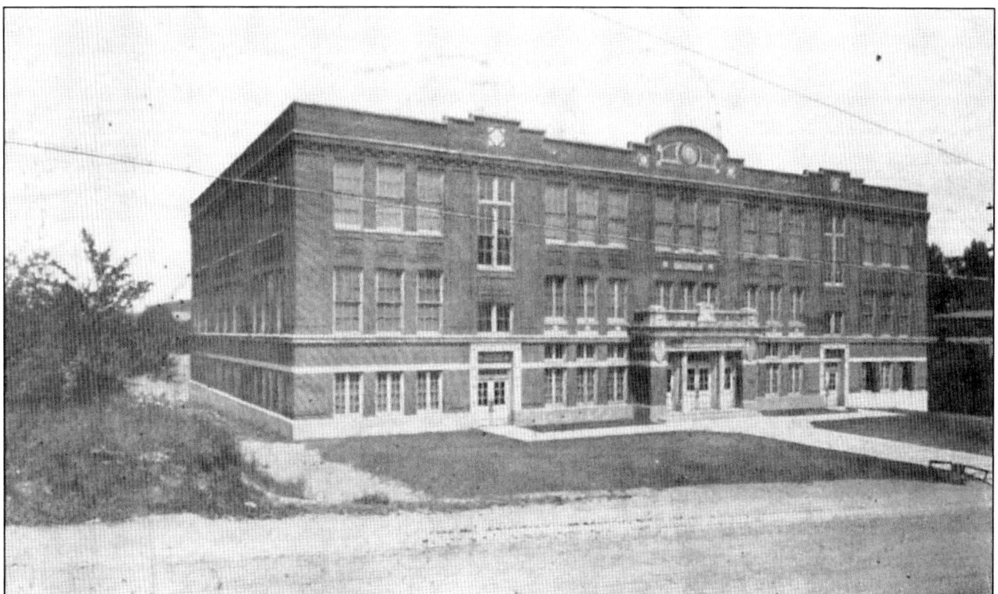

The Schuylkill Haven High School building, *c.* 1931. Opened in September 1917, this structure was used for many years as a secondary school; it later housed classes for the lower grades.

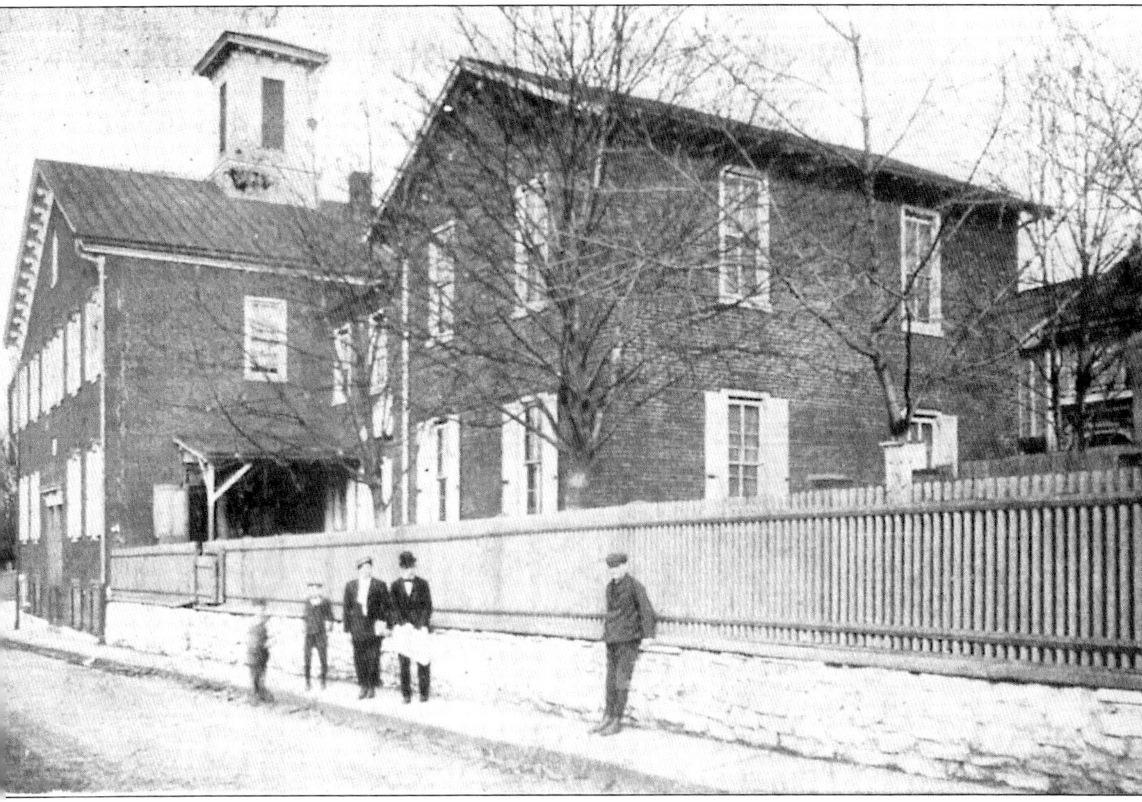

The South Ward Public School of Schuylkill Haven. In 1900, a brick building with two rooms was built on Canal Street in the South Ward. A few years later the structure was remodeled and rooms were added.

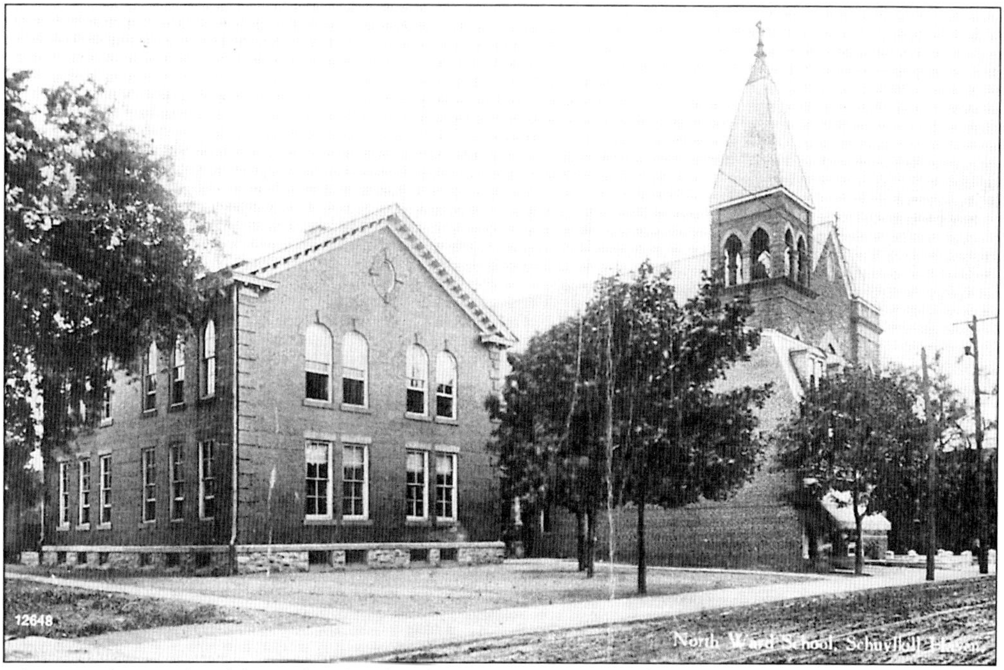

The North Ward Public School. The first North Ward School, which consisted of a one-story frame building, was constructed in 1874. Later, a building of four rooms was built on the same site.

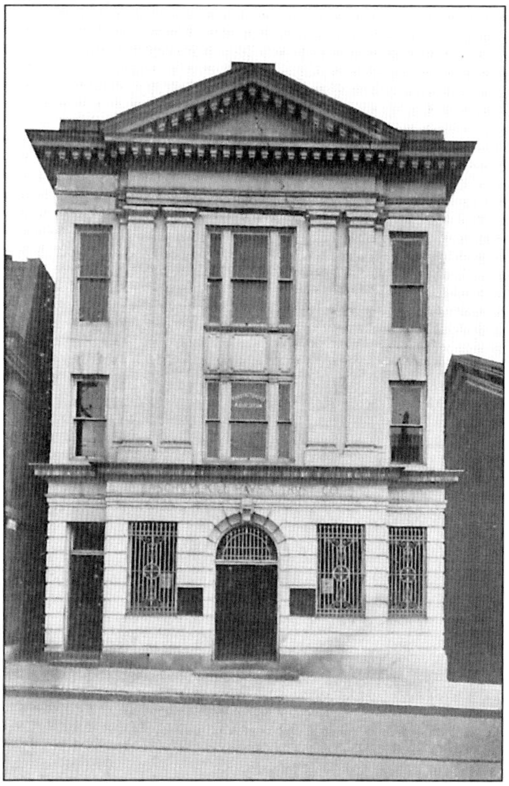

The Schuylkill Haven Trust Company Bank, c. 1913. On January 25, 1910, the Schuylkill Haven Trust Company was established as a permanent institution in Schuylkill Haven.

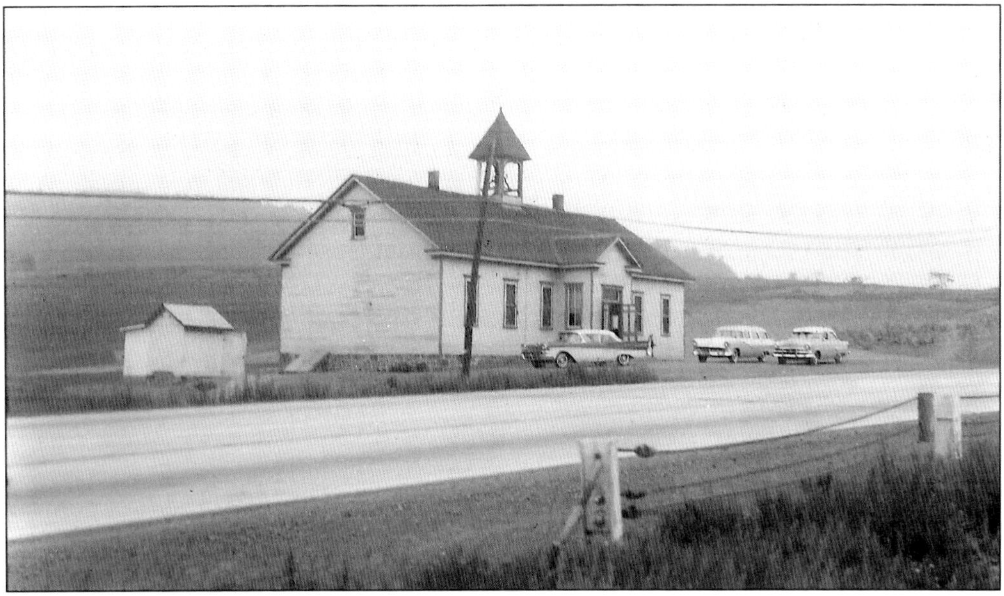

The Pinedale Schoolhouse in Deer Lake, *c.* 1961. The original school at Pinedale was made of logs and stood on the site of the more recent Deer Lake Motel complex. This image shows the later structure, which served as a school until 1961. In October 1960, John F. Kennedy, a U.S. senator at the time, stopped at the Pinedale School while campaigning for the presidency. During his visit to the school, Kennedy wrote, "Knowledge is Power" on the chalkboard.

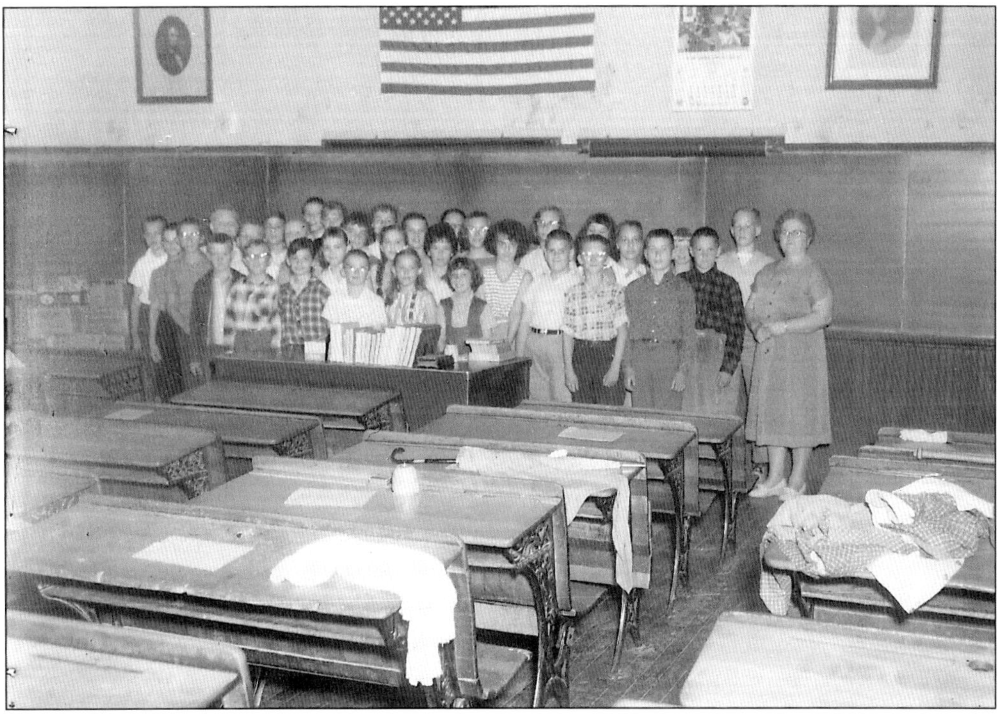

The last students to attend the Pinedale School in Deer Lake, June 9, 1961. Grace Meck is the teacher pictured here. Note the old-fashioned wooden school desks and the portraits of Lincoln and Washington that traditionally adorned most early classrooms.

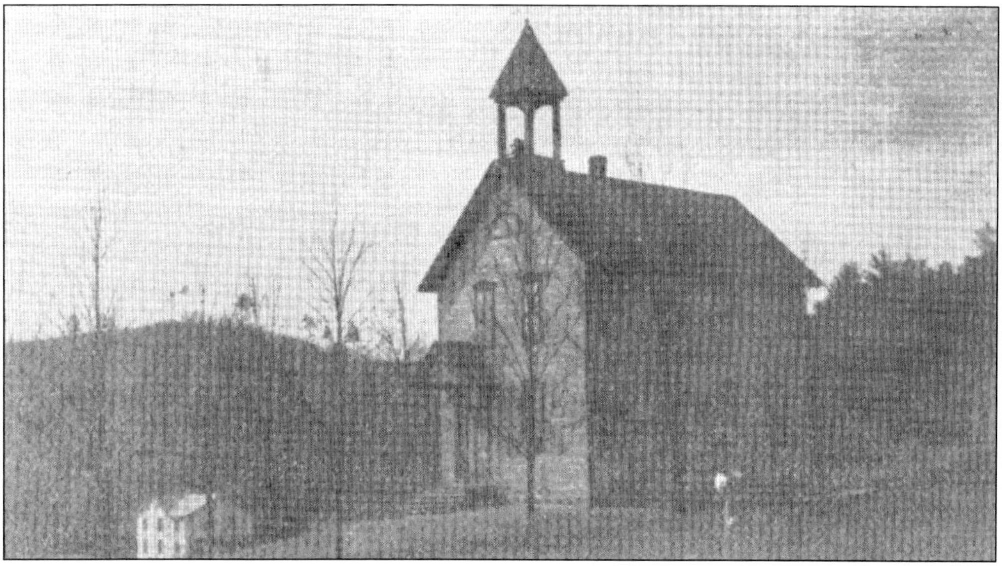

The New Ringgold Schoolhouse. Country schools such as this one were quite common in Schuylkill County. Schuylkill was the first county in the state to adopt the School Bill of 1834, establishing a system of free education. In the East Brunswick Township, where this school was located, there were ten public schools managed similarly to the one in New Ringgold. At that time, schools were built approximately 3 miles apart, the maximum distance children were required to walk in order to attend classes.

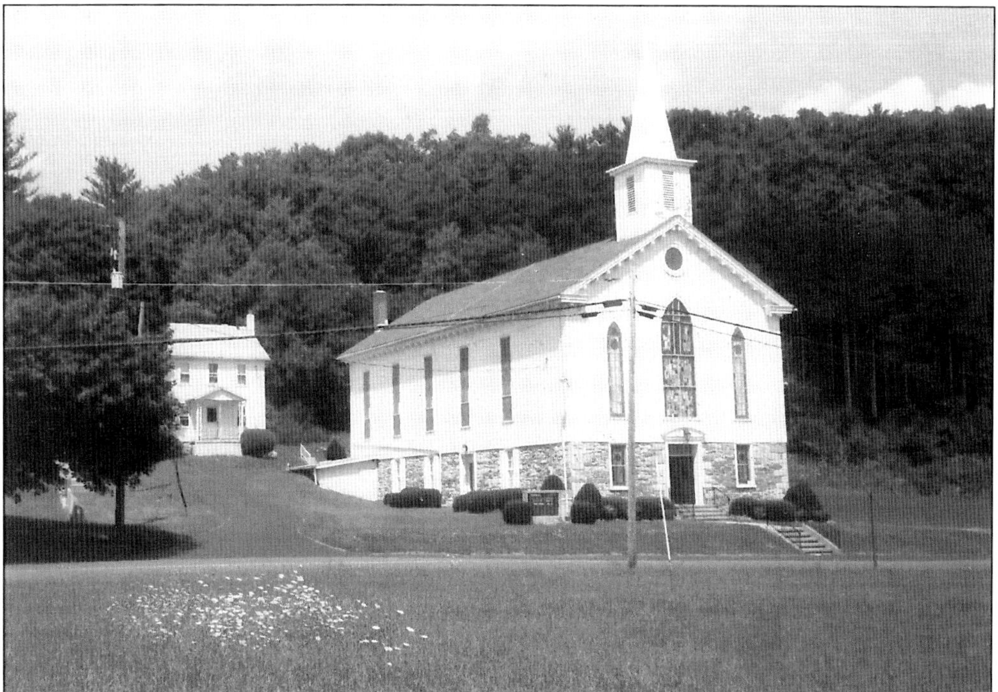

Friedens Church near New Ringgold. This church was organized in 1796, but the settlers who made up the Reformed congregation arrived as early as 1756 and worshiped with the Lutheran congregation until 1796.

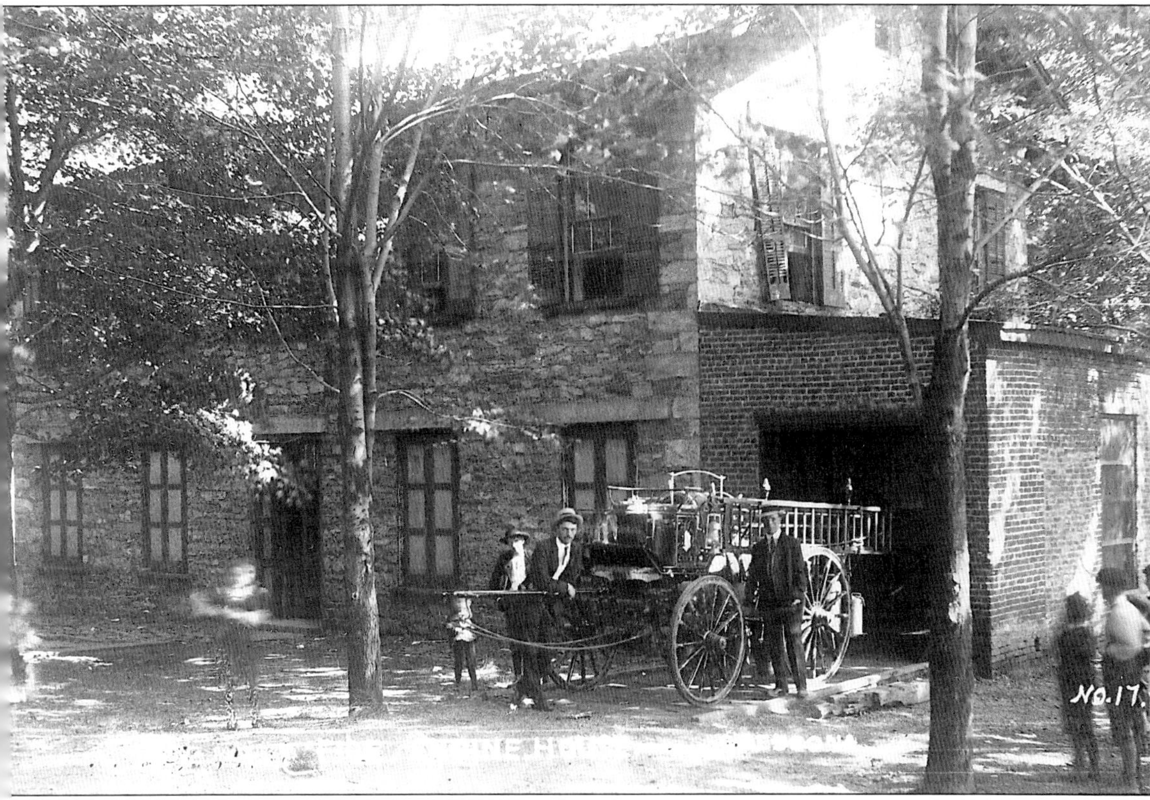

The No. 1 Fire Company of Cressona. This stone structure, located on Front Street, was originally the Mine Hill Railroad Office Building; it later became a horn factory, the American Legion headquarters, and eventually a storehouse.

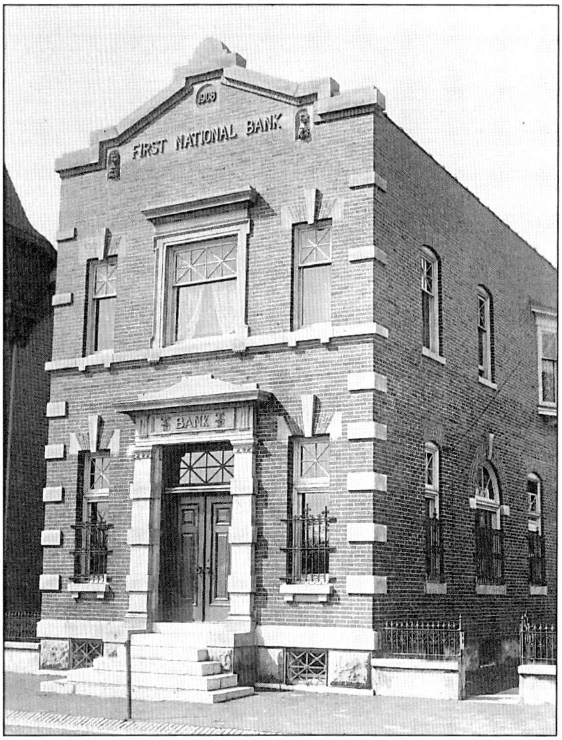

The First National Bank in Cressona. This bank, located on Sillyman Street, later became the Pennsylvania National Bank.

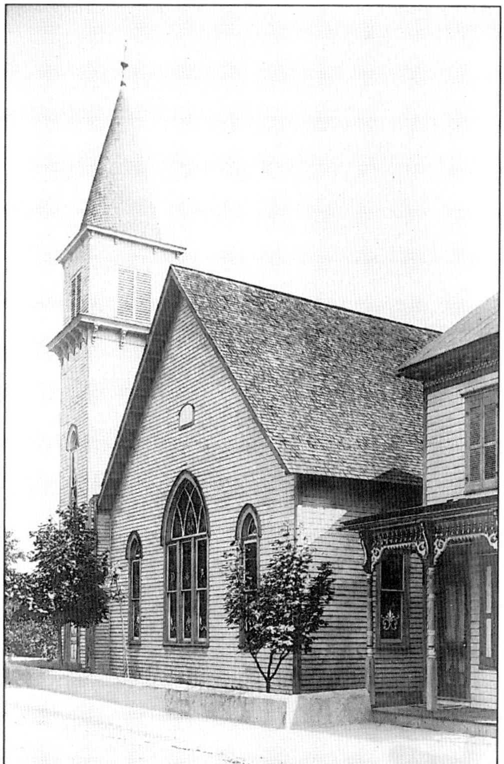

The United Evangelical Church of Cressona. This church was completely destroyed by fire on November 19, 1920. A new building was erected on the same site and dedicated on November 21, 1921, one year and one day after the fire.

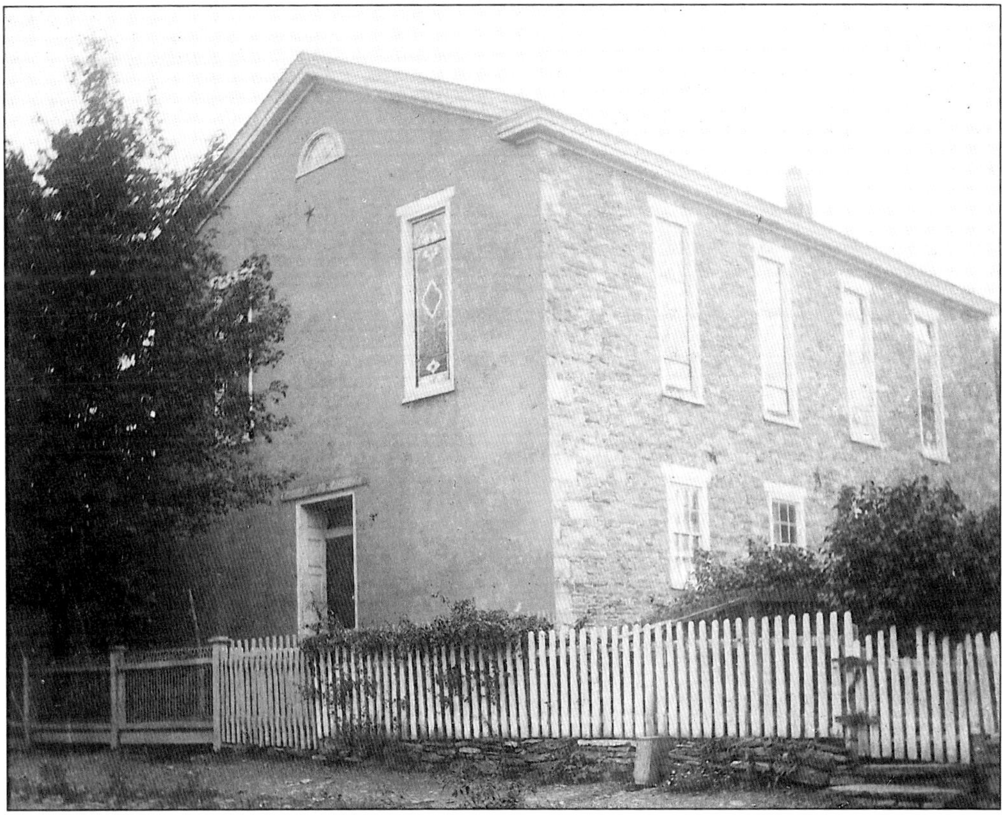

Cressona's Methodist church as it looked in the late 1800s. It is the oldest church in Cressona.

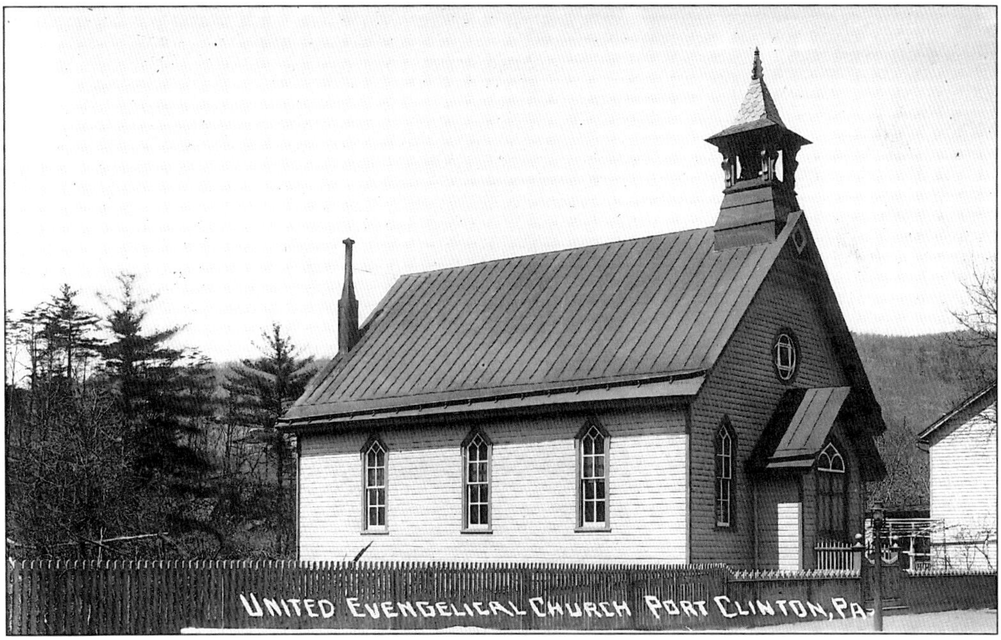

The United Evangelical Church in Port Clinton. This structure was built in 1894 and was later destroyed in a fire.

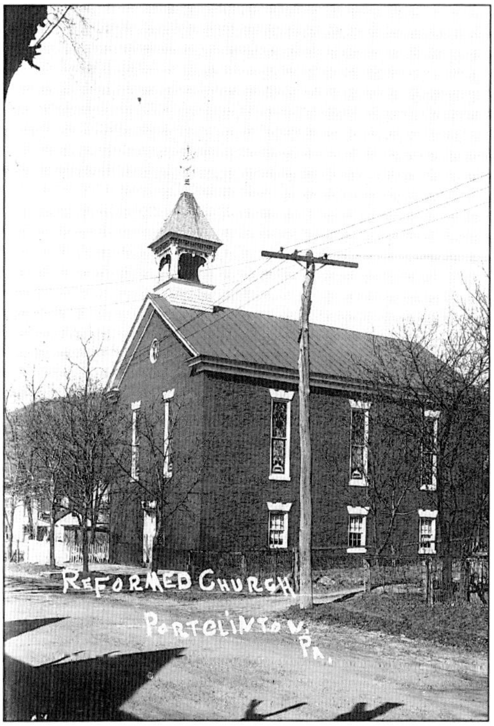

The Reformed Church in Port Clinton. This church was built in 1868 and still stands today.

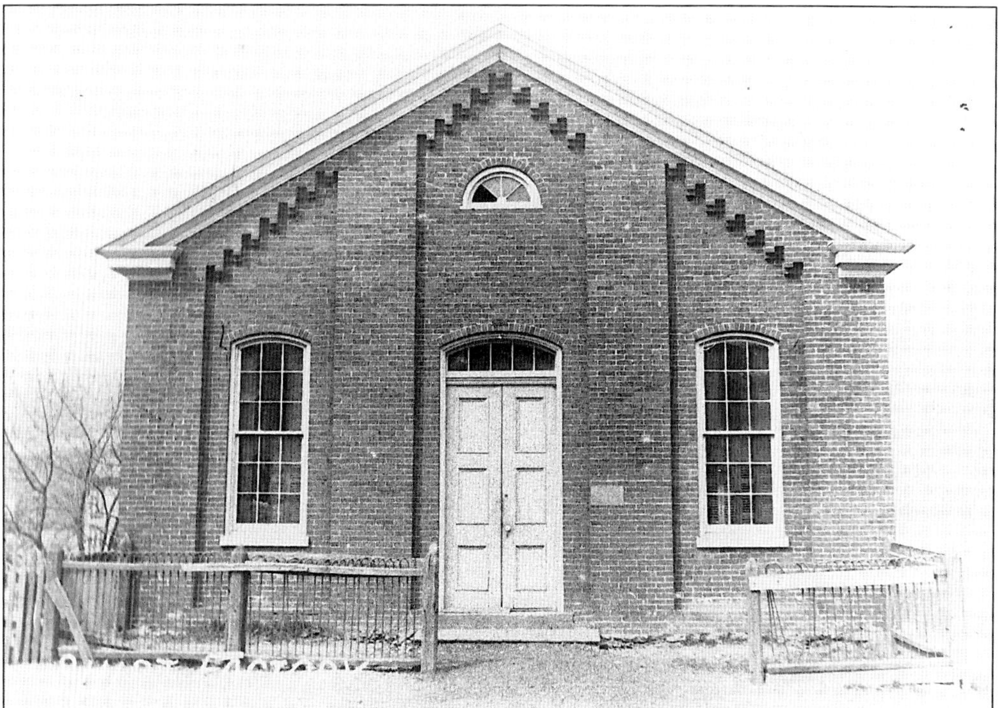

A versatile building. This brick structure in Port Clinton, along Route 61, served the community in a variety of ways. Through the years it was a shirt factory, church, private residence, and most recently, an antique shop.

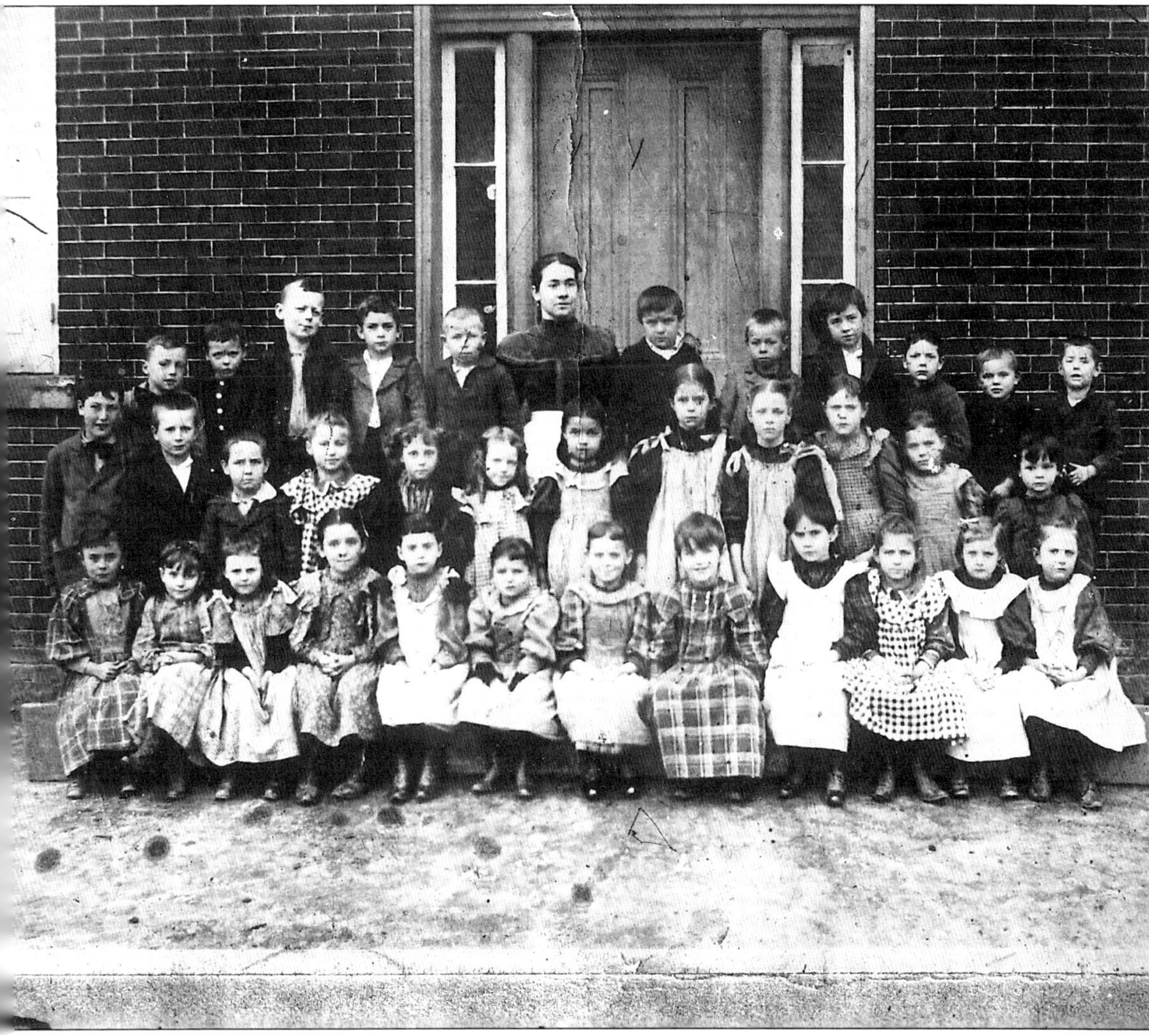

A group of students posing in front of the old schoolhouse in Port Clinton. The school, which today serves as a museum and library, held two classes, one for first grade through fourth grade and another for grades five and six.

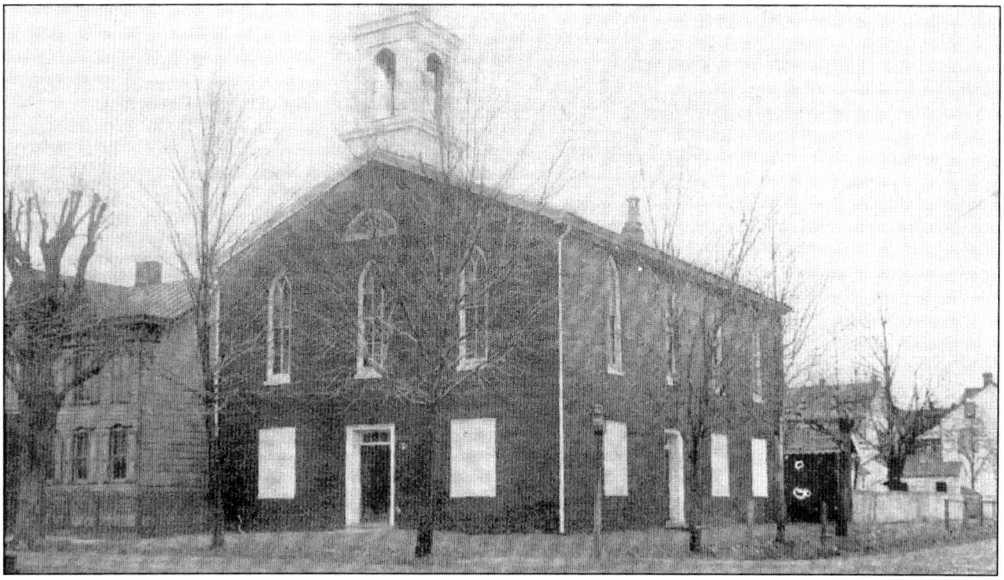

The Salem United Methodist Church in Orwigsburg. On November 10, 1819, a public meeting for the purpose of instituting the first Bible Society of Schuylkill County was held in Orwigsburg. In 1826, the original Salem Church was built on Independence Street and was the first church of any denomination to be erected within the borough limits. The second Salem Church, shown in this image, was built 1834–35.

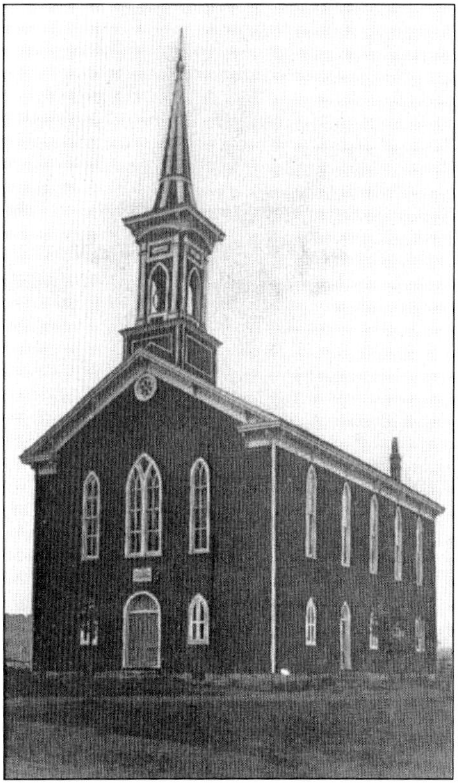

The historic Red Church, near Orwigsburg. This photograph shows the fourth and current Red Church. Some of the wood from the previous church, which was built in 1803, was utilized in this church, built in 1883.

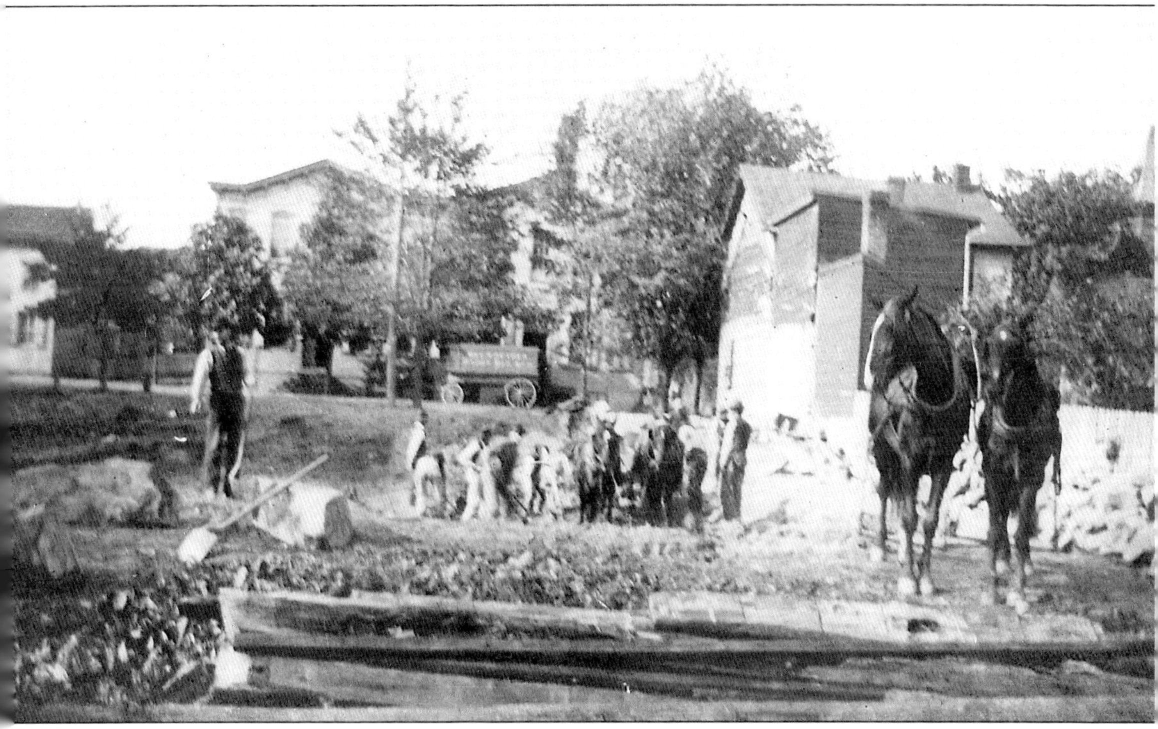

The site of St. John's Reformed Church in Orwigsburg. This photograph shows the primary stage of the church's construction at its East Market Street location. Note the primitive manner in which excavation took place.

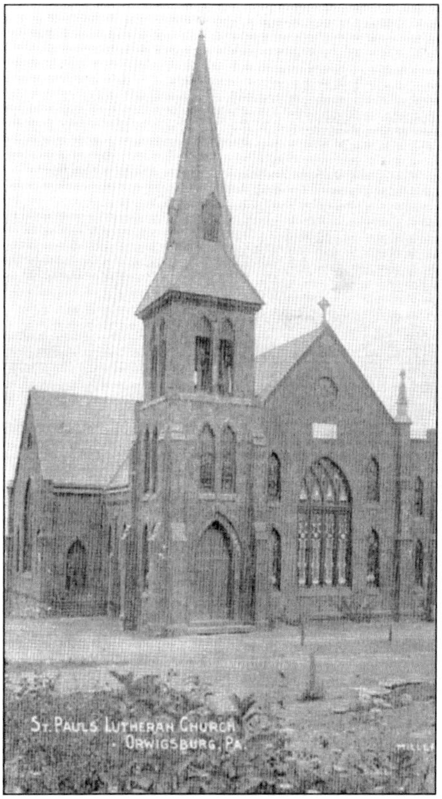

St. Paul's Lutheran Church in Orwigsburg. This church, located on North Warren Street, was organized and consecrated in 1844.

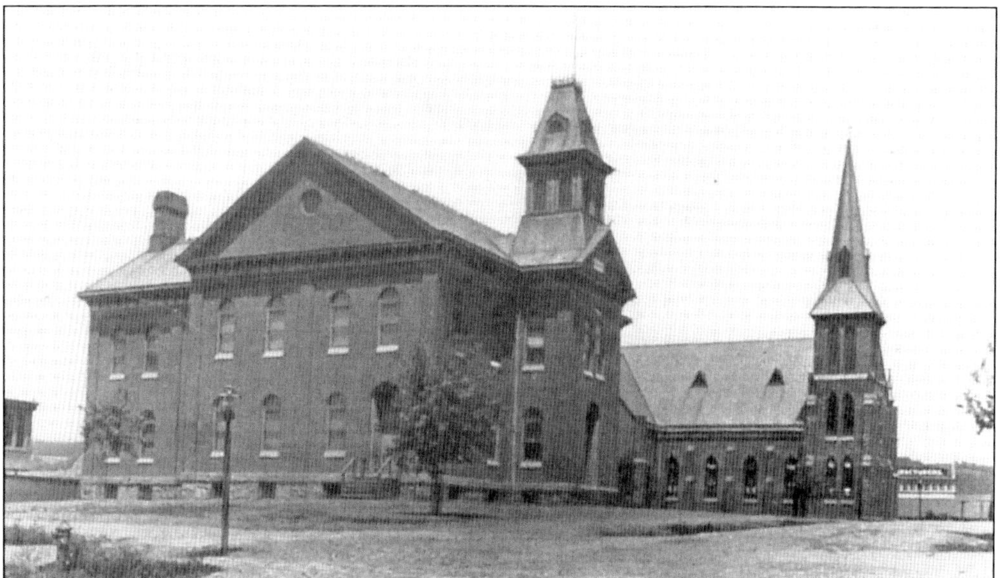

The Orwigsburg Public School building. Built in 1889, this building served as a high school until 1911. It was also used as a grammar school in later years until it was designated as Orwigsburg's Borough Hall. St. Paul's Lutheran Church can also be seen in this image.

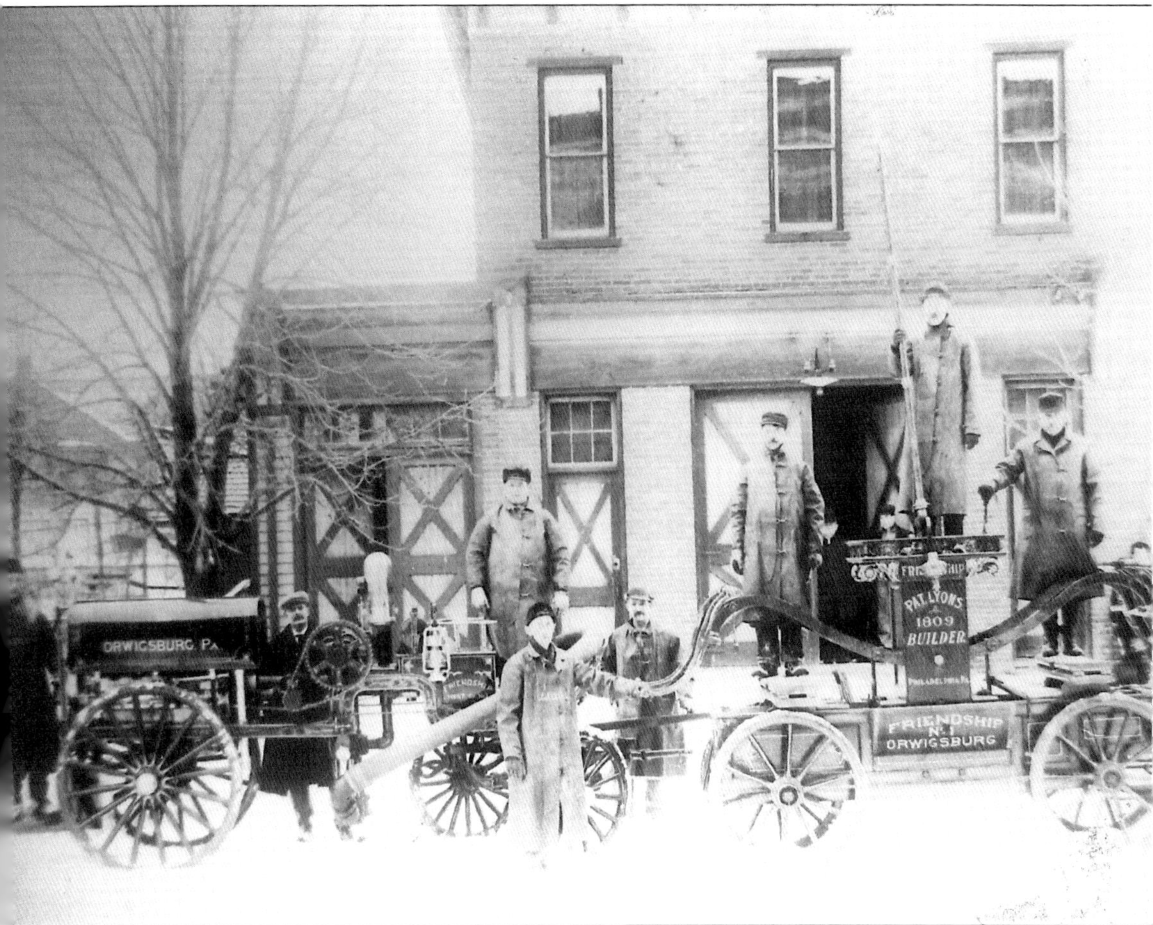

The Friendship Hose Company, No. 1, *c.* 1911. Orwigsburg's fire company, the Friendship Hose Company, was in existence as early as 1813, when it was referred to as the "Orwigsburg Fire Company." The building in this image, located on east Mifflin Street, was constructed in 1891 and is now the home of the Orwigsburg Historical Society. Note the early fire apparatus: on the left is the Howe Engine #100, the first gasoline powered engine, and on the right is the 1809 Pat Lyons Handpumper, currently on permanent loan and display at Fireman's Hall Museum in Philadelphia.

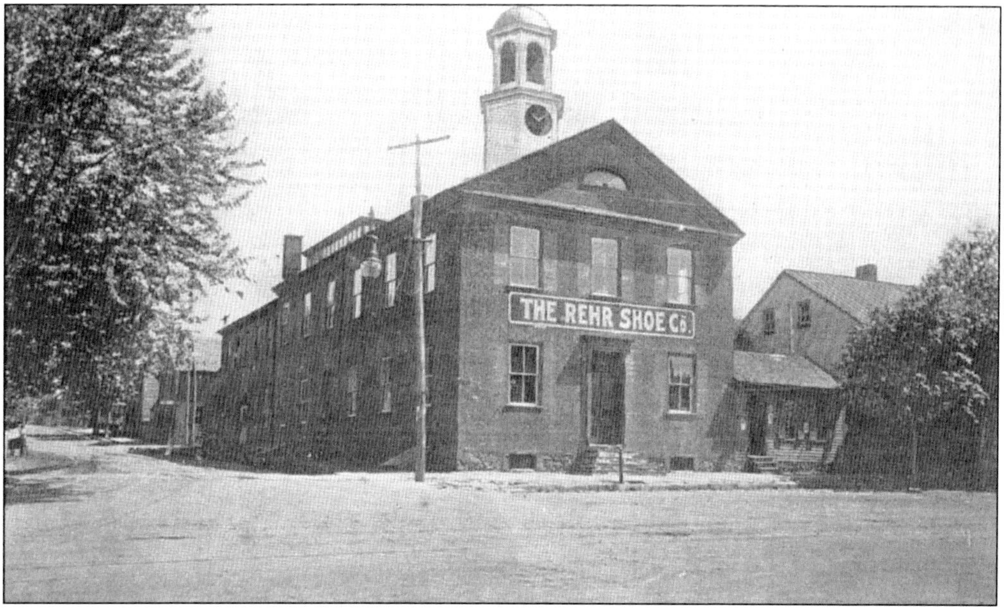

The first official courthouse of Schuylkill County. Built in 1815 along East Market Street in Orwigsburg, this structure served as the county's seat of government until 1851. In 1854, the building was opened as a co-ed seminary, known as the Arcadian Institution. It closed in 1864 and later became the Rehr Shoe Company. The building was completely demolished in 1941, with only the clock and bell escaping destruction.

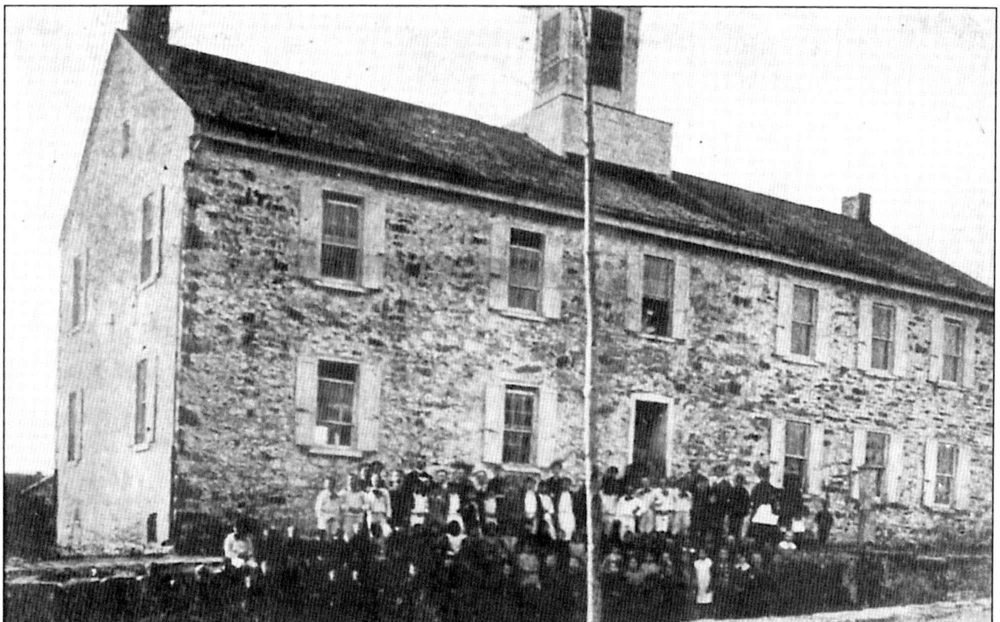

The first jail of Schuylkill County, located in Orwigsburg. Built in 1814 of field stone, this structure housed the county's jail until 1852, when a new jail was erected in Pottsville. The old jail was utilized as a school building until 1869.

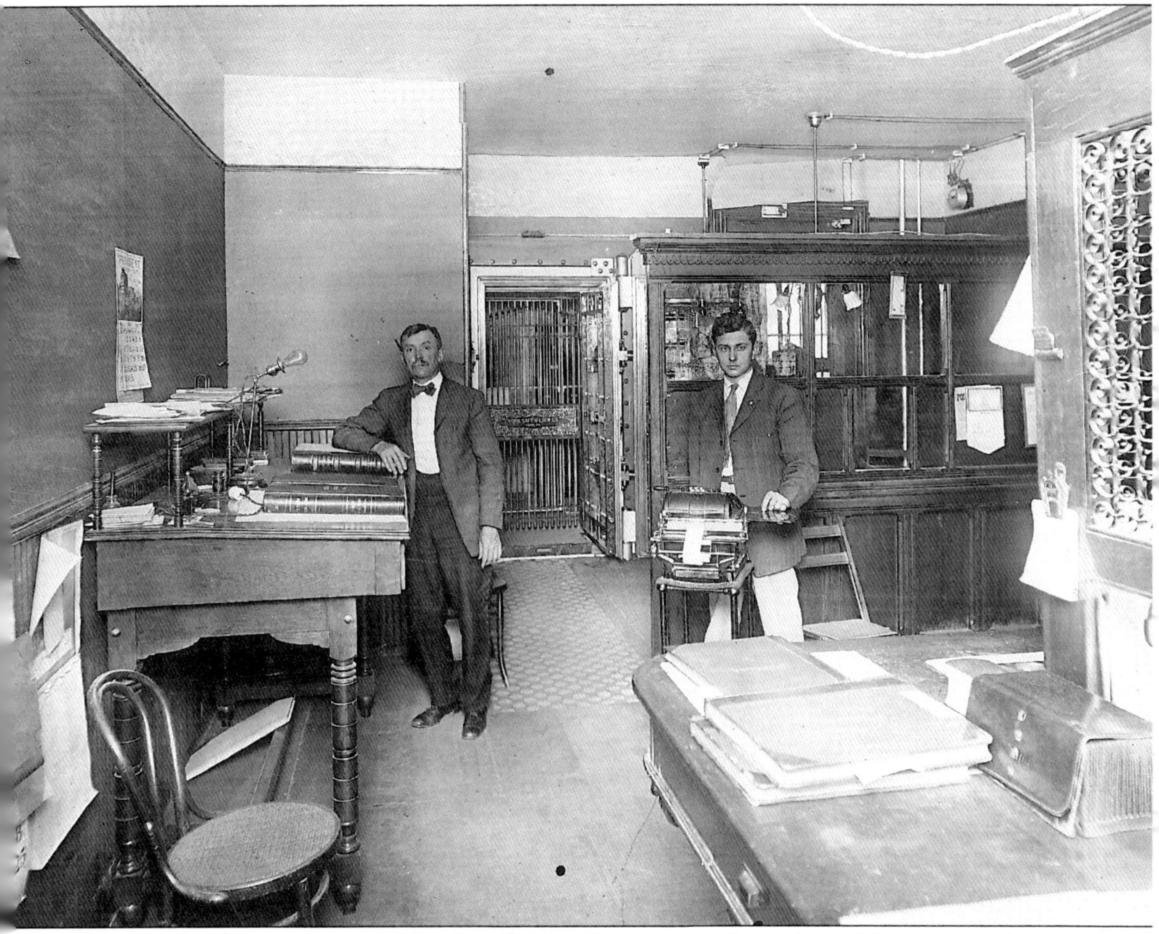

The interior of the First National Bank and Trust Company in Orwigsburg. This image, taken in 1911, shows the inner office area and vaults.

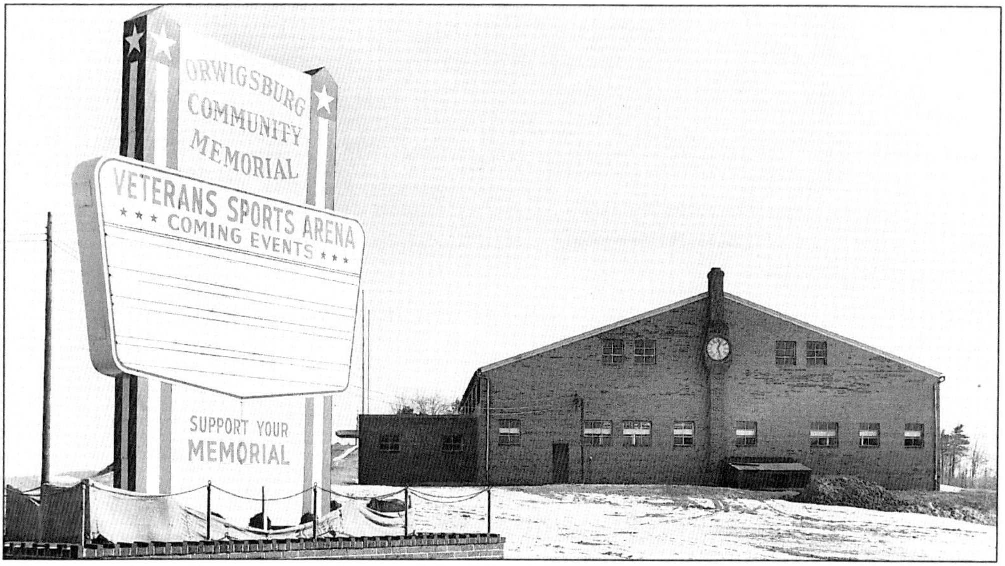

The Orwigsburg Community Memorial Building, c. 1960. Dedicated in 1950, this building was intended to be a tribute to all Orwigsburg veterans. Through the years it has been used for sporting events and social gatherings. The clock, which can be seen on the side of the building, was originally located in the tower of the Schuylkill County Courthouse when it was located in Orwigsburg.

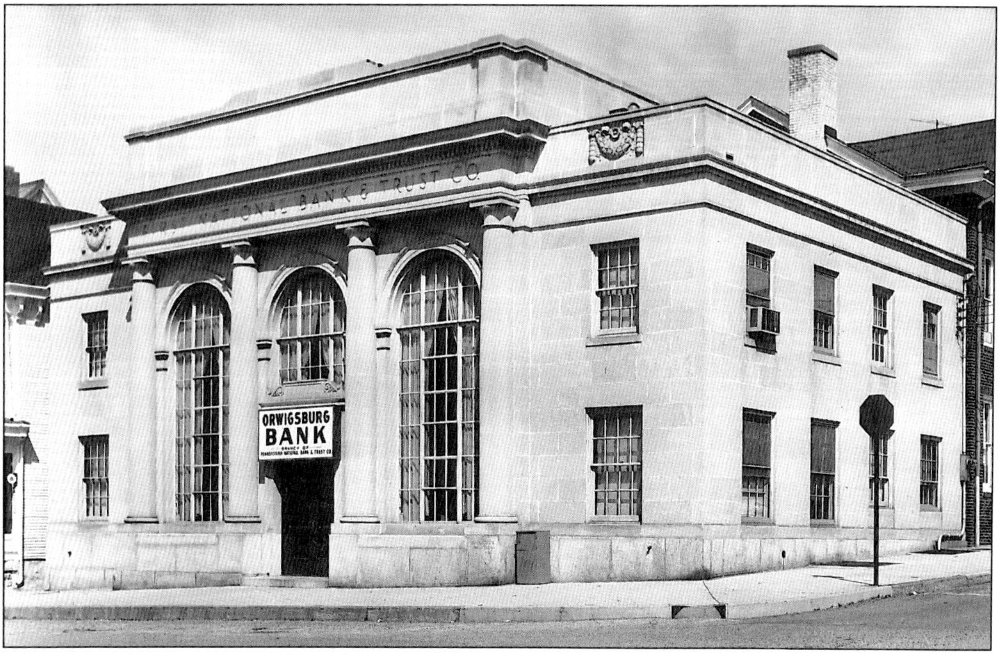

The Pennsylvania National Bank and Trust Company, c. 1963. The First National Bank of Orwigsburg opened for business on September 23, 1890, in a corner room located at Wayne and Market Streets. In 1898, the bank moved to a new building on Center Square, and in 1927, the institution moved to the corner of Market and Warren Streets. The bank merged with the Pennsylvania National Bank of Pottsville in 1962 and is still located on the corner of Market and Warren Streets.

Three

Transportation

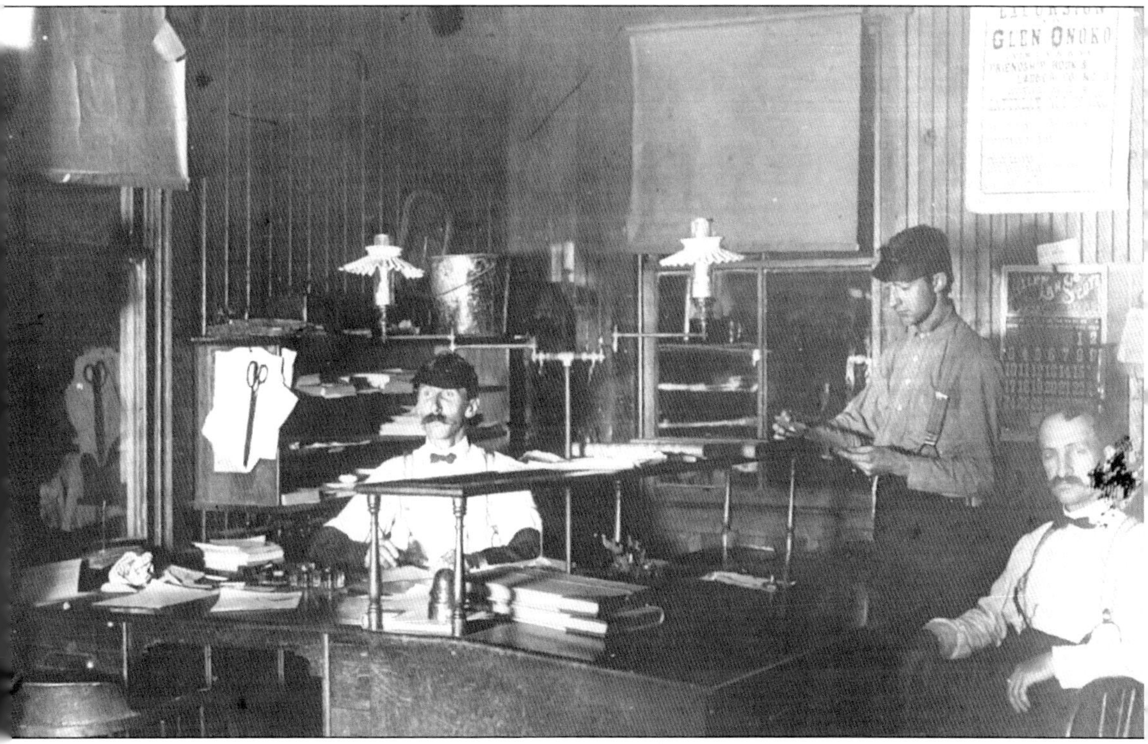

The Philadelphia and Reading Coal and Iron Company shipping office at Cressona, c. 1906. Pictured, from left to right, are George Reiger, Charles Eiler, and Ed Fessler.

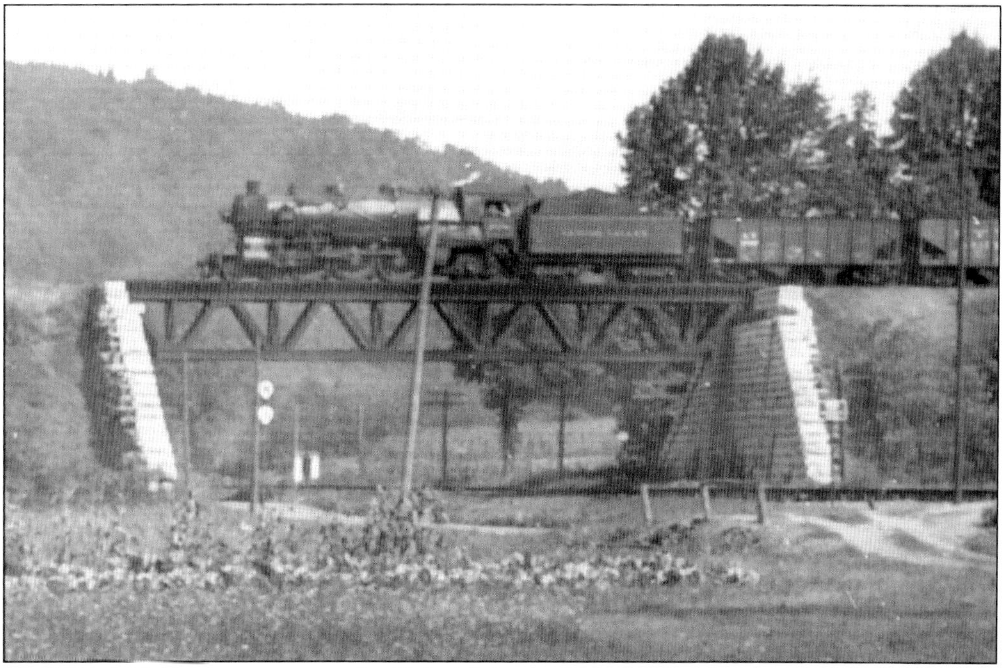

The Lehigh Valley train crossing the Philadelphia and Reading Railroad at Rauch's en route to Orwigsburg and Pottsville, *c.* 1947.

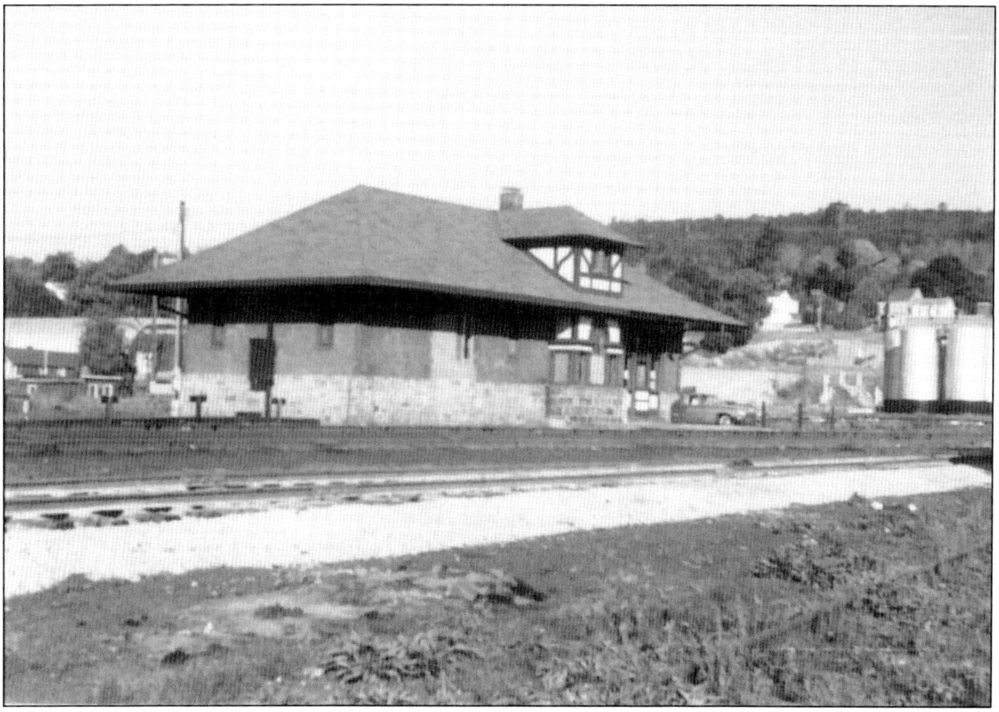

The Philadelphia and Reading Railroad station in Cressona, *c.* 1962.

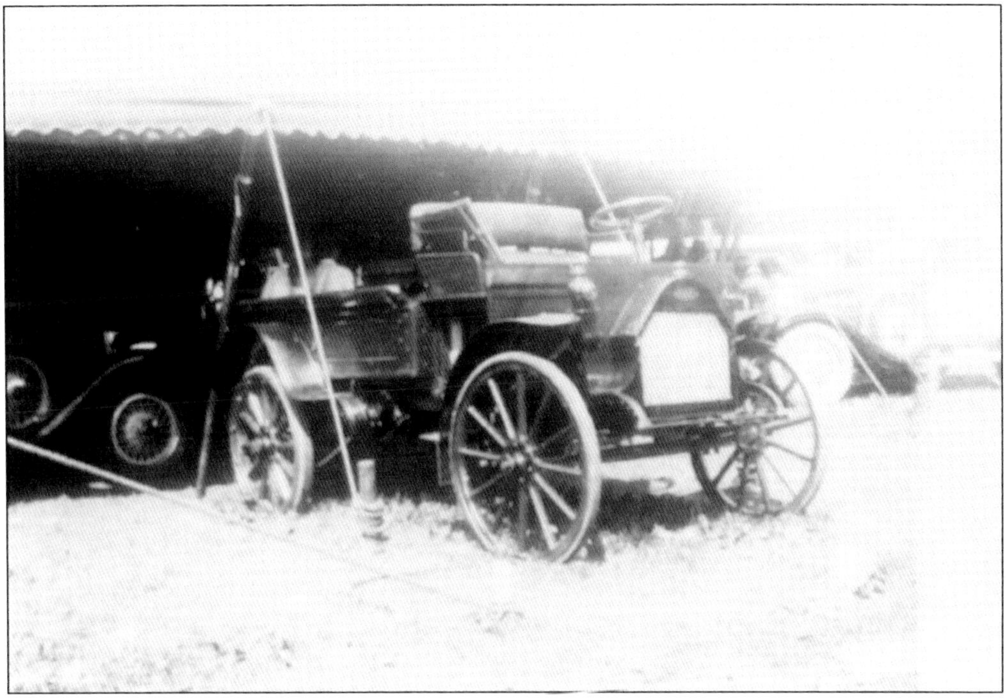

An old Reo truck, c. 1928. This truck was displayed by one of the local car dealers at the Schuylkill County Fair held in Cressona.

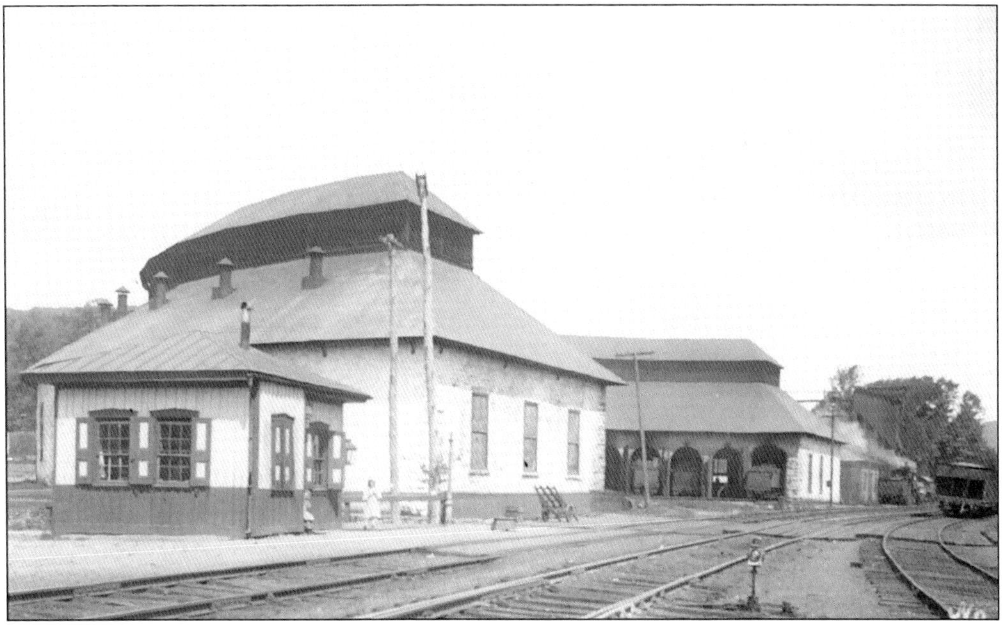

The Pennsylvania and Reading Railroad Depot and Roundhouse, located in Cressona, c. 1900. The roundhouse, situated near the intersection of Sillyman and Wilder Streets, was built in 1867.

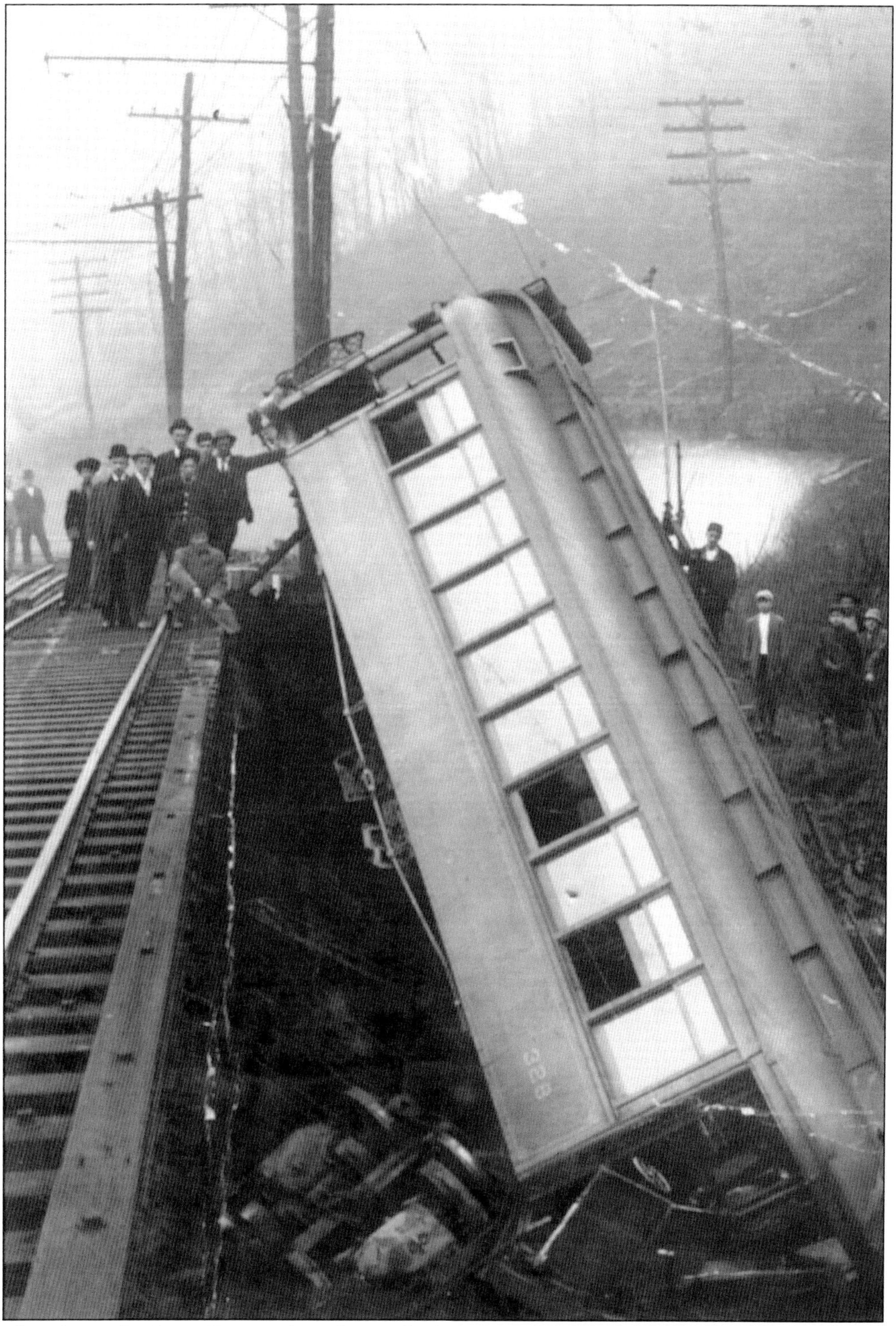

The aftermath of a trolley accident that took place on December 25, 1911, at Cape Horn, near Cressona. Out of the 35 passengers aboard, no one was seriously injured.

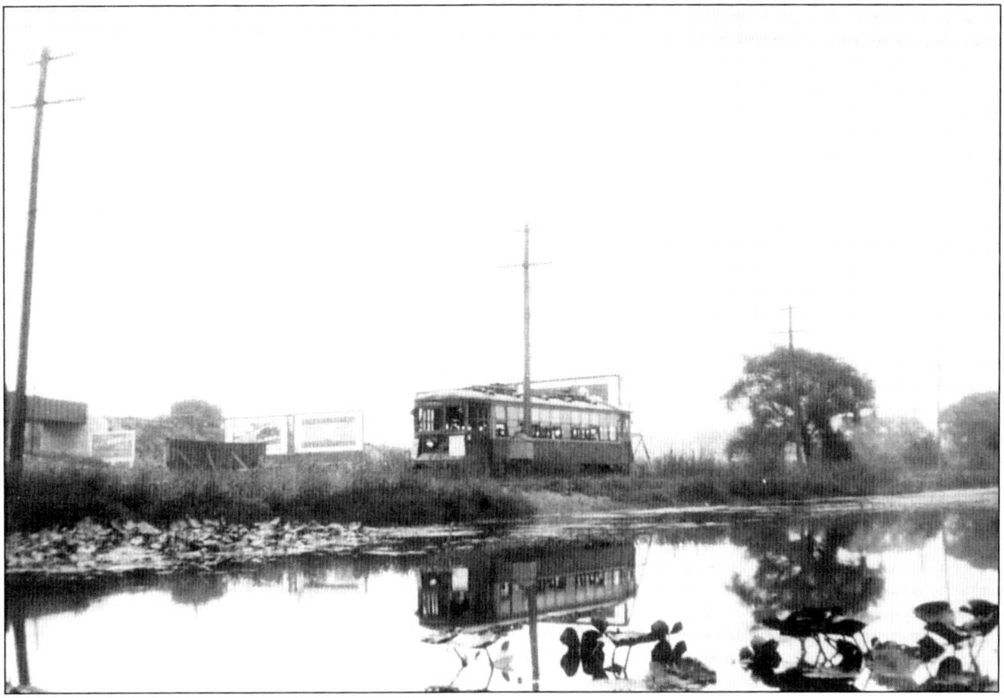

A view in Cressona, along Connors Crossing, on the last day of trolley operation in 1932.

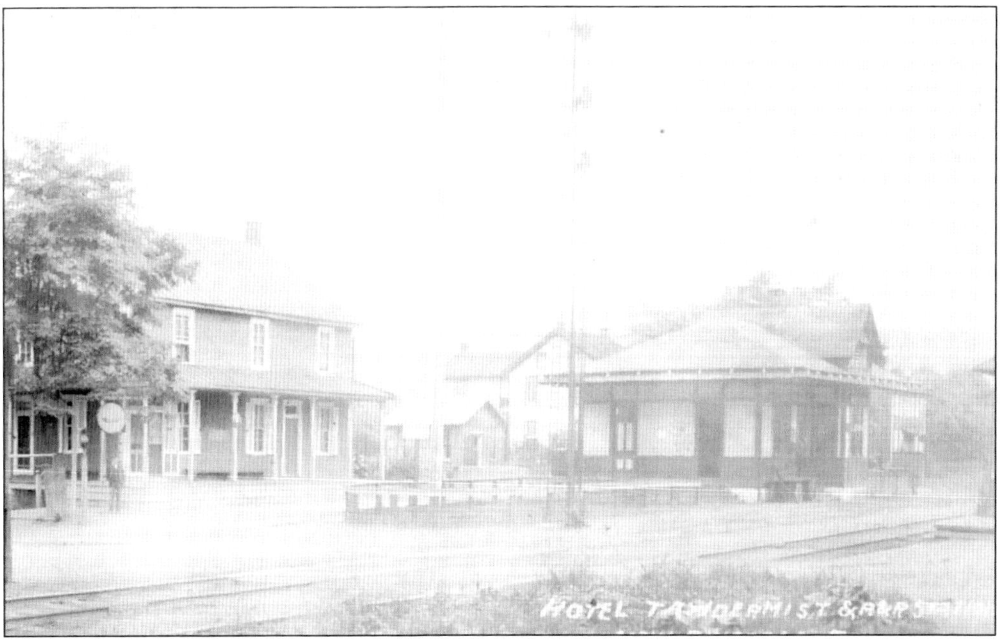

The Philadelphia and Reading Railroad station in New Ringgold. The hotel and taxidermist shop are also visible in this image. All three buildings have since been demolished.

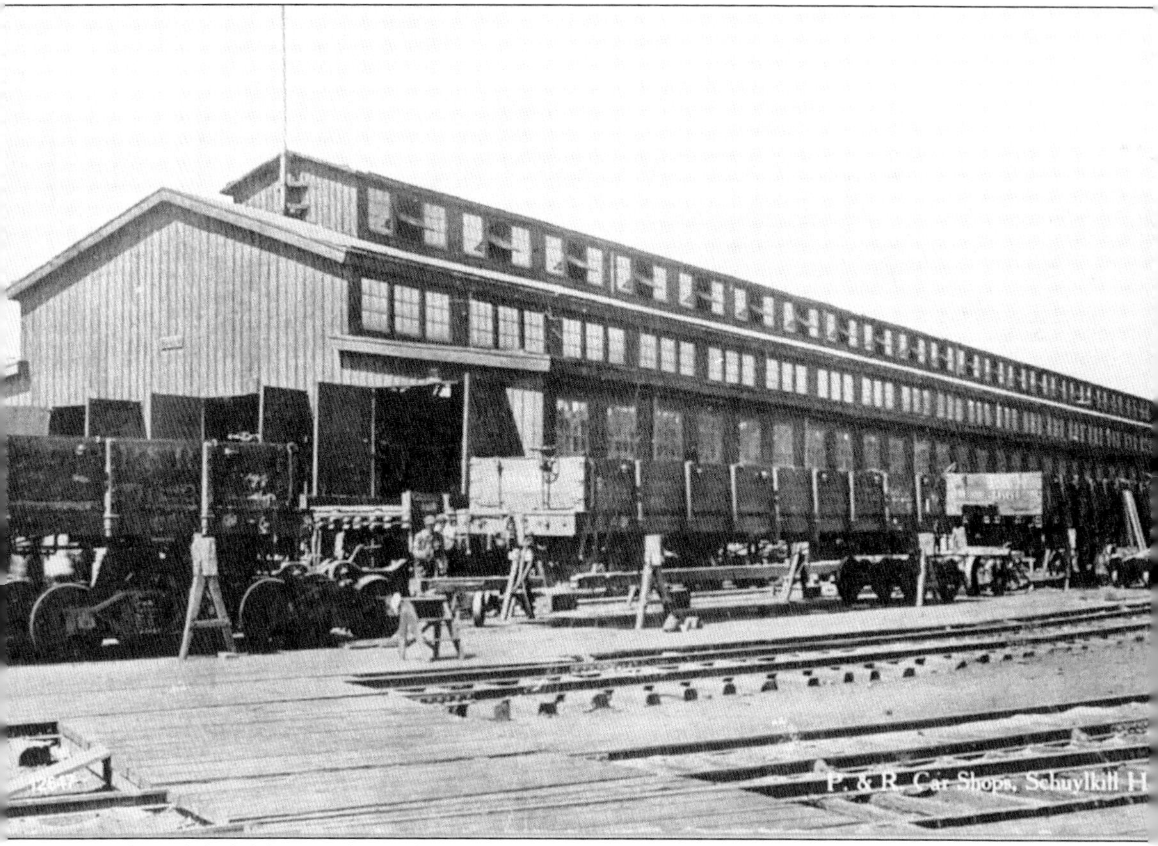

The Philadelphia and Reading Railroad Car Shops in Schuylkill Haven, *c.* 1913. The Philadelphia and Reading Railroad was opened for traffic through Schuylkill Haven in 1842. Around the same time, the company established this car shop for repairs. As of 1925, the shop still employed several hundred workers.

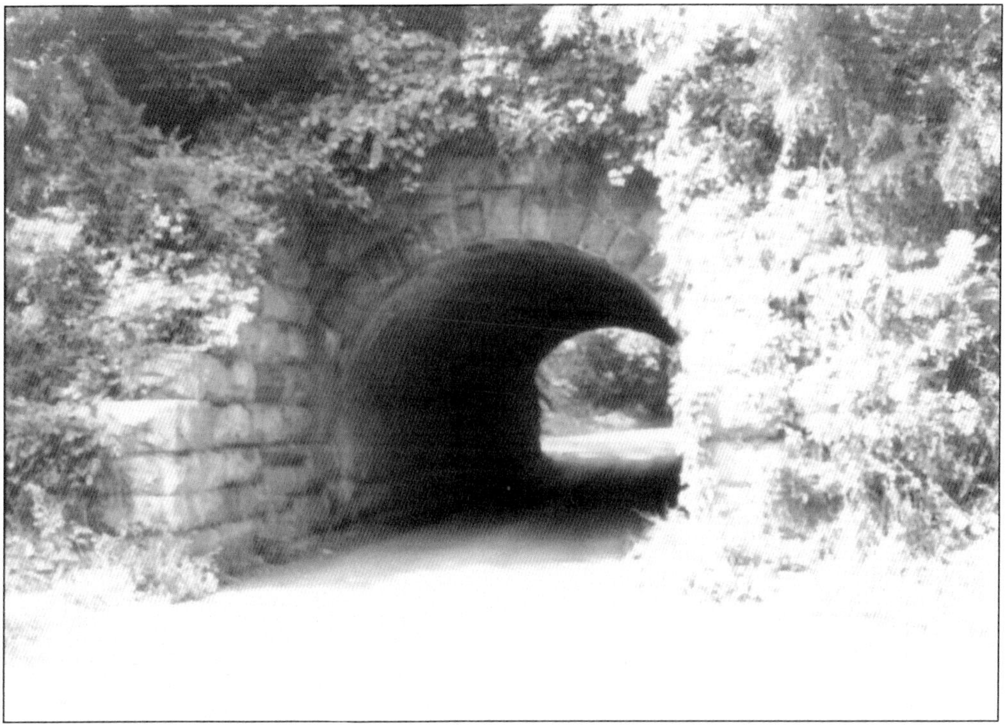

The hand-built railroad arch, a familiar landmark along Memorial Drive near Schuylkill Haven. Italian stonemasons built several of these arches for the Pennsylvania and Reading Railroad in the late 1800s. Fashioned after similar structures in Europe, these "works of art" are now in danger of being removed.

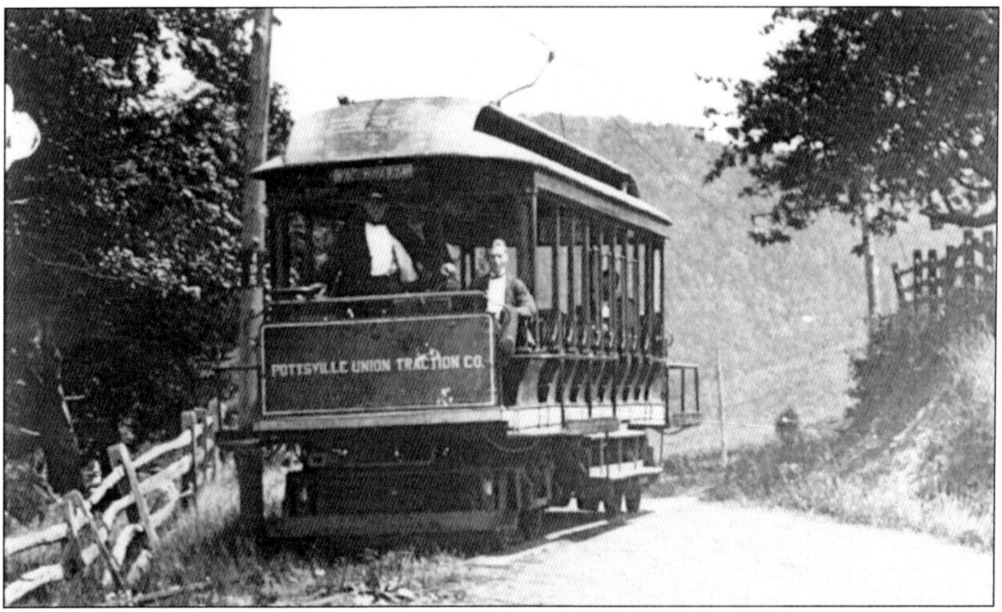

The "Highball" at Adamsdale Park. This trolley was part of the Orwigsburg line.

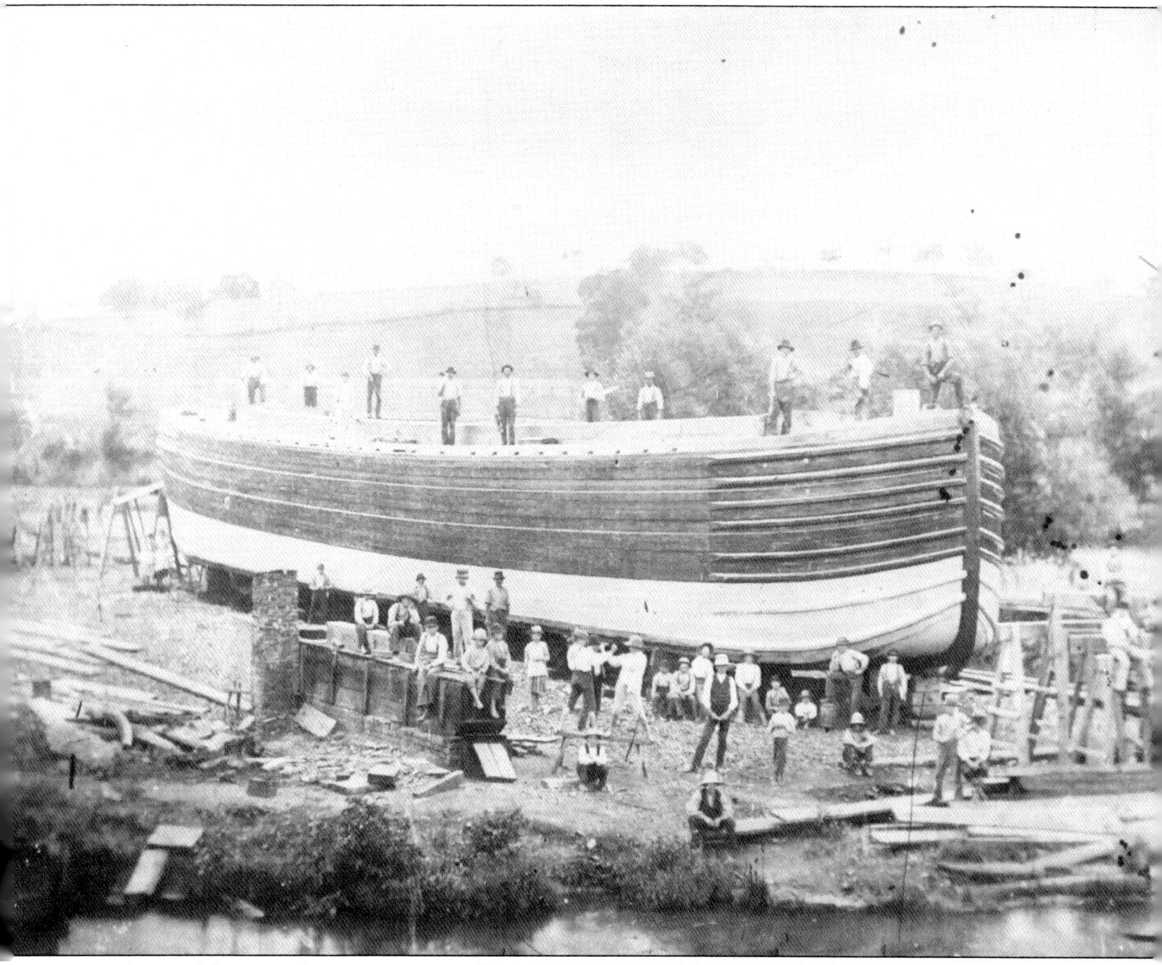

A canal boat under construction. This 200-ton canal boat was built at the Schuylkill Haven Boat Yard.

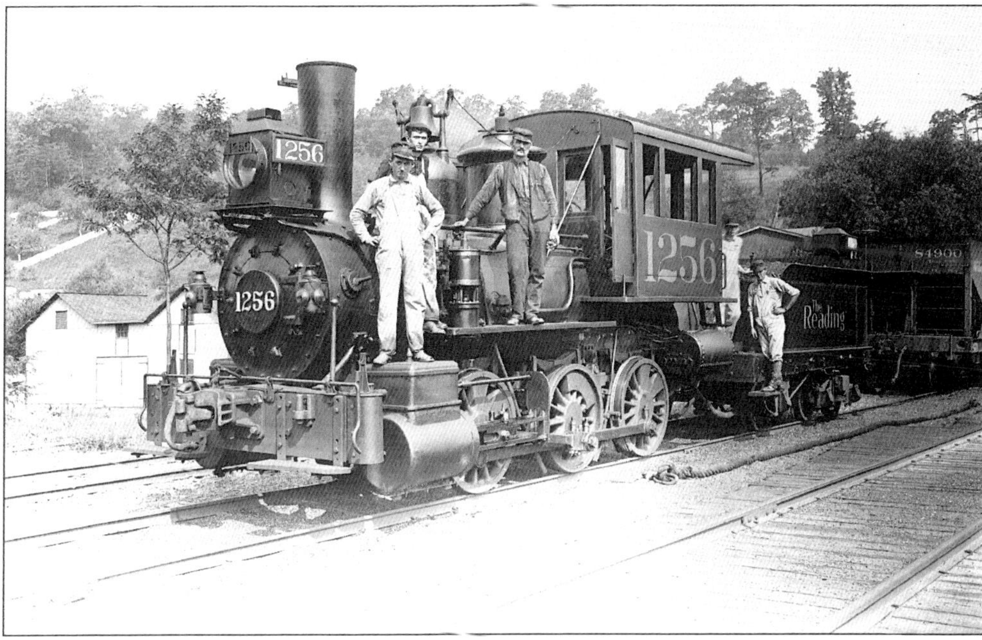

The Reading Railroad's stately No. 1256 engine in Port Clinton, seen while hauling coal in the early 1900s.

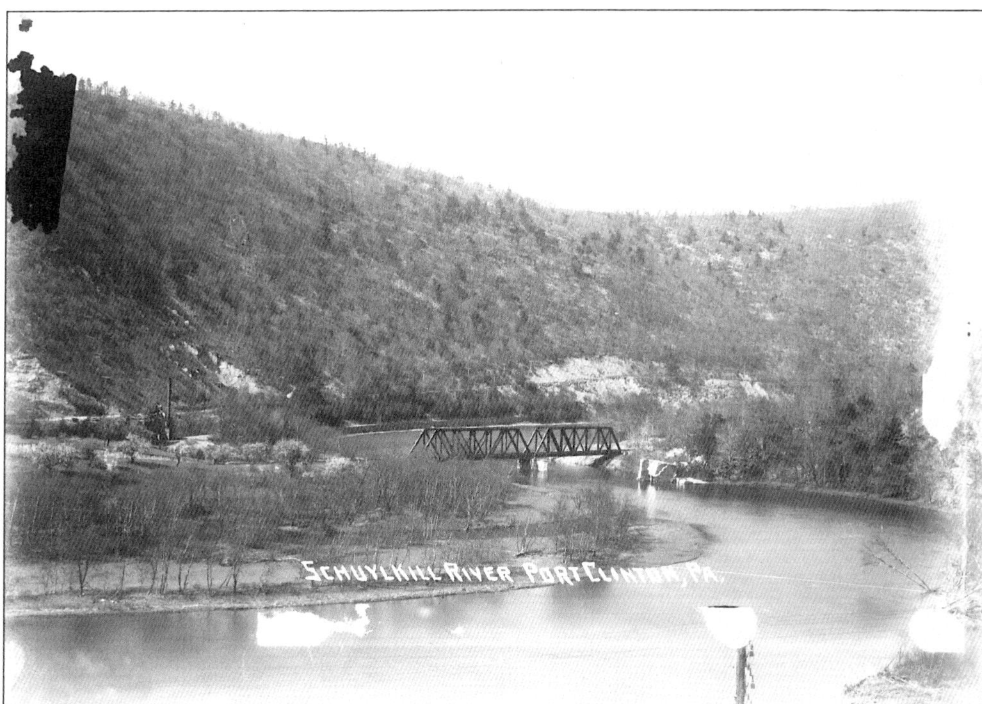

A view of the Schuylkill River in Port Clinton. The town of Port Clinton was settled at the confluence of the Schuylkill and Little Schuylkill Rivers.

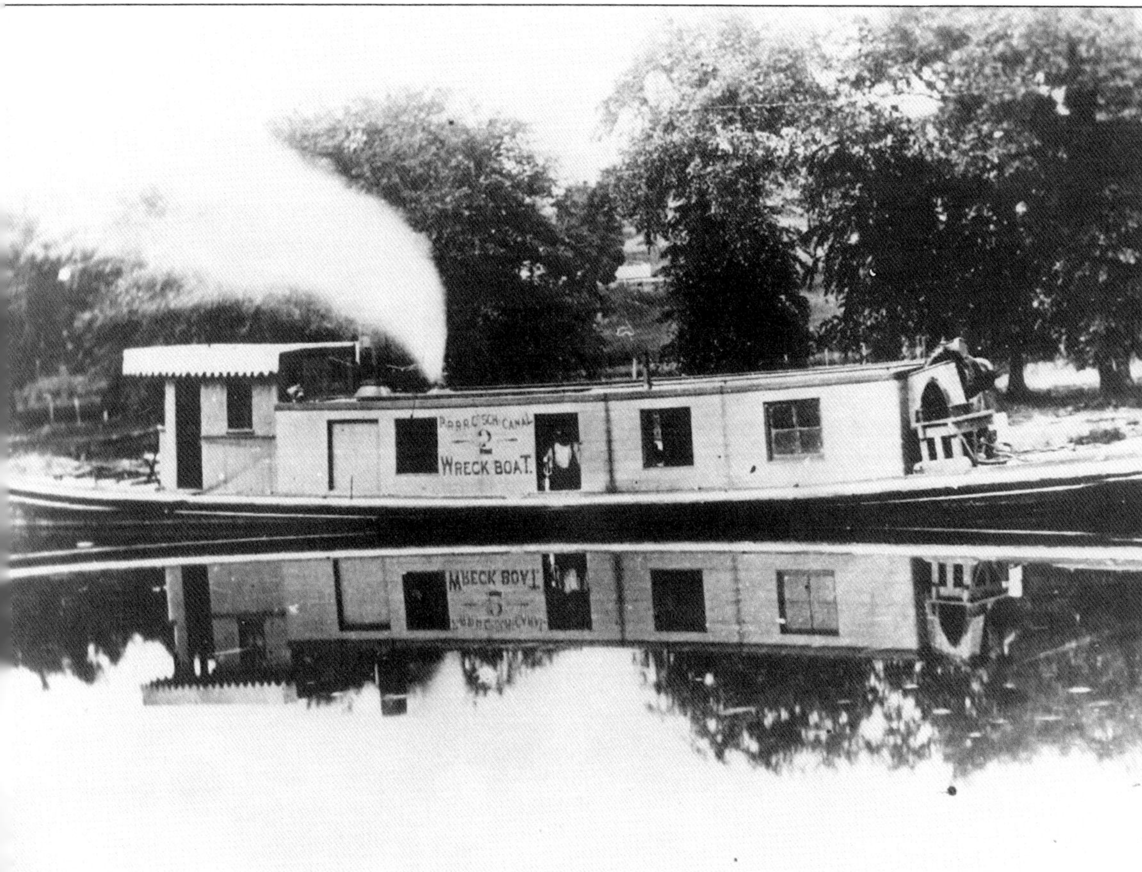

Wreck Boat No. 2 on the Schuylkill Canal. From 1815 until 1825, the Schuylkill Navigation Canal Company developed and constructed a water route from the anthracite coal fields in northern Schuylkill County through the Blue Mountain barrier. In 1870, the Philadelphia and Reading Railroad Company signed a long-term lease for the Schuylkill Navigation Company's holdings.

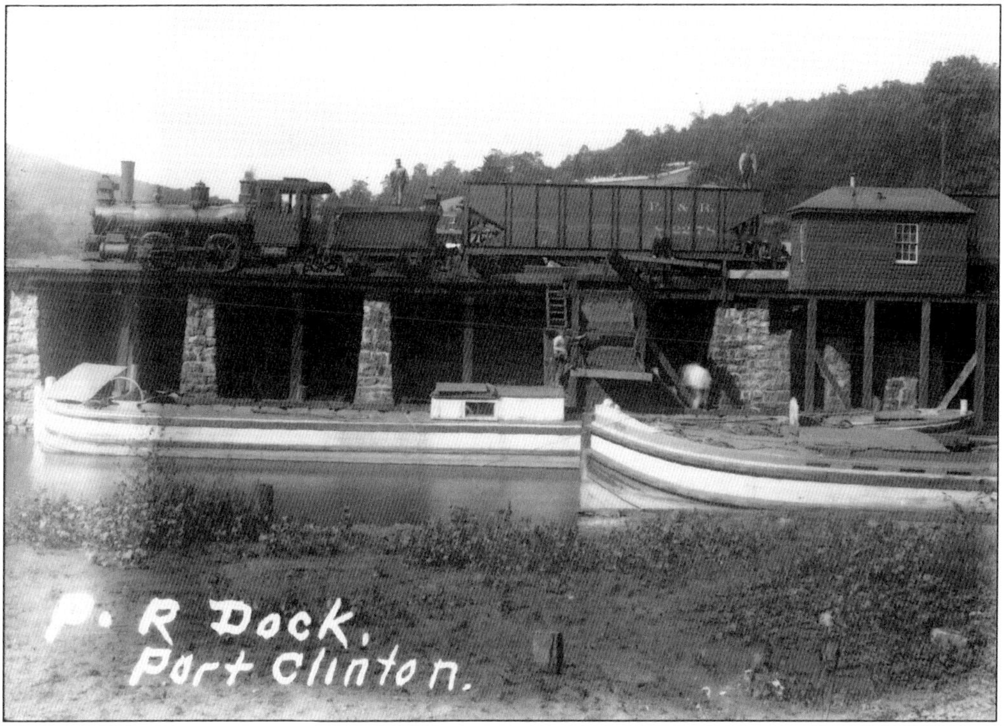

The Philadelphia and Reading Railroad dock in Port Clinton, *c.* 1905. This unusual photograph shows coal being loaded onto the canal boats from the coal cars.

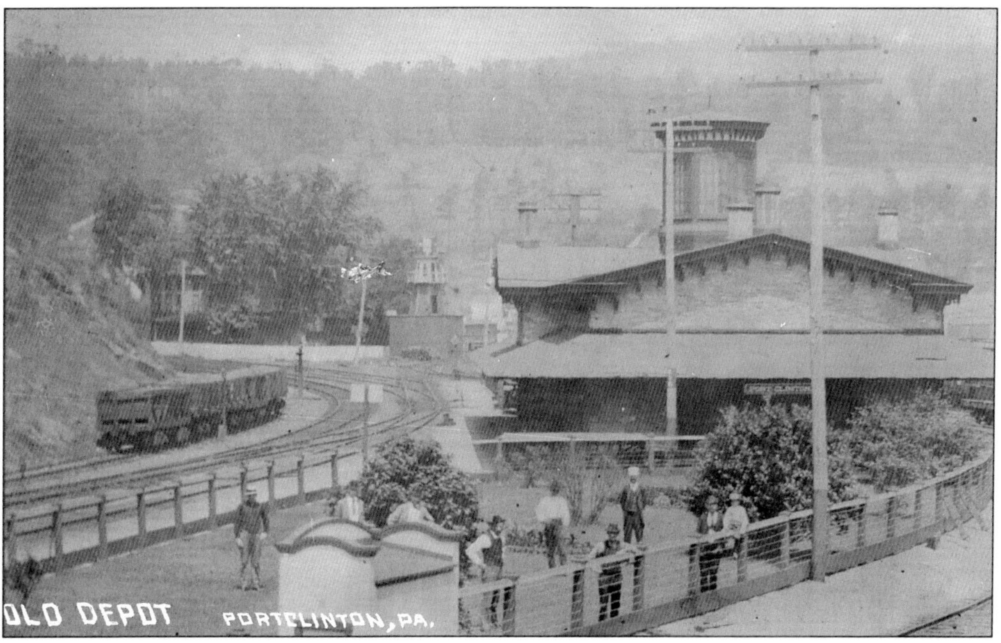

The old train depot in Port Clinton.

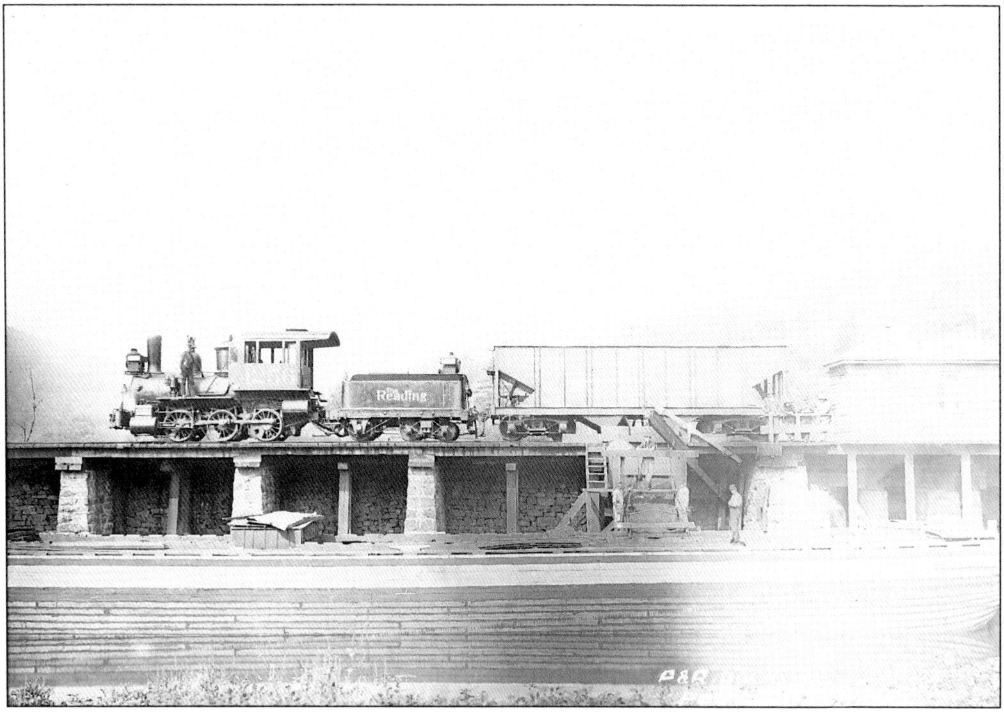

Engine No. 1256 at the loading chutes in Port Clinton. Coal fields were serviced by the Little Schuylkill Railroad, which terminated at the loading pens in Port Clinton.

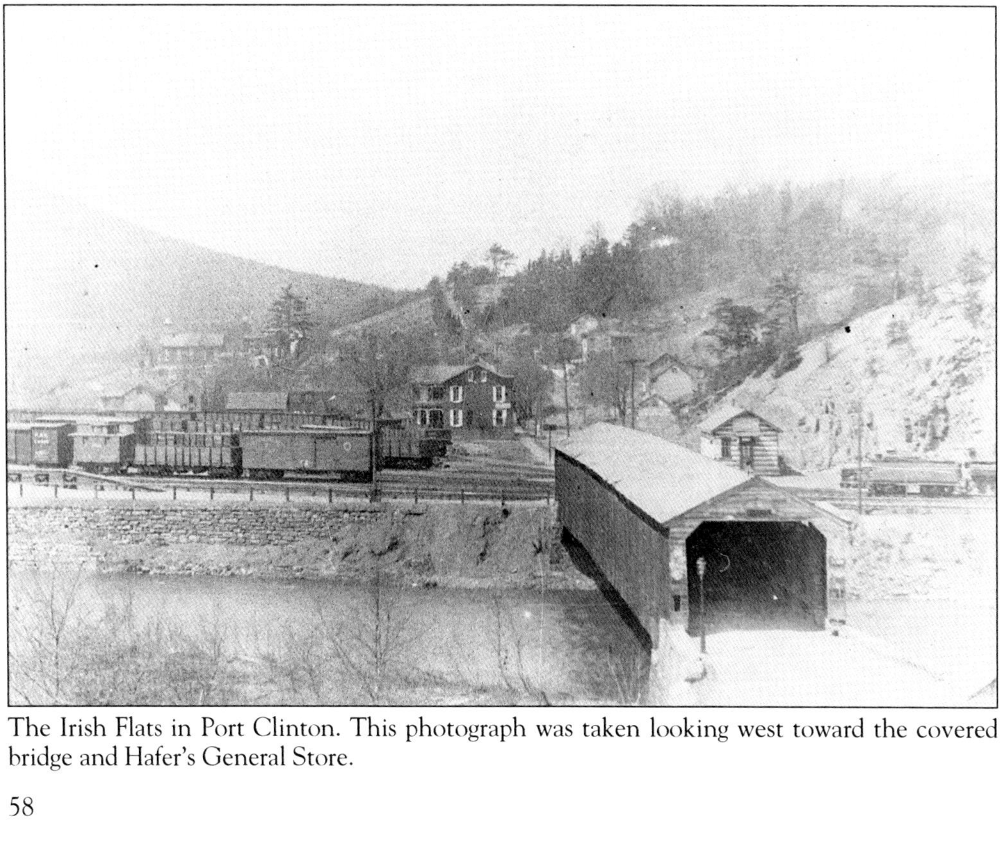
The Irish Flats in Port Clinton. This photograph was taken looking west toward the covered bridge and Hafer's General Store.

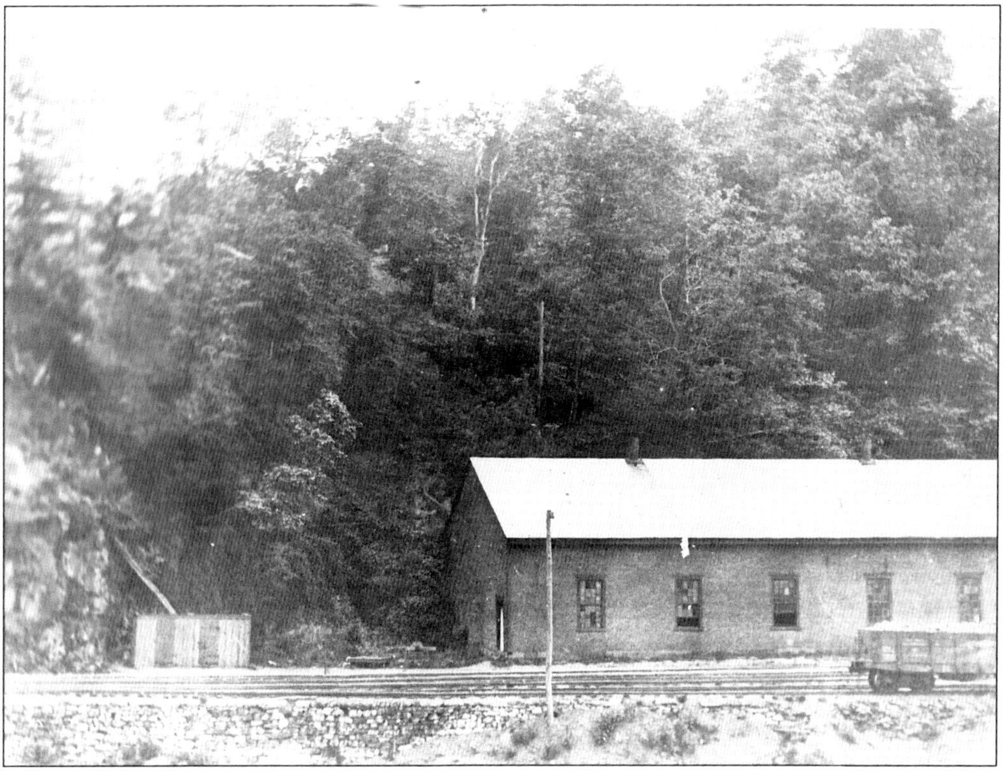

The engine works and turntable on the Little Schuylkill River. This image was photographed behind the schoolhouse in Port Clinton.

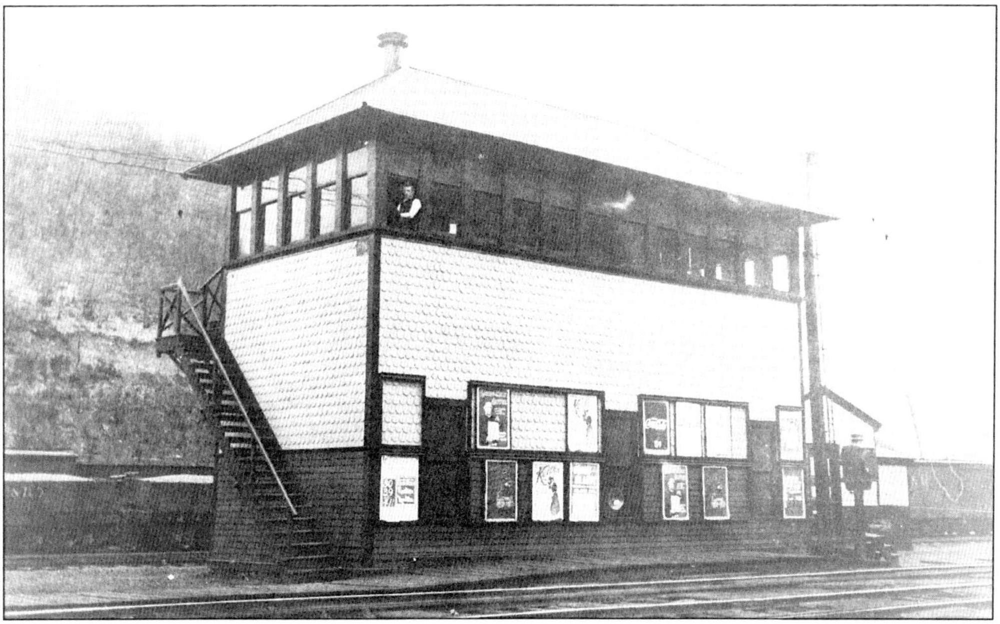

The Philadelphia and Reading Railroad tower in Port Clinton. In 1842, the Philadelphia and Reading Railroad passed through the Gap and the town of Port Clinton on its way to the Pottsville coal fields. Note the interesting advertising posters on the side of this structure.

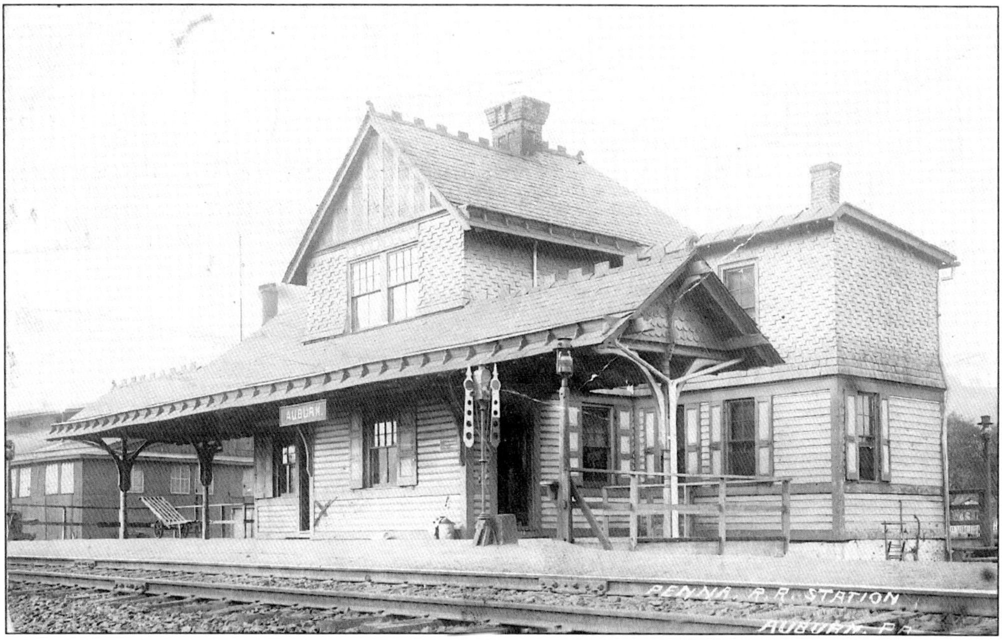

The Pennsylvania Railroad Station in Auburn. The Schuylkill Valley Division of the Pennsylvania Railroad was completed on July 6, 1886.

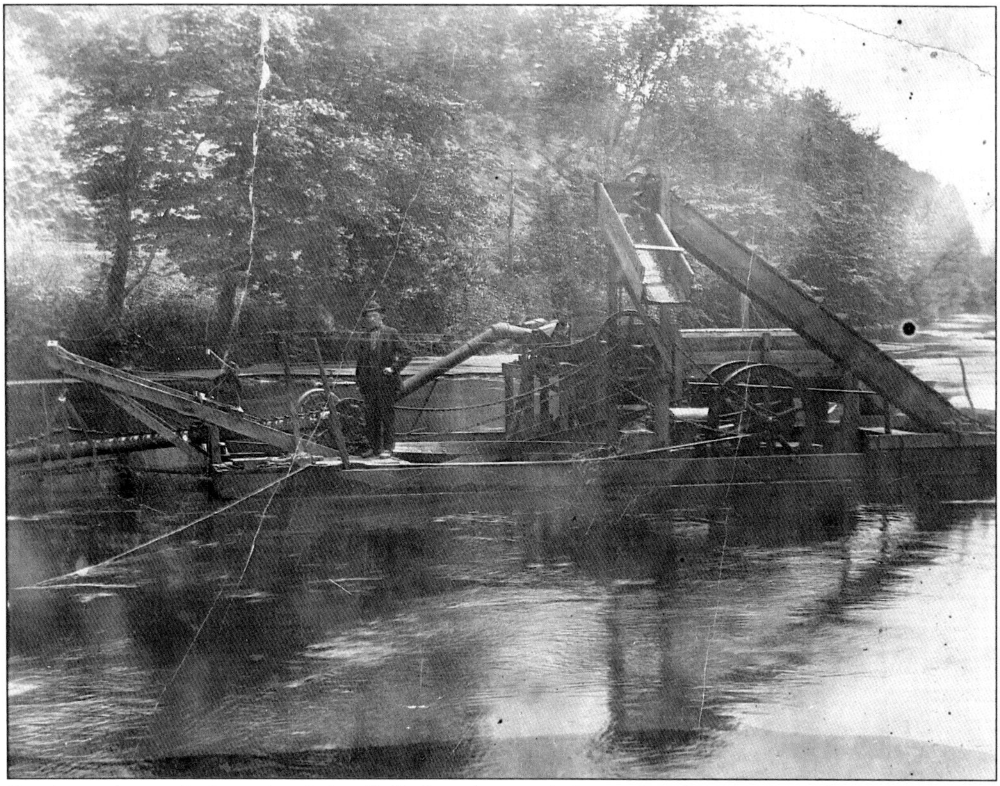

Dredging for coal along the Schuylkill Canal near Auburn. Dredges were used to remove coal and other obstructions within the canals.

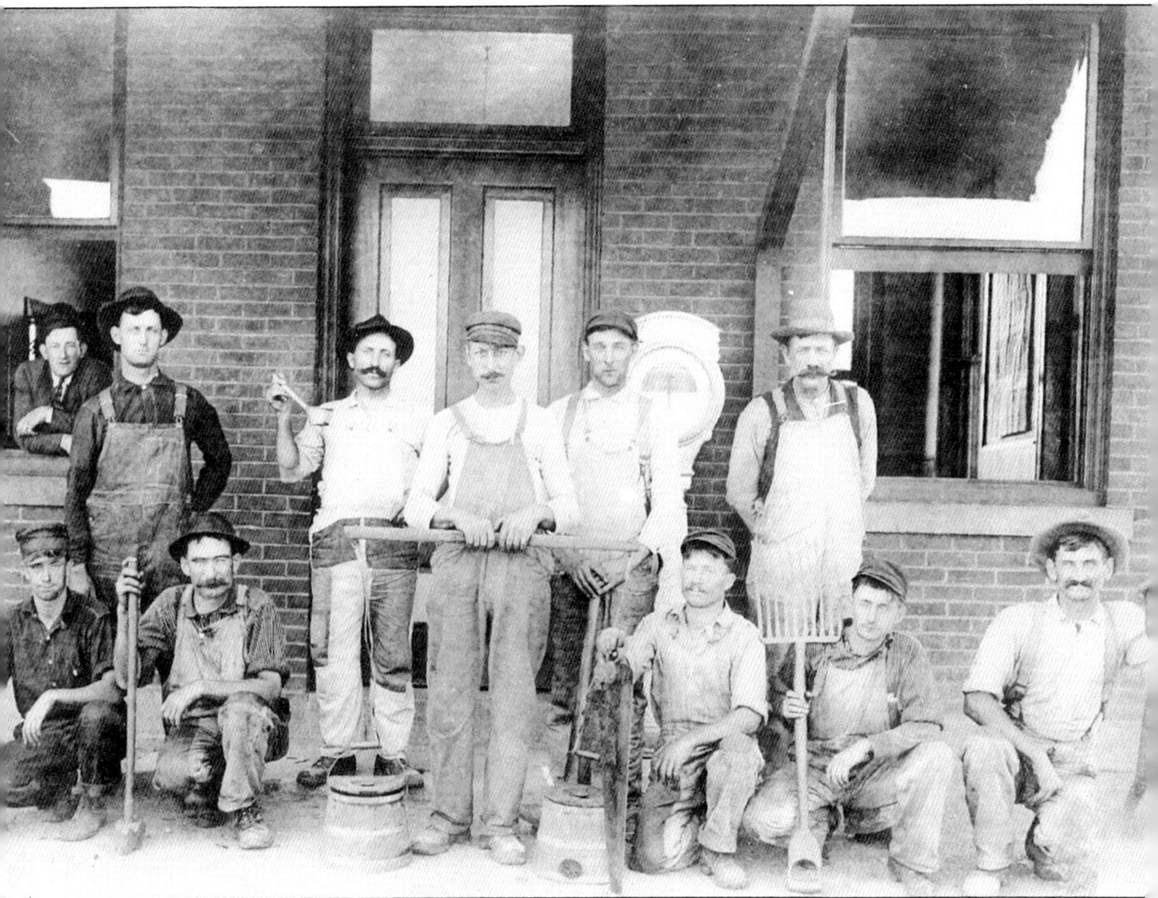

A Reading Railroad crew at the Auburn station. This photograph was taken during the 1920s and includes the following gentlemen: (kneeling) Walter Brensinger, Harry Miller, Blossie Long, Olin Eckart, and William Petry; (standing) Charles (the agent), Will Wenrich, Andy Santella, Charles Leonard, Daniel Metz, and Henry Long.

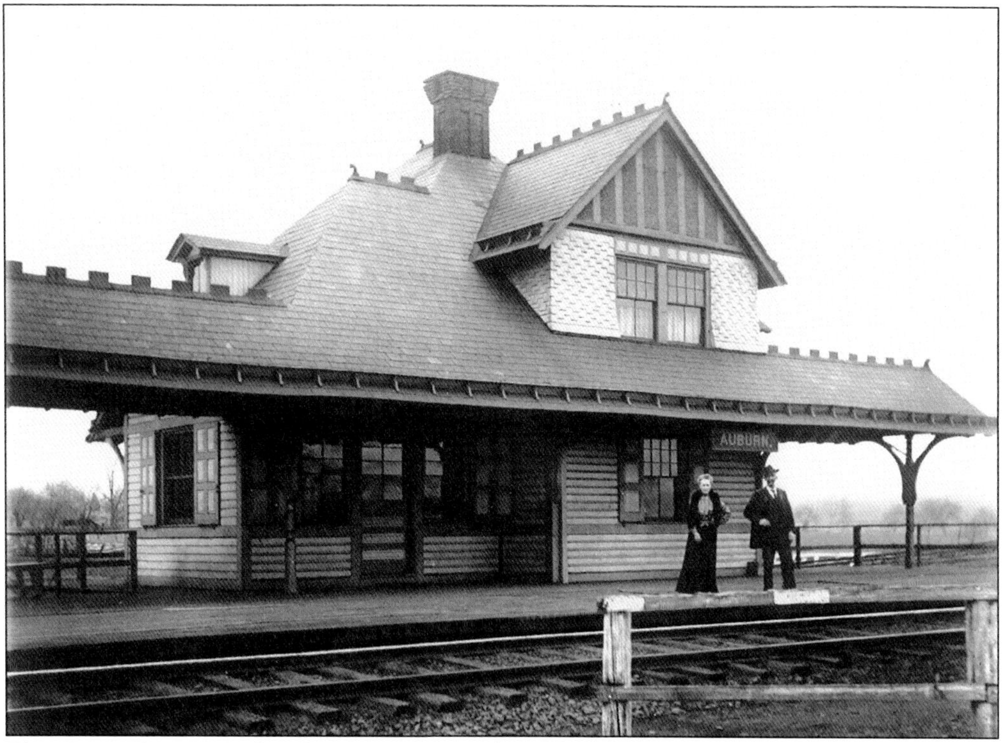

The Pennsylvania Railroad Station in Auburn. Due to the introduction of railroads, the population in Auburn increased dramatically. The Schuylkill Valley Division of the Pennsylvania Railroad was completed on July 6, 1886.

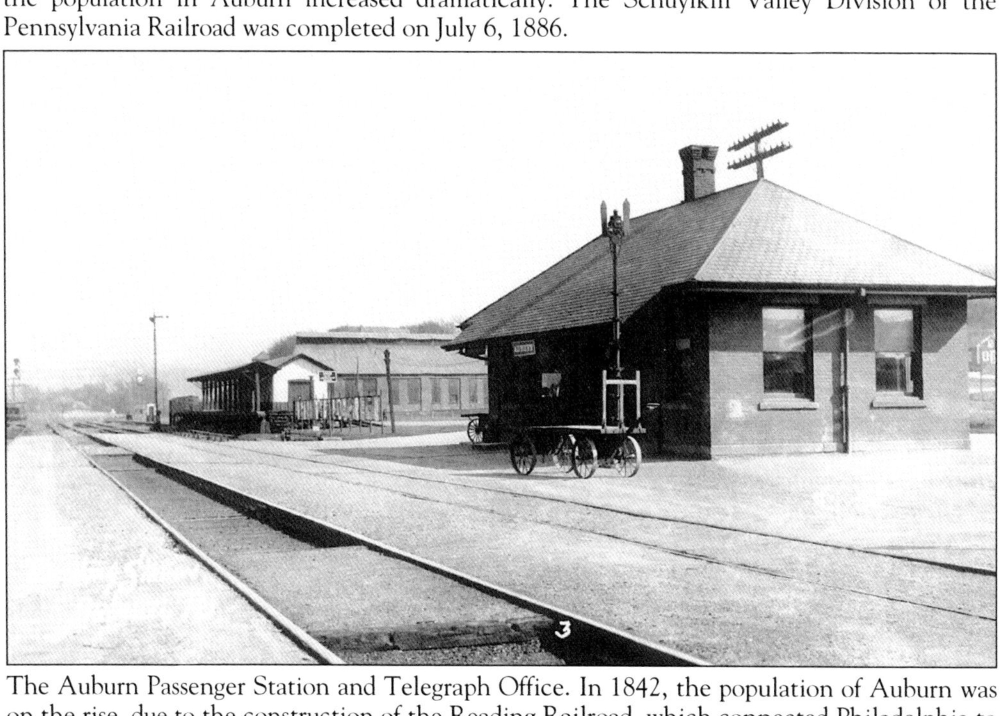

The Auburn Passenger Station and Telegraph Office. In 1842, the population of Auburn was on the rise, due to the construction of the Reading Railroad, which connected Philadelphia to Pottsville. In 1857, Auburn was incorporated as a borough.

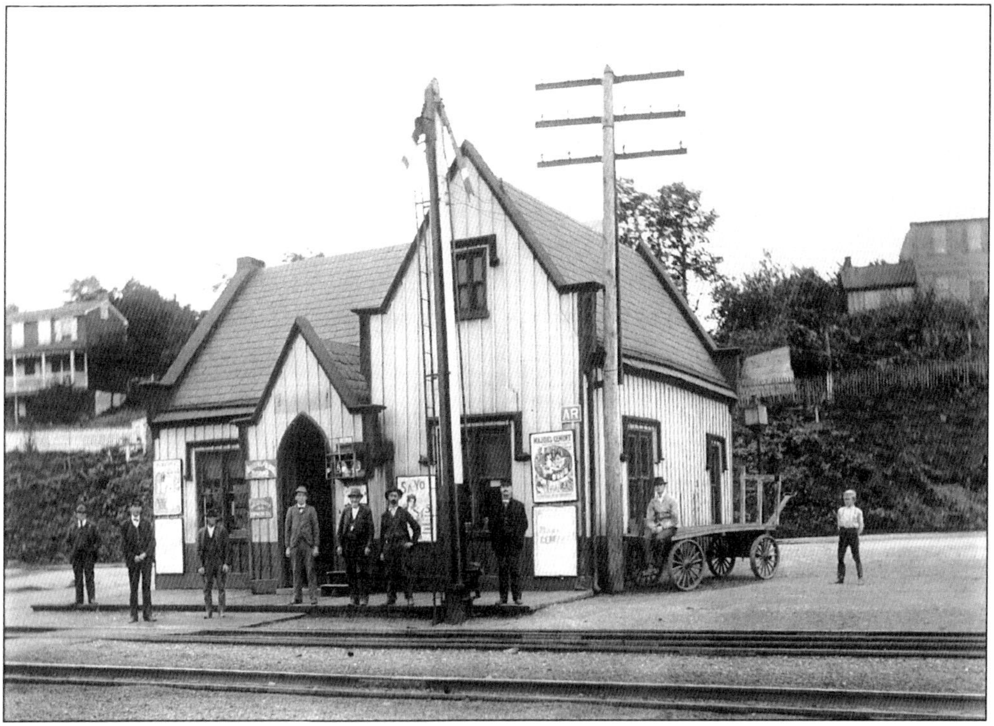

The Schuylkill and Susquehanna Railroad Station in Auburn. The Schuylkill and Susquehanna Railroad, built in 1854, connected Auburn with Pine Grove and Harrisburg. This station was Auburn's first.

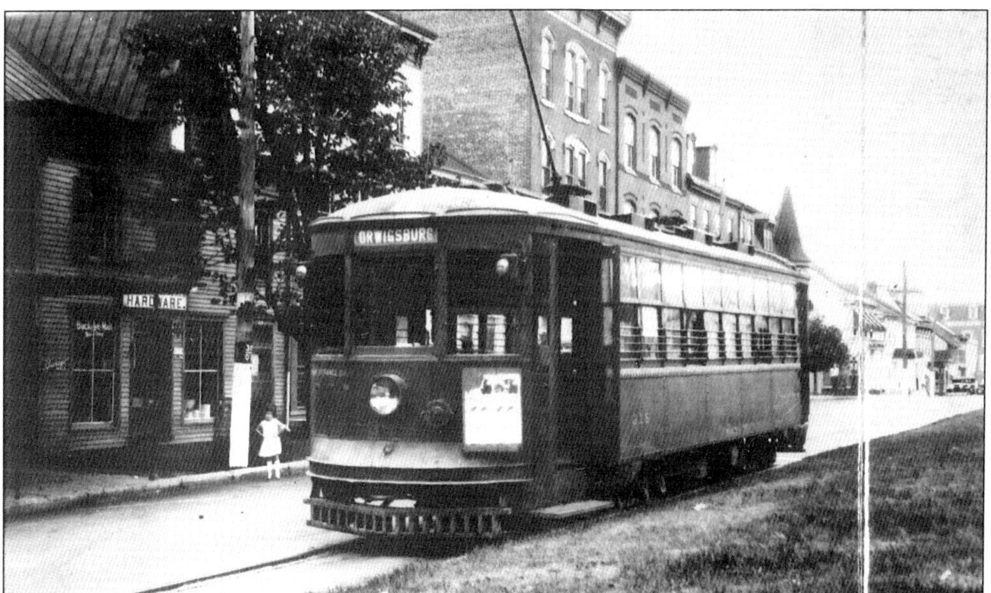

The No. 315 trolley on Center Square in Orwigsburg. This image was taken on September 7, 1930, the last day of operation.

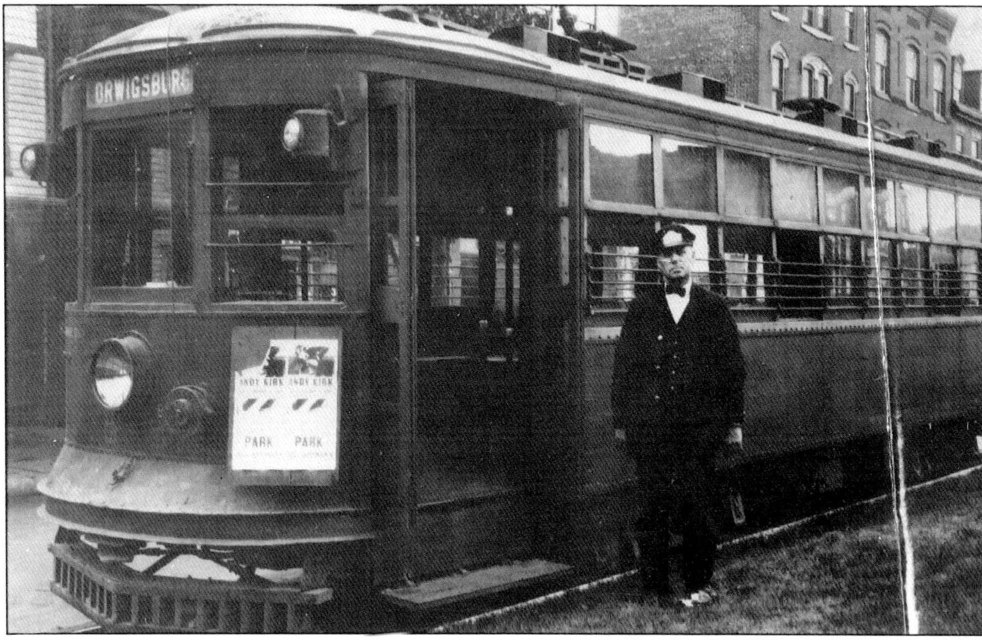

A trolley that had stopped along Center Square in front of the Arcadian Hotel, which was the end of the circuit in Orwigsburg, 1930. The system never extended to the end of East Market Street.

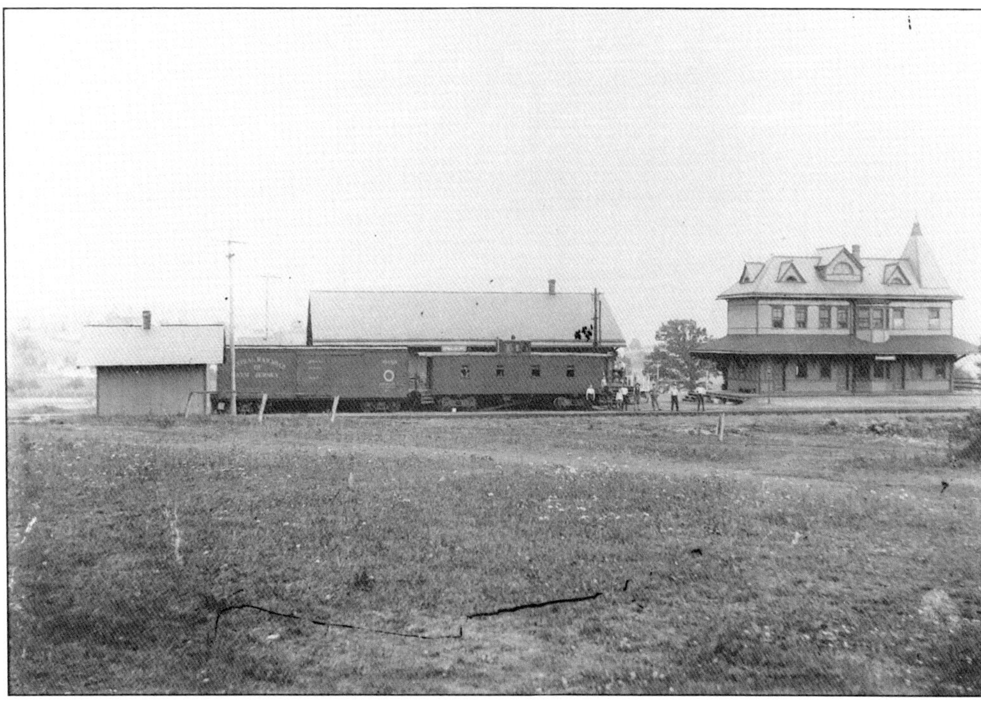
The Lehigh Valley Train Station in Orwigsburg. In 1890, the Lehigh Valley Railroad opened its Lizard Creek branch, the first railway leading into Orwigsburg. Passenger service, however, was never outstanding and eventually ended in 1925. The last freight run took place in April of 1953. This structure was one of the Lehigh Valley Railroad's most ornate stations.

Four

Business and Industry

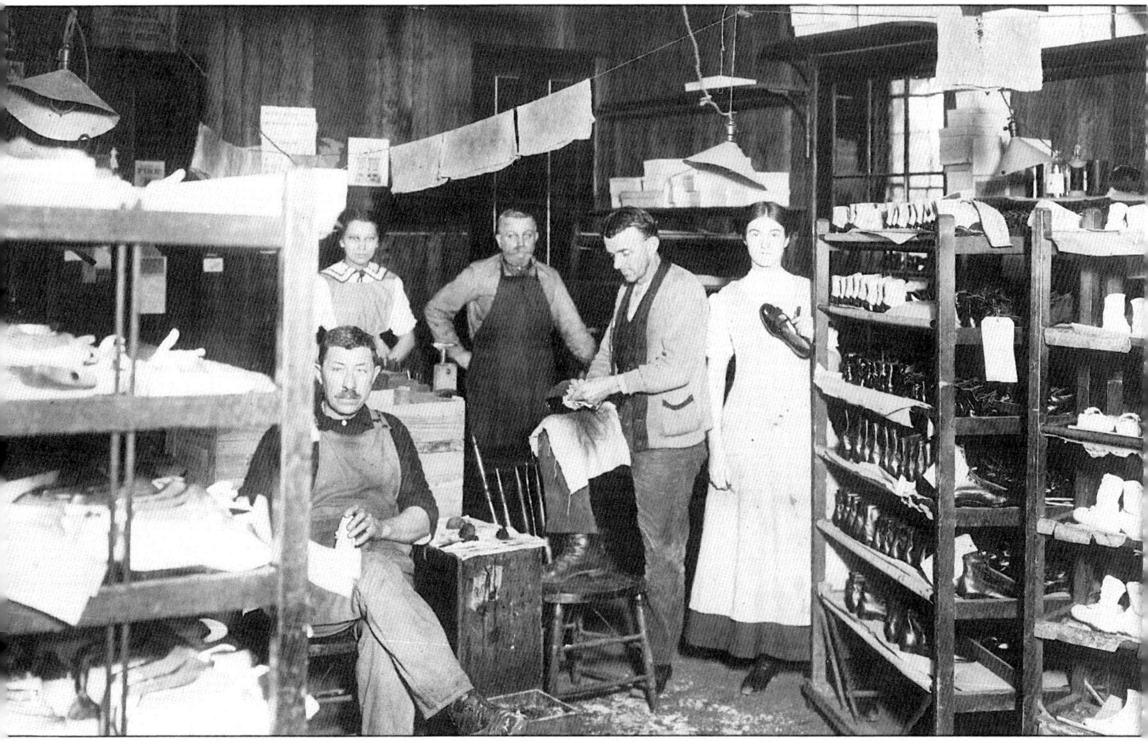

The interior of a typical shoe factory in Orwigsburg. Orwigsburg's step into the age of industrialism began with the development of the shoe-manufacturing industry. After the establishment of the Orwigsburg Shoe Manufacturing Company in 1873, many others quickly formed and prospered throughout the late 1800s and early 1900s. In addition, knitting mills and cigar manufacturing also contributed to Orwigsburg's economy during this time.

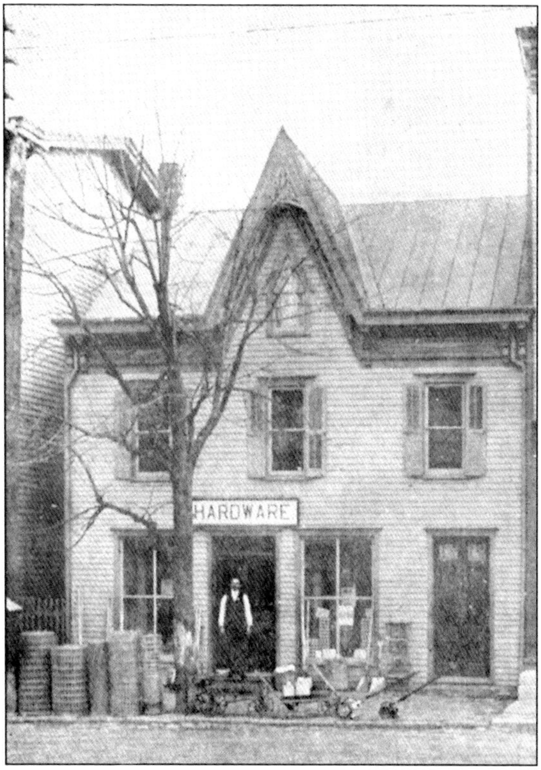

Adams Hardware Store in Orwigsburg, c. 1913. John Adams opened his hardware store on Centre Square around 1910. Years later his son Chester took over the business and moved the store to East Market Street.

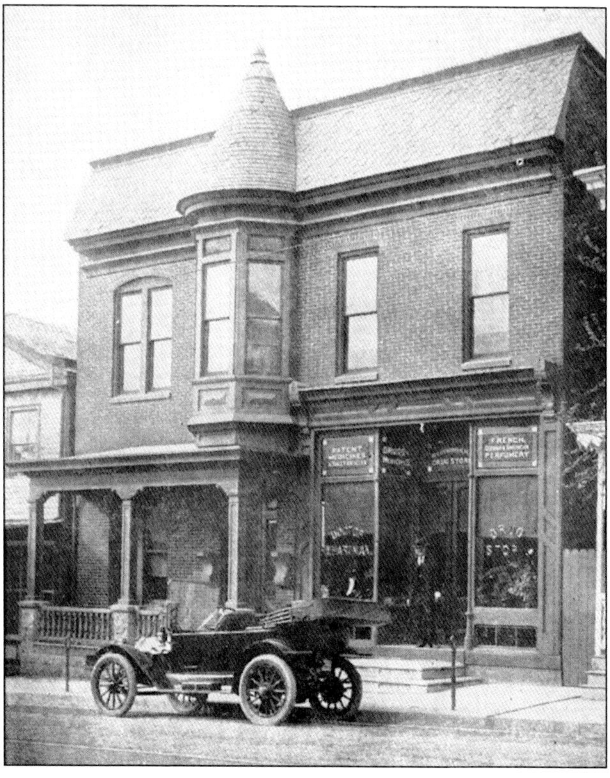

The residence and pharmacy of Dr. H.Y. Hartman in Orwigsburg, c. 1913. Dr. Hartman operated a successful medical practice, as well as a pharmacy on West Market Street. It was common at that time for doctors to prepare their own remedies and to own and operate the local drugstore.

The S.R. Kepner Cigar Store, c. 1913. Well into the early 1900s, cigar manufacturing was big business in Orwigsburg. Established in 1883, the cigar factory of S.R. Kepner manufactured a number of well-known brands of cigars. At the height of manufacturing, 35 people were employed and 8,500 cigars were made daily.

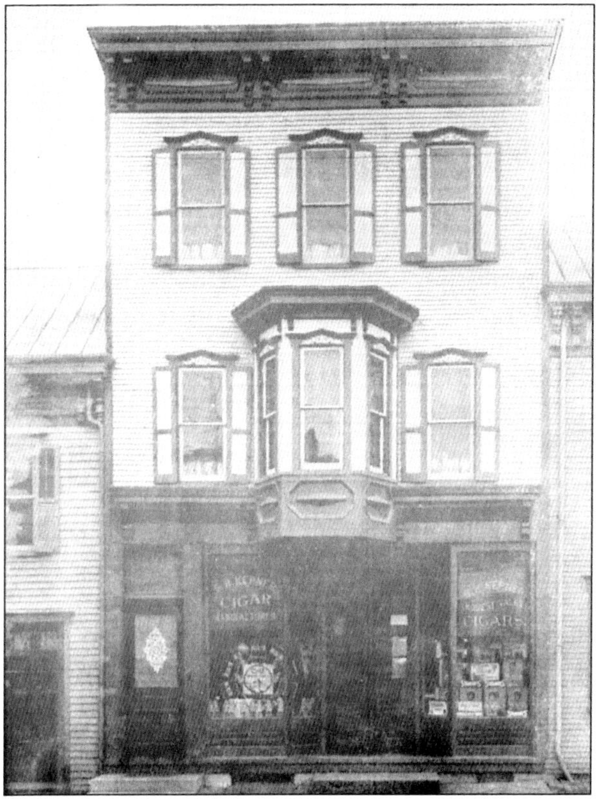

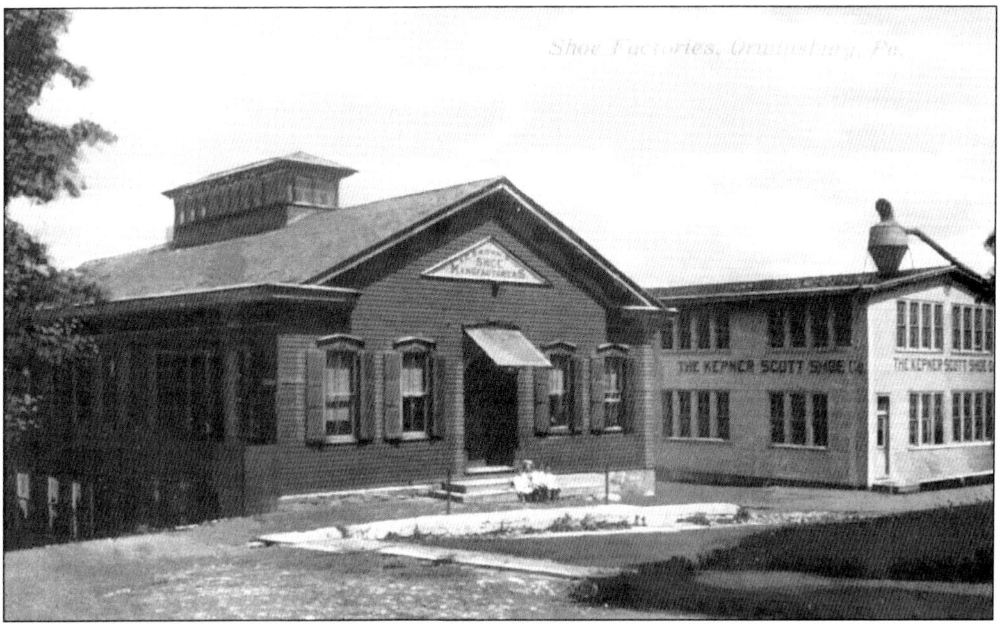

The A.E. Brown and the Kepner Scott shoe manufacturing companies. In 1883, Albert E. Brown created the A.E. Brown Shoe Manufacturing Company in partnership with P.W. Feglay. Shoes from their enterprise were sold all over the country. In 1885, W. Clinton Kepner formed the Kepner Scott Shoe Company in cooperation with the firm Beck, Haeseler and Company.

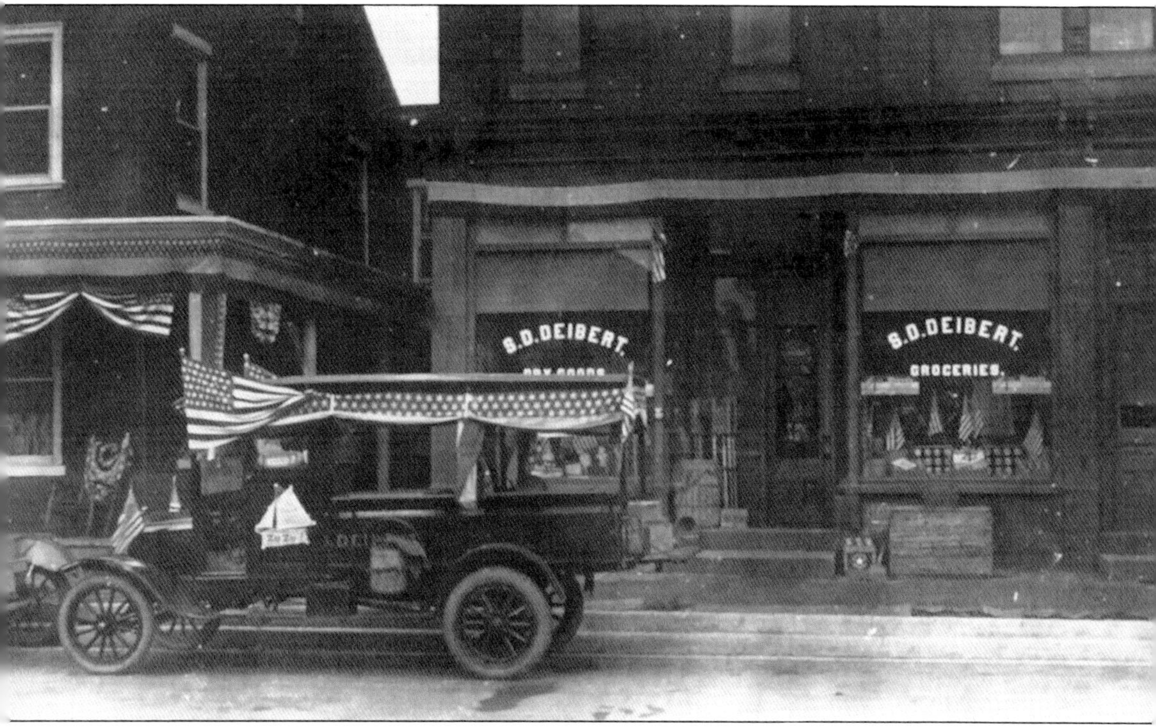

S.D. Deibert Grocery and Dry Goods Store, located on East Market Street in Orwigsburg, c. 1913. Since travel was limited, general stores, such as this one, were very common in towns throughout Schuylkill County.

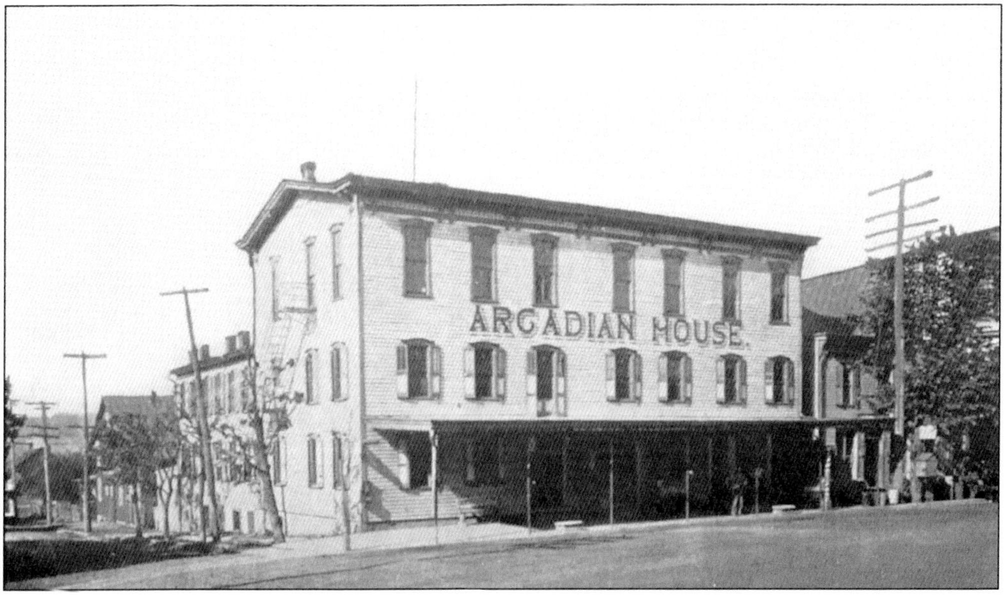

The Arcadian House in Orwigsburg, *c.* 1916. Located on the east end of Centre Square, this was Orwigsburg's largest and most popular hotel during the late 1800s and early 1900s. Until recently, this building was the home of the Orwigsburg Public Library.

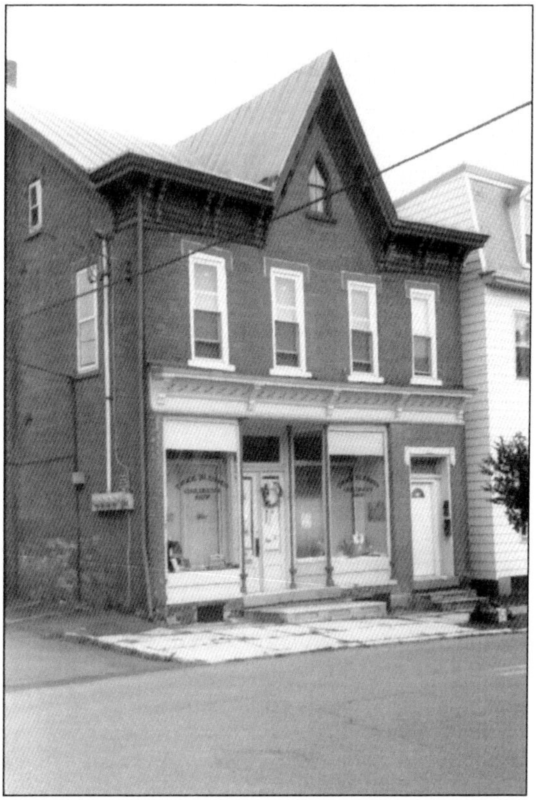

Andrew Heim's general store. This structure has changed very little since it served as a general store in the early 1900s. Located on South Liberty Street in Orwigsburg, it still houses a retail business today.

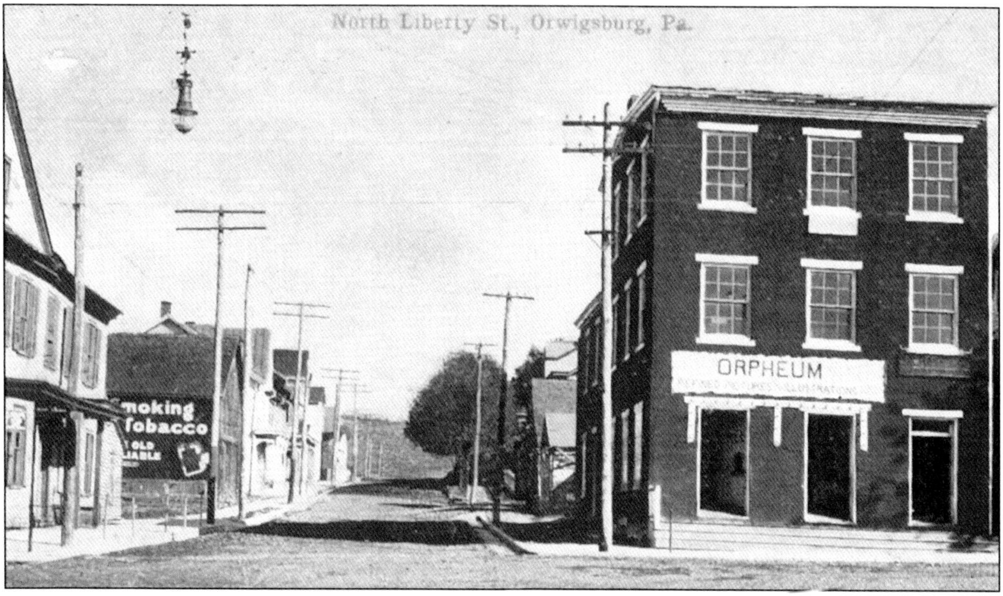

The Orpheum Theatre on North Liberty Street, Orwigsburg. Around 1900, Charles Greenawalt and William Freed started showing motion pictures at this location. In 1912, Arlington Edwards opened his Orpheum Theatre showing *A Fool There Was*, starring Theda Bara. The theater remained a popular entertainment spot for many decades.

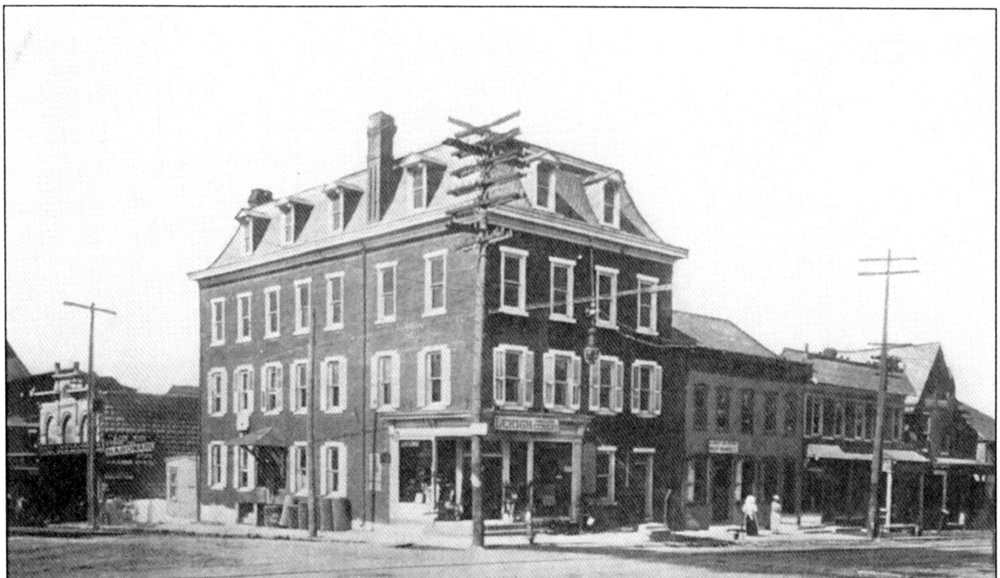

The Odd Fellows' Building, Orwigsburg. Grace Lodge No. 157 was organized March 19, 1846. The building, located at the west end of Centre Square, still stands today and is home to a hair salon.

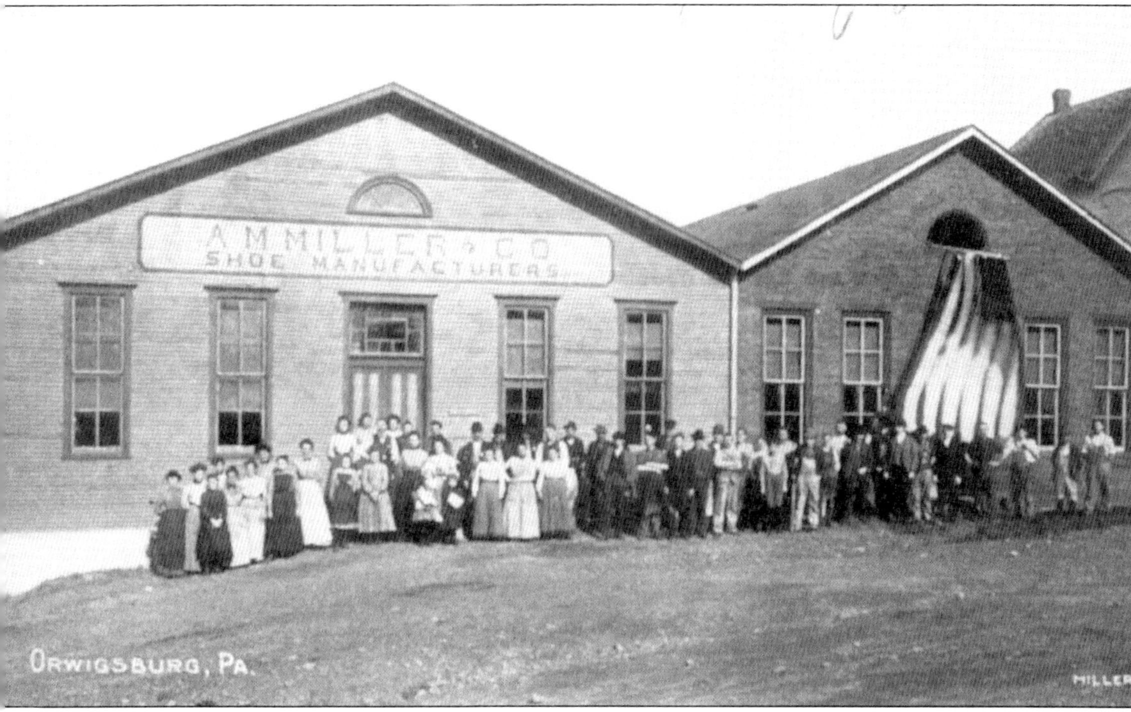

A.M. Miller & Company in Orwigsburg. Established in 1891, this shoe-manufacturing firm made ladies' and children's shoes. In 1913, the business was capable of producing six hundred pairs of shoes daily.

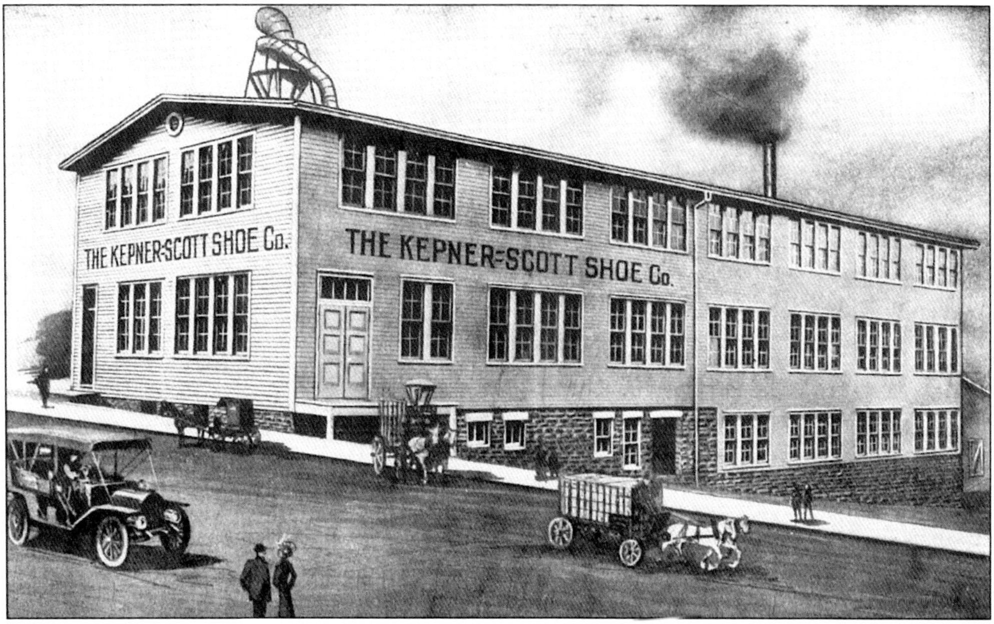

The Kepner Scott Shoe Company, Orwigsburg. In 1885, W. Clinton Kepner formed this company as a partnership. Today, children's shoes are still manufactured under the same name. This sketch shows the factory during the early 1900s.

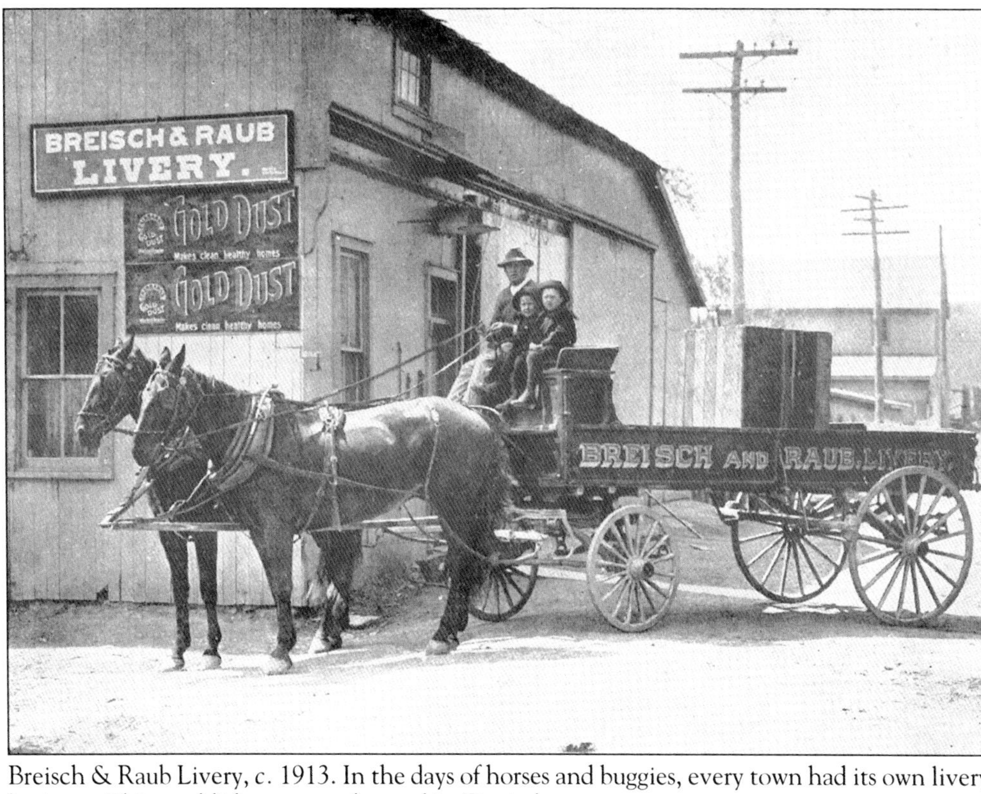

Breisch & Raub Livery, *c.* 1913. In the days of horses and buggies, every town had its own livery business. This establishment was located in Orwigsburg.

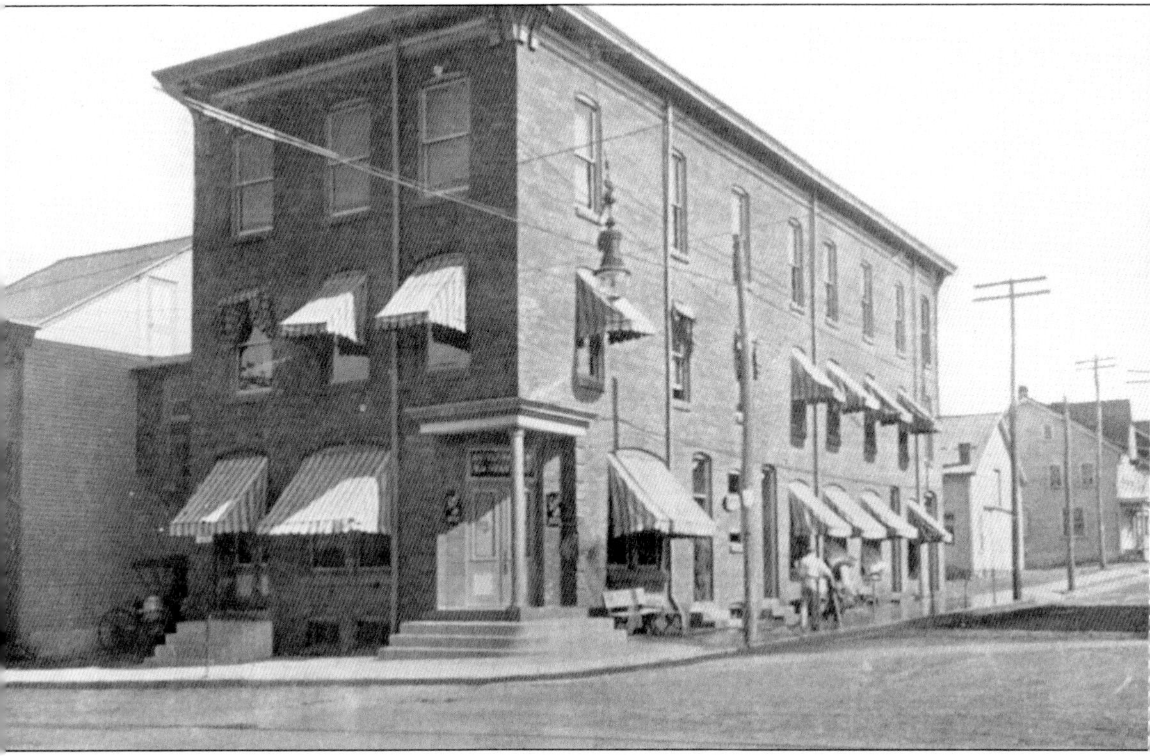

The Harlem Hotel in Orwigsburg, c. 1915. Located on the corner of Liberty and Market Streets, this popular inn and eatery was established in 1892 by D.R. Schall. Changing very little through the years, the structure is still a restaurant and tavern. The daily rate for a night's stay in 1898 was $1.50!

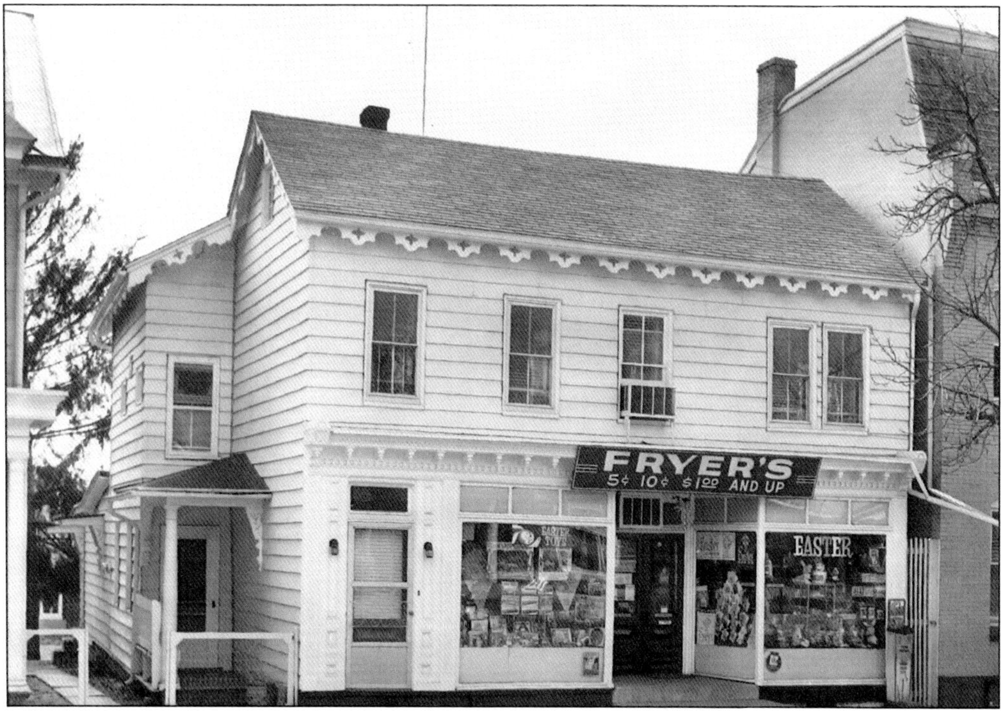

Fryer's 5 & 10, *c.* 1965. Formerly the site of Vost's variety store, this building, located on East Market Street in Orwigsburg, has continually served as a store since the early 1900s. In 1954, it was purchased by George and Esther Fryer and has been owned and operated by the same family ever since.

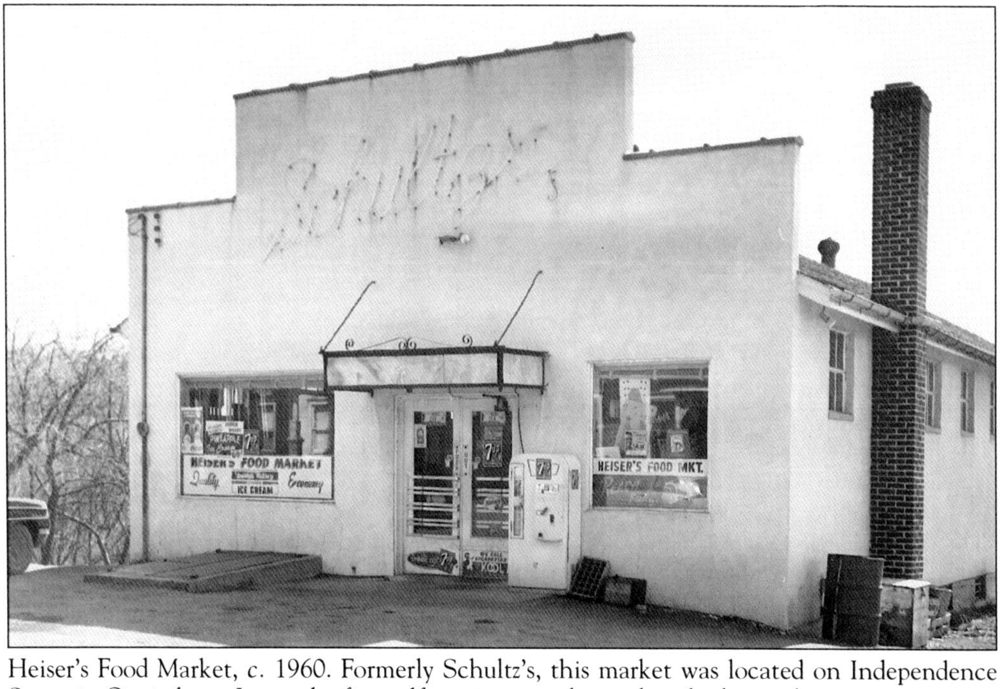

Heiser's Food Market, *c.* 1960. Formerly Schultz's, this market was located on Independence Street in Orwigsburg. It was the first self-service store located in the borough.

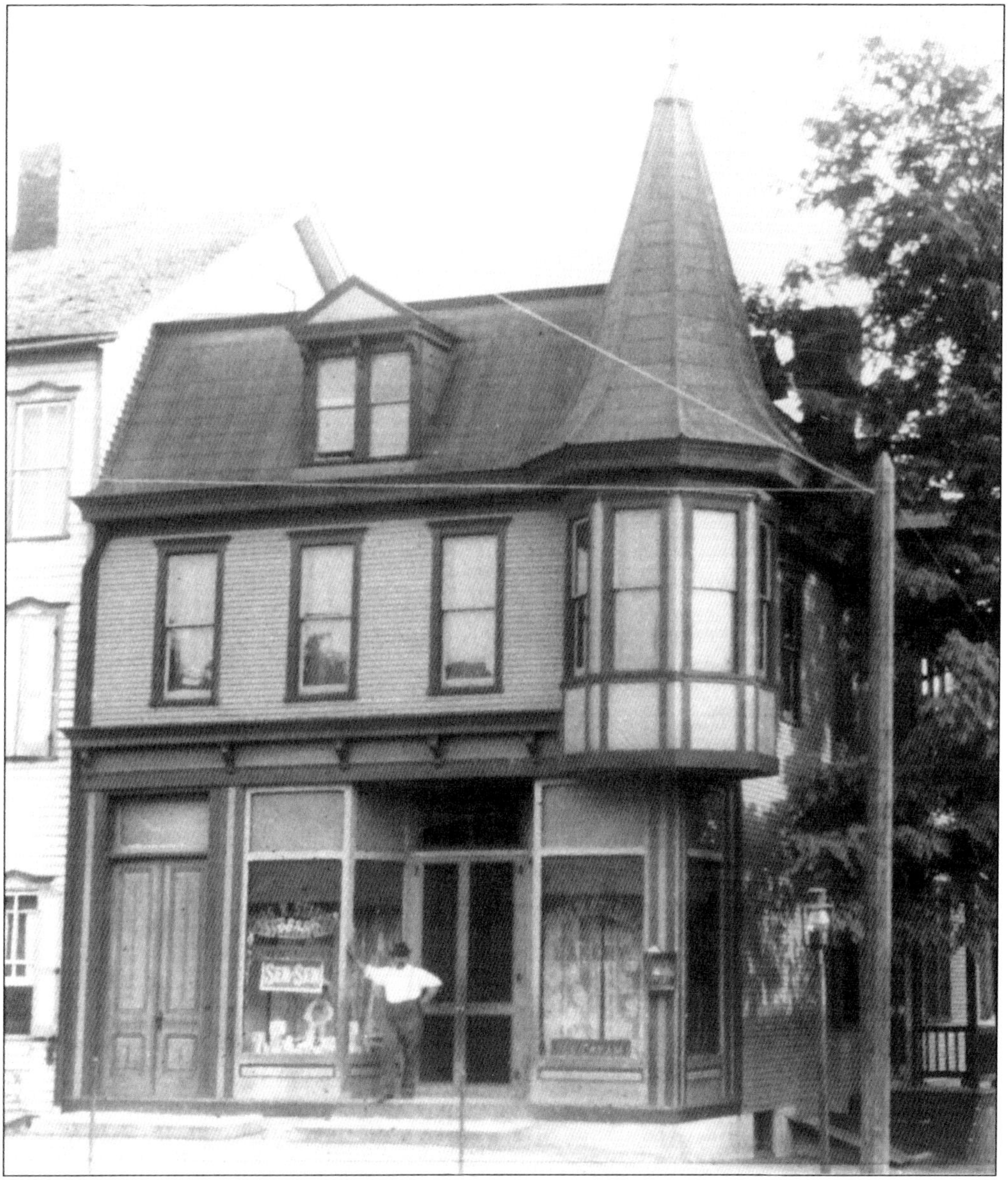

Charles W. Staele, baker and confectioner, c. 1898. This building, located on the corner of Market and Warren Streets, has always been home to some type of retail business. In later years it was owned by Herman G. Miller, who also operated a confectionery business.

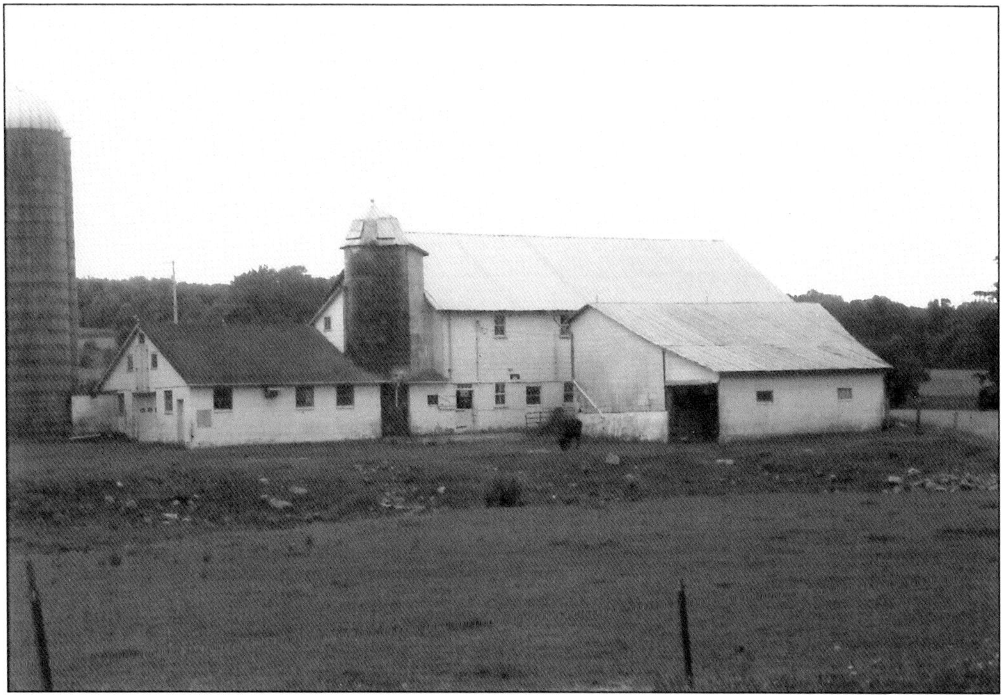

The Kunkle Farm. This landmark farm and cold storage barn was founded by Jonas Kunkle. The farm, which is still a working farm, provided fresh fruits and vegetables throughout the county.

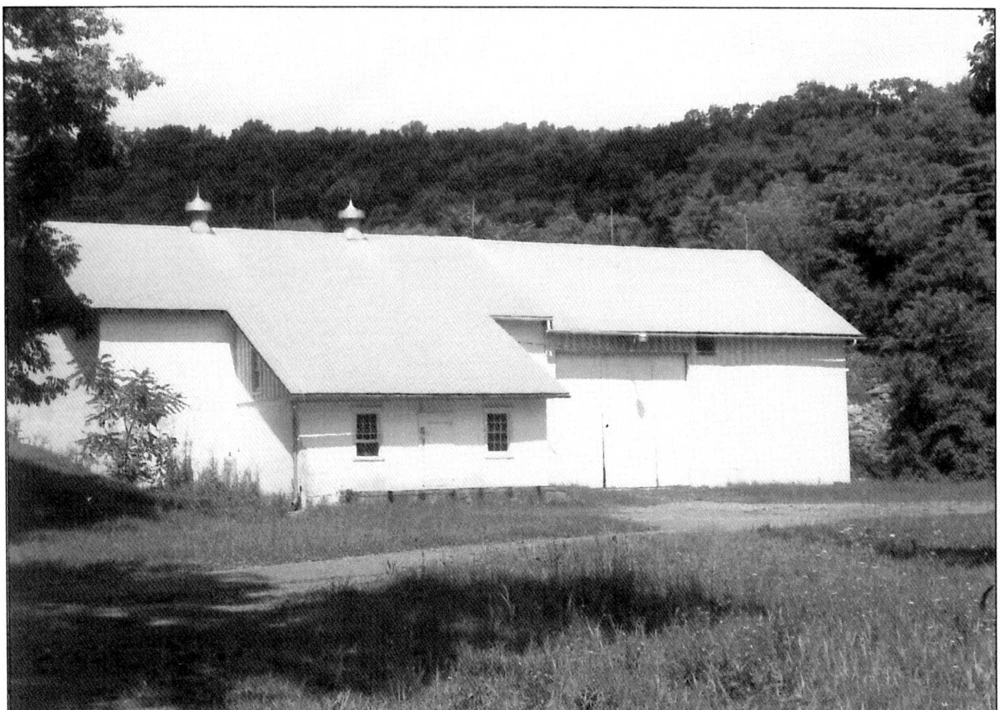

Kunkle's storage plant. Jonas Kunkle built one of the first cold storage plants at Kunkle's Dam near McKeansburg. It was used for storing fruits and vegetables.

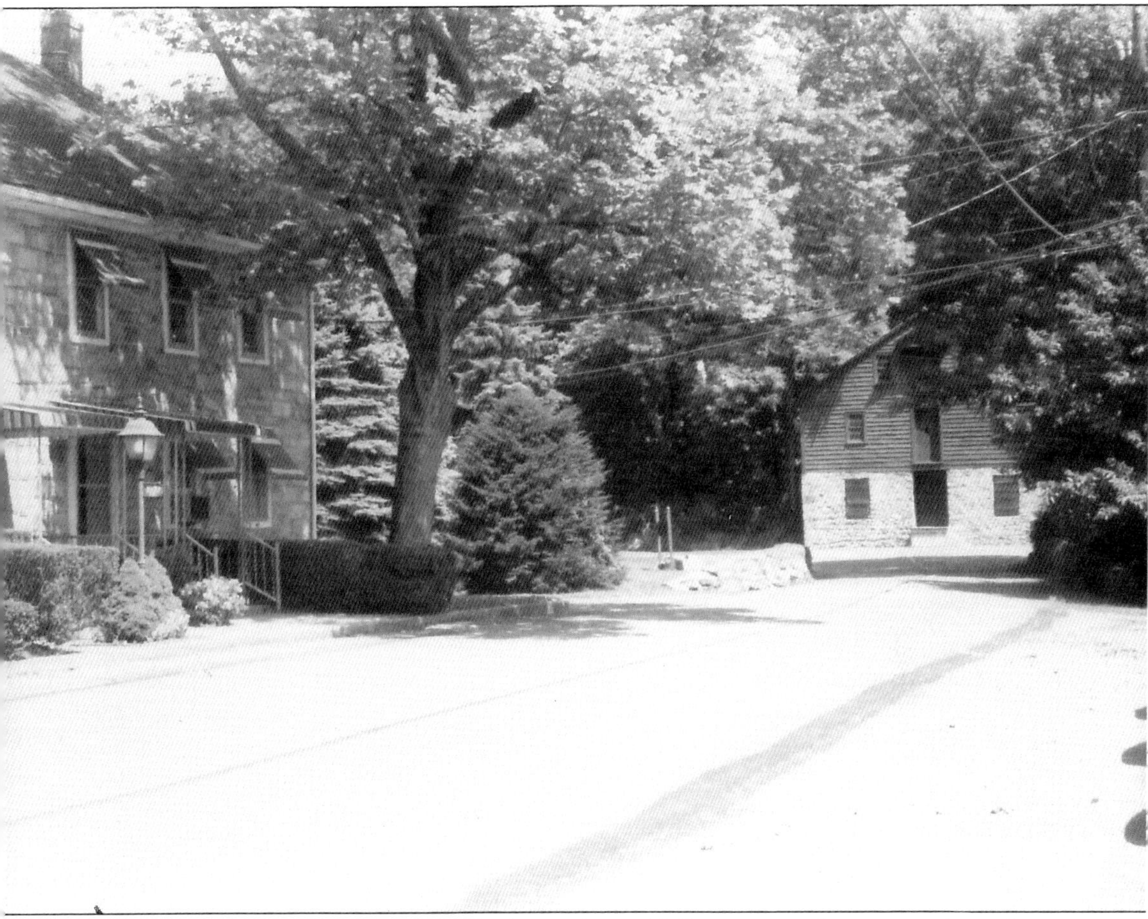

A stagecoach stop near New Ringgold. As early as 1769, stagecoaches stopped on the Catawissa Trail at this hotel and tavern. Today, known as Smith's Country Inn, this original structure still serves as a restaurant and tavern. The old gristmill, which can be seen in the background of this image, was built prior to 1842. Known as Witman's Mill, the facility was in full operation until 1938.

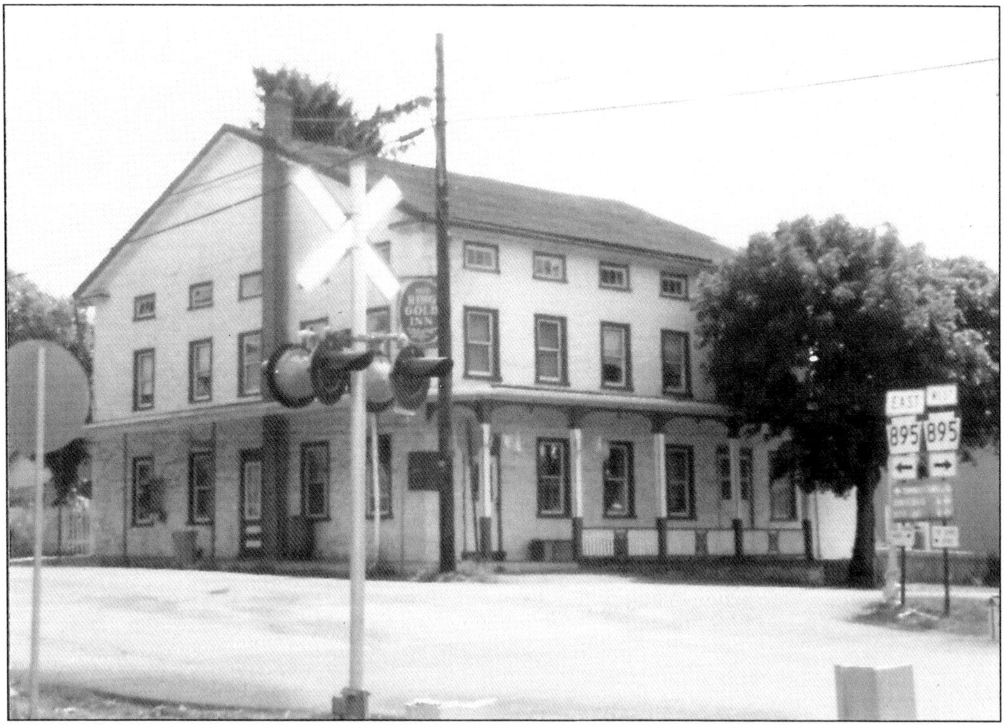

The Ring Gold Inn. This tavern, located in New Ringgold, served as a tavern and rest stop for weary travelers for many years.

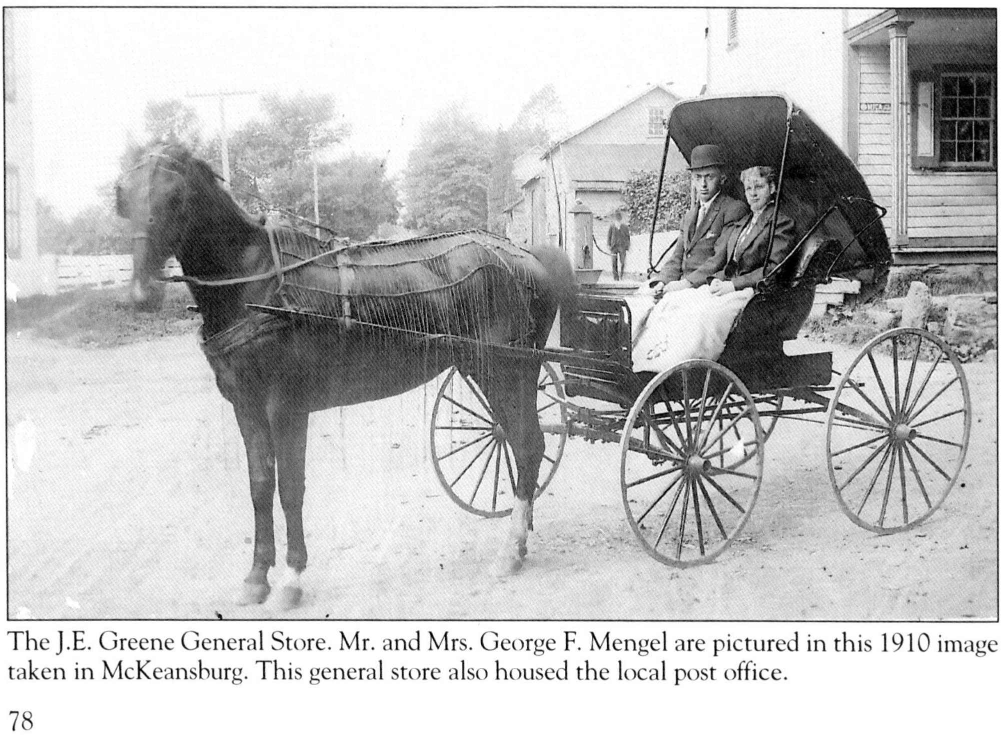

The J.E. Greene General Store. Mr. and Mrs. George F. Mengel are pictured in this 1910 image taken in McKeansburg. This general store also housed the local post office.

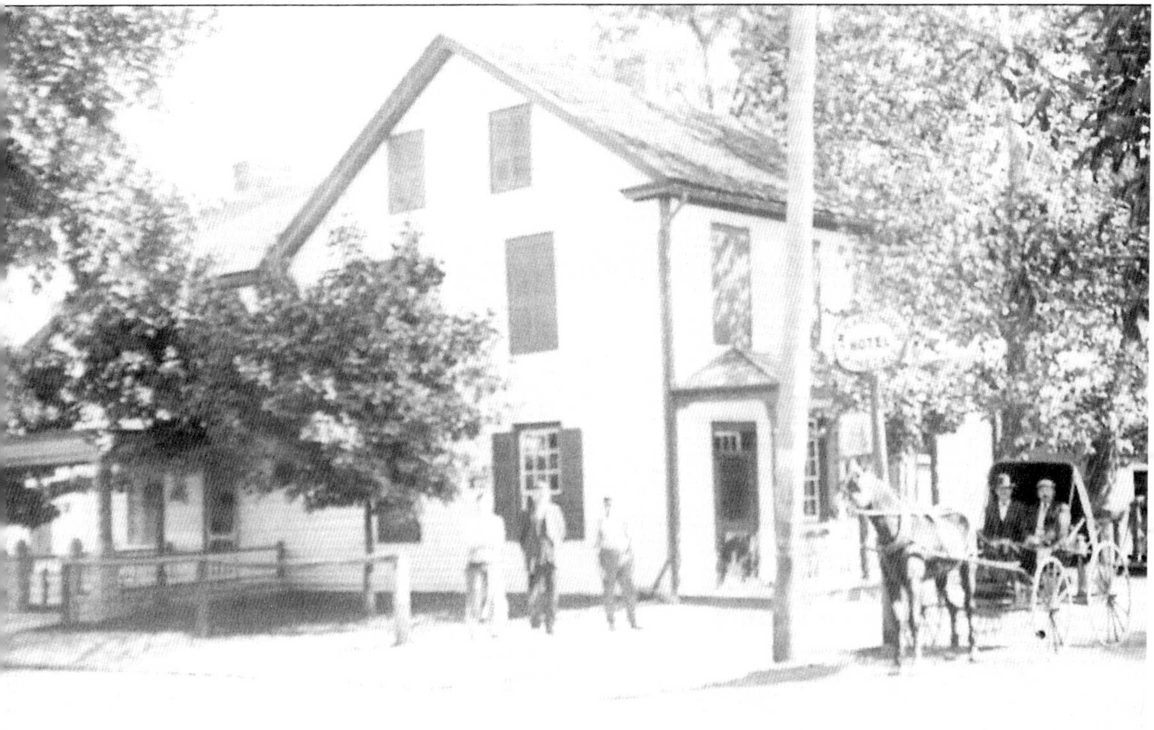

The Pinedale Hotel, Deer Lake, during the late 1900s. The hotel was owned and operated by J.M. Hardinger.

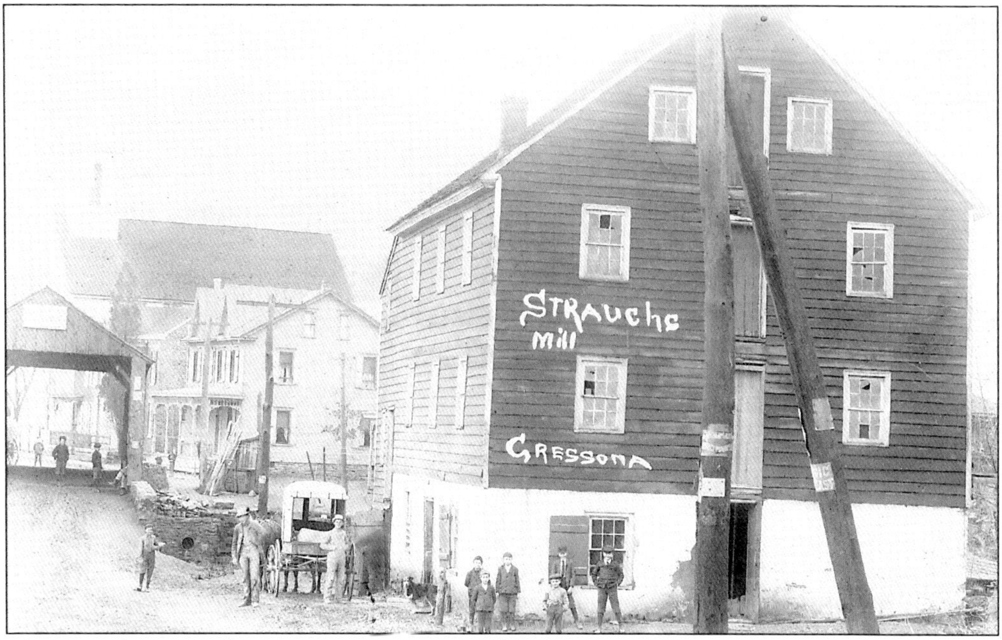

The Strauch Gristmill in Cressona. Isaac Strauch, a boatman on the Schuylkill Canal, built this gristmill, which was operated by four generations until it was eventually sold and torn down in the 1970s. Note the covered bridge over the west branch of the Schuylkill River.

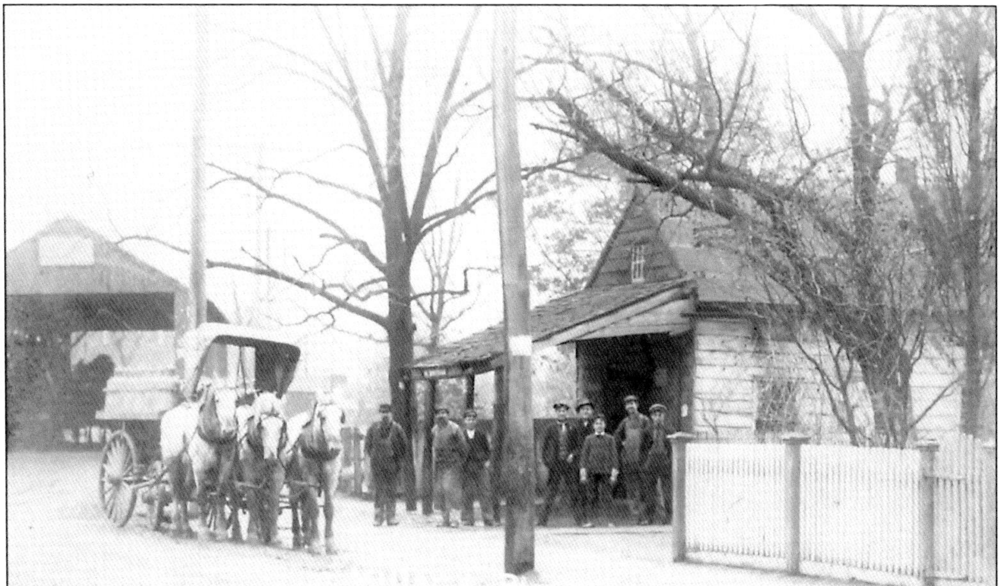

Mayberry's Blacksmith Shop on Pottsville Street in Cressona, c. 1900. This image also shows the covered bridge over the Schuylkill River.

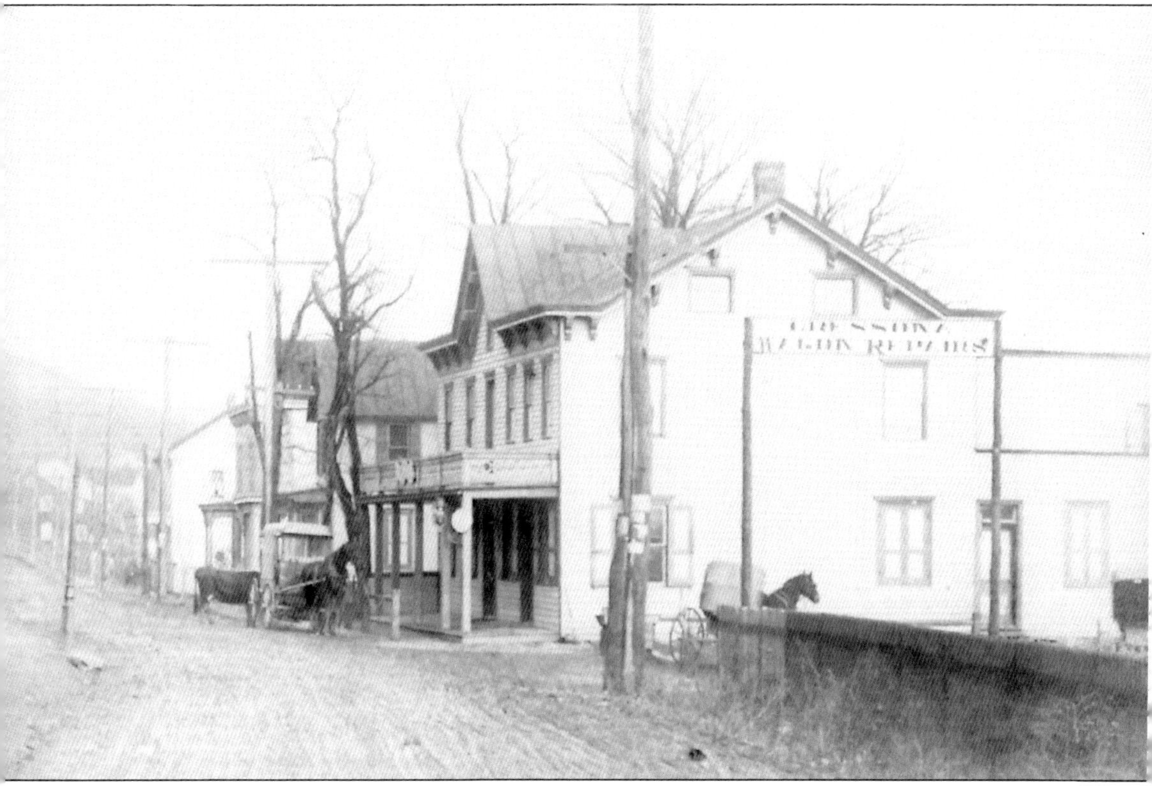

A view of Pottsville Street in Cressona. In earlier years this area was known as Cressona Park; hence the hotel in this image was named the Park Hotel. The hotel had a number of owners and today is operated as a restaurant, the Hubert Inn. Note the Cressona Wagon repair sign also in this photograph.

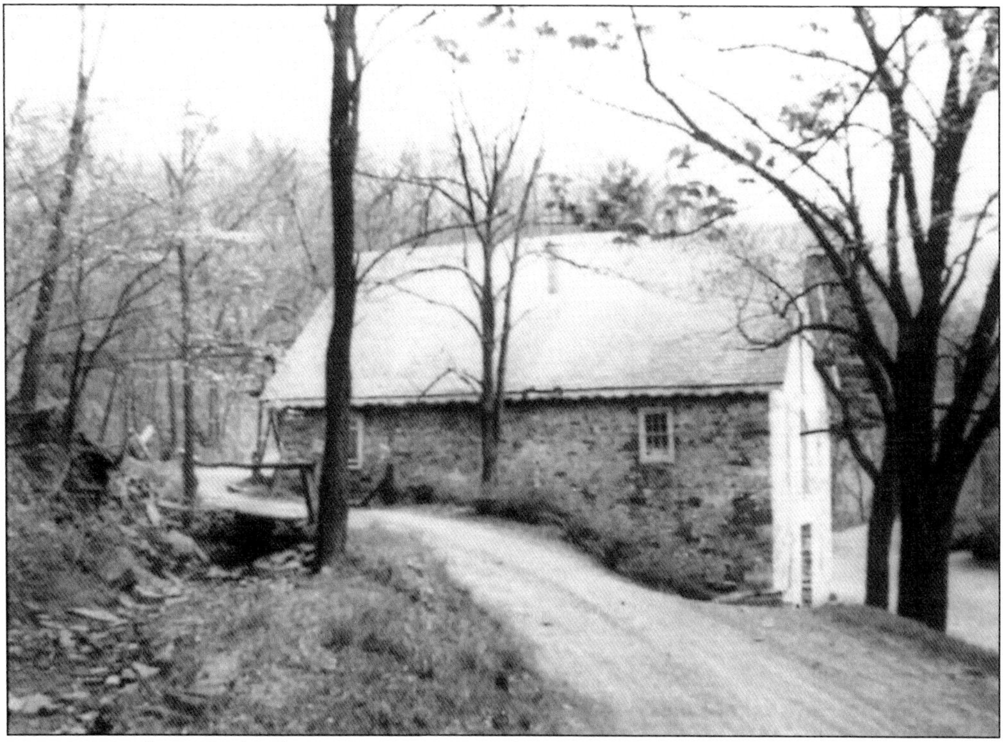

Mengle's Mill in Beckville, near Cressona. The original mill, built in 1820, was run by waterpower and produced cider, flour, and feed. First held by the Beck estate, it was purchased by S.E. Mengle Sr. in 1919 and run by the Mengle family until 1963, when it was sold to the B & M Milling Company.

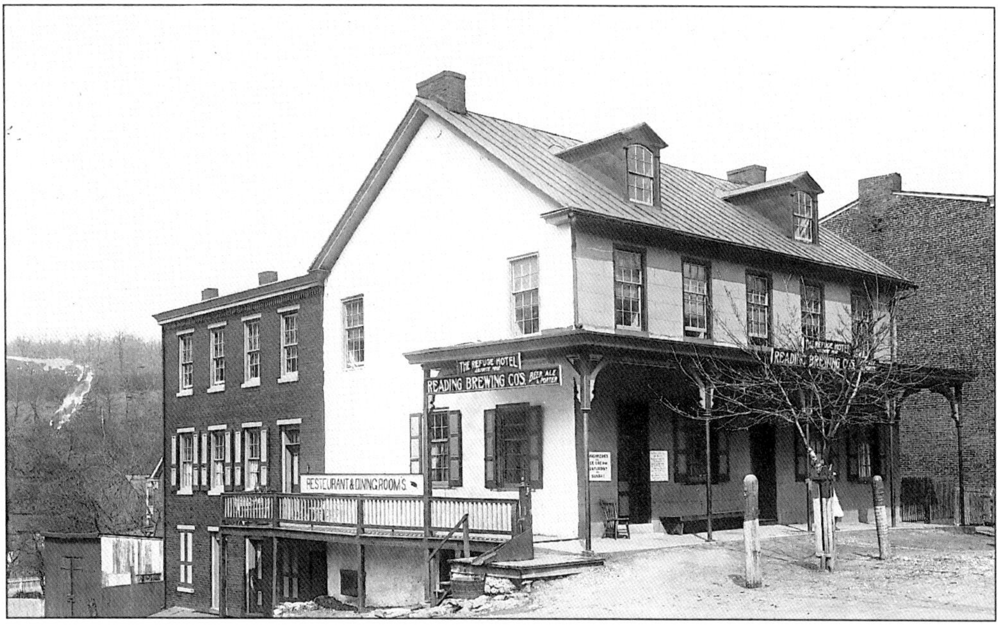

The Refuge Hotel in Port Clinton. This hotel was a favorite stop along the old Centre Turnpike.

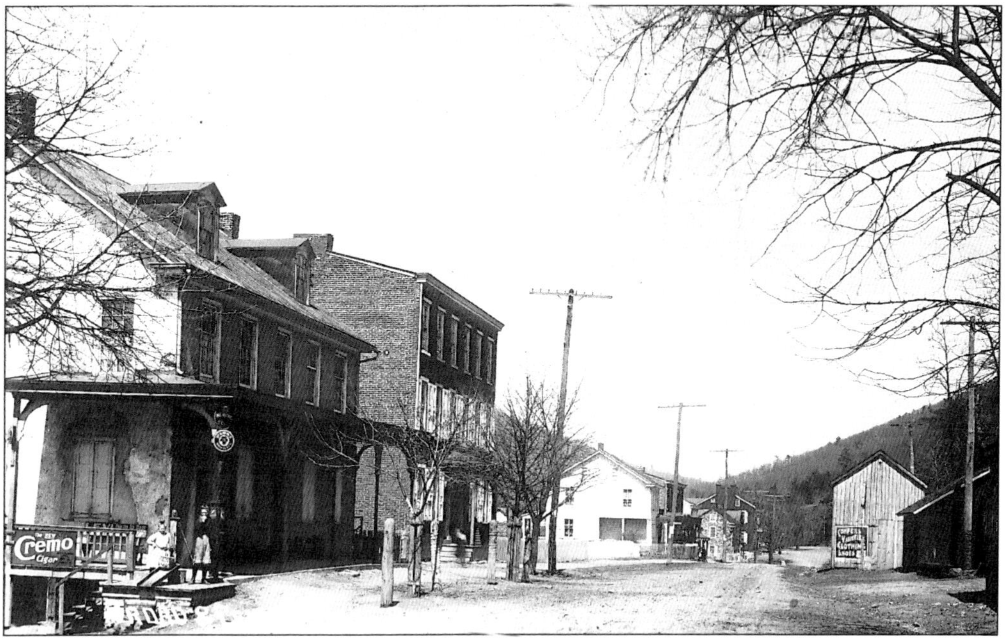

A view of Broad and Centre Streets in Port Clinton. This view, looking north, shows the Centre Turnpike, known today as Route 61.

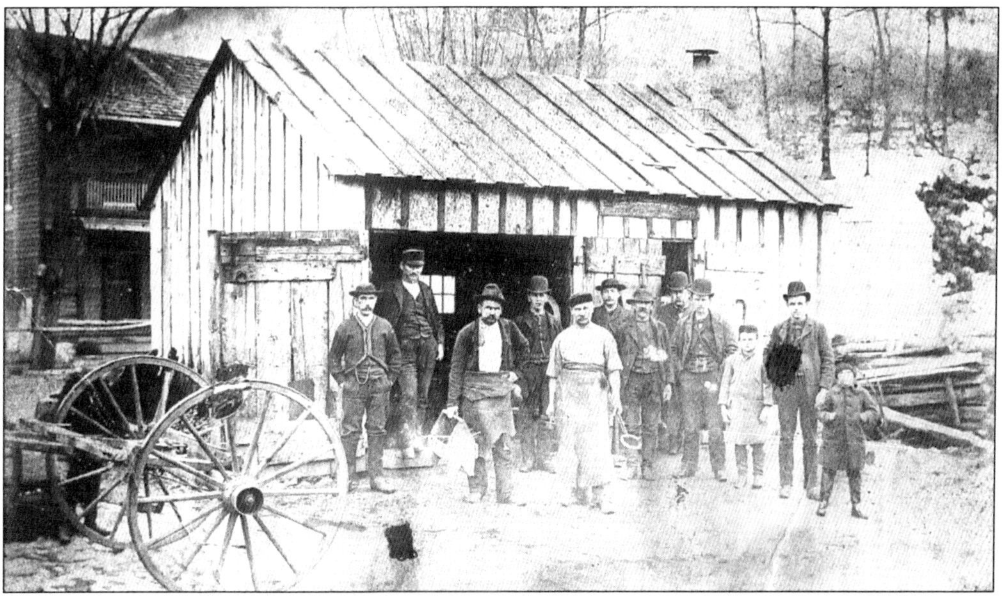

The Blacksmith Shop in Port Clinton. This primitive shop was located at Clinton Street and the Centre Turnpike.

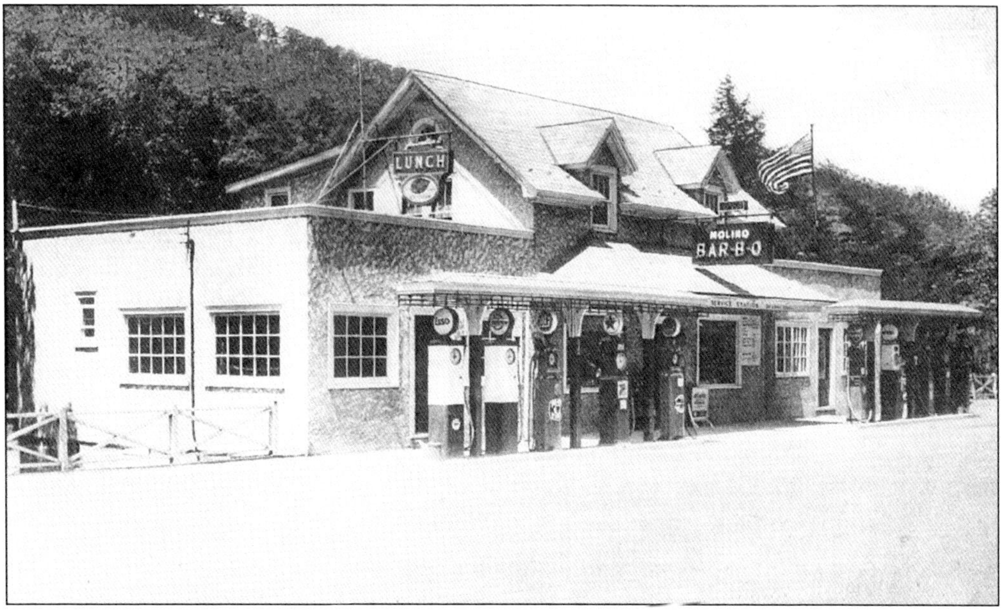

The Strouse & Beck Molino Service Station near Port Clinton. This image shows an exterior view of the popular rest stop. Today the Three C's restaurant stands on this site.

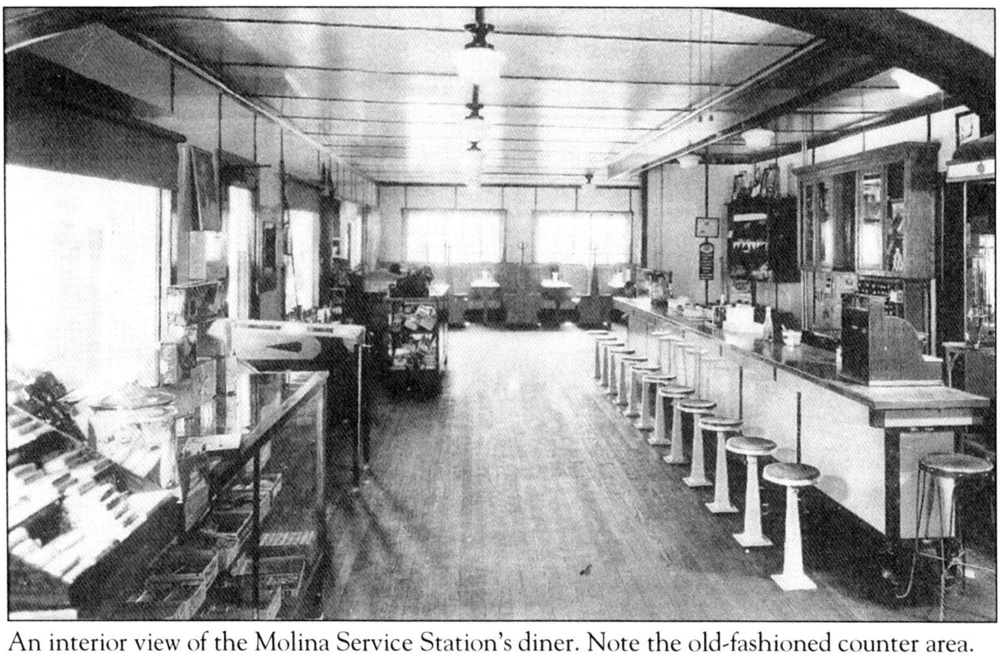

An interior view of the Molina Service Station's diner. Note the old-fashioned counter area.

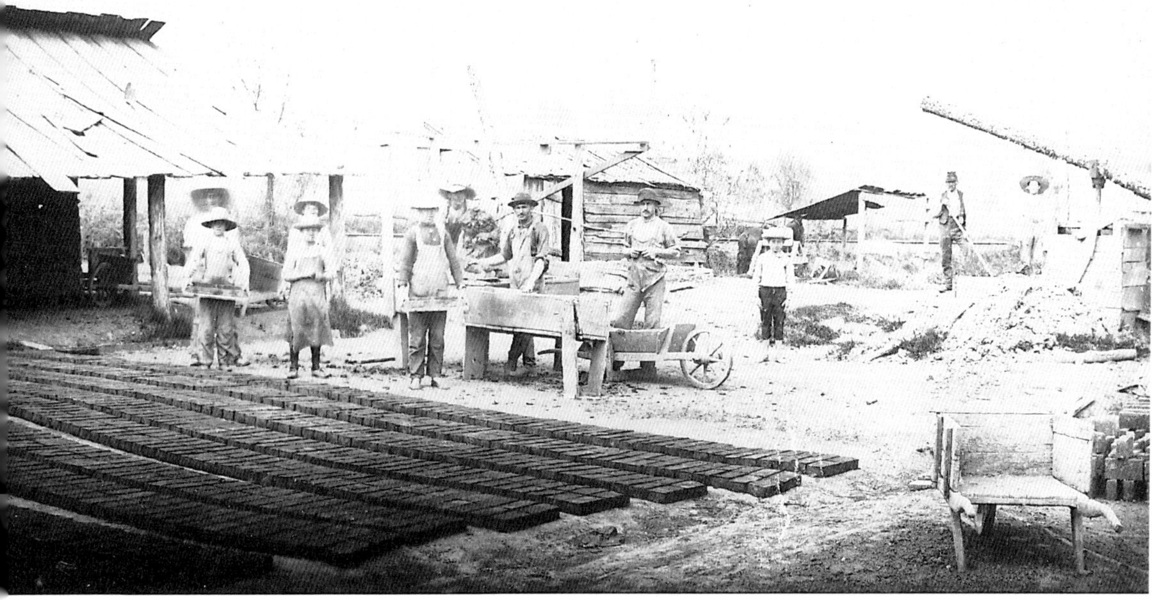

The brickyard located at Molino, near Port Clinton. In the 1800s, bricks were made by hand, and many children worked alongside the adult employees, as can be seen in this photograph.

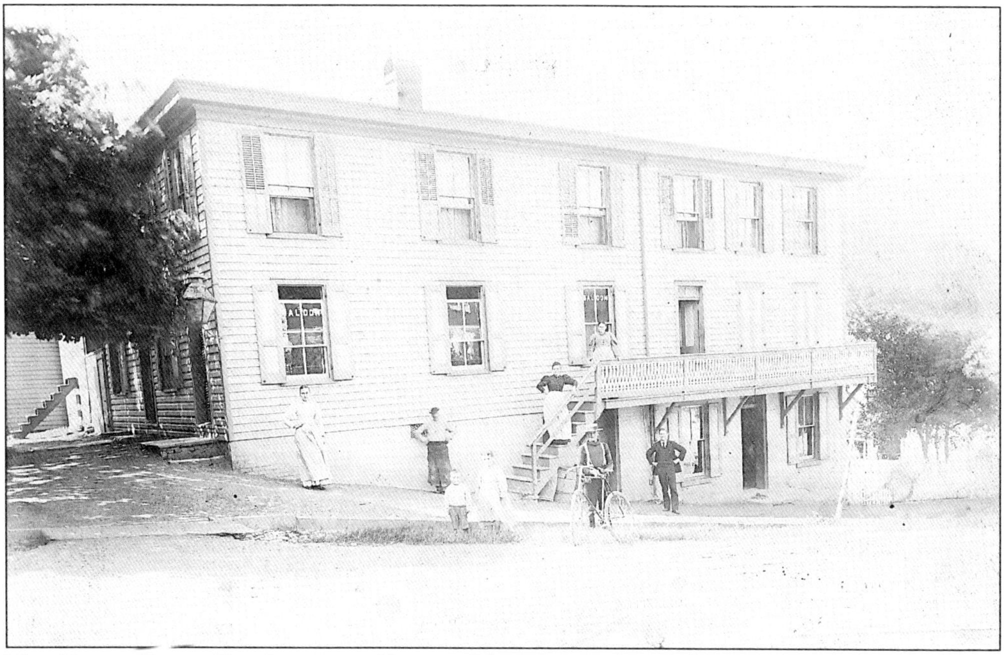

The Union House Hotel in Port Clinton. This popular hotel, located at Broad and Centre Avenues, provided food, drink, and lodging for travelers, railroaders, and canal workers. Today it is still in operation under the same name.

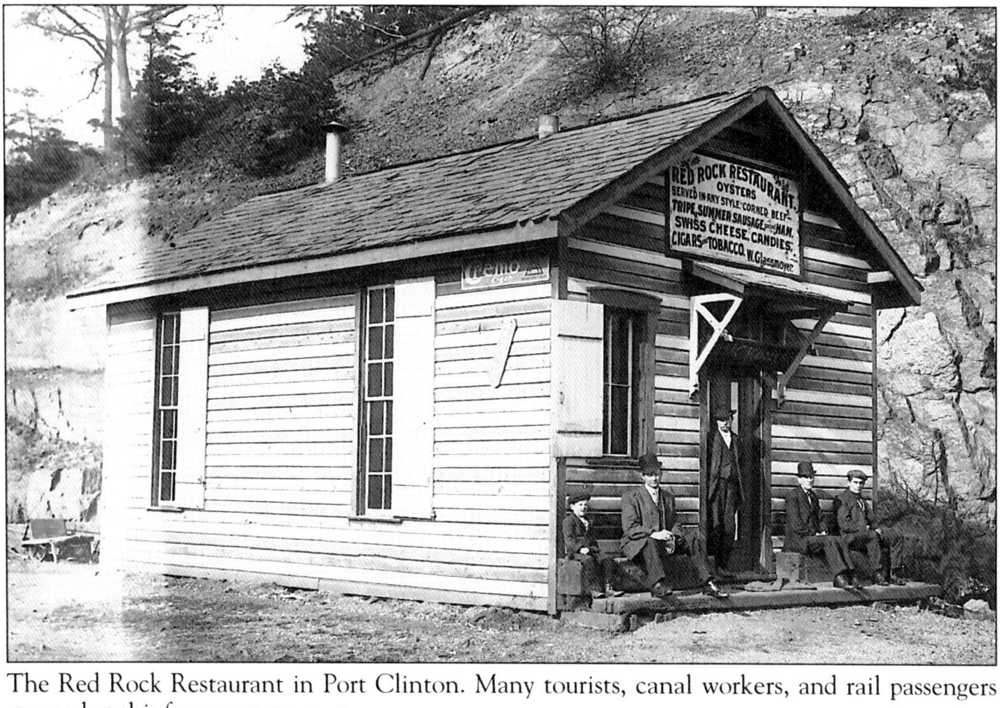

The Red Rock Restaurant in Port Clinton. Many tourists, canal workers, and rail passengers stopped at this famous restaurant.

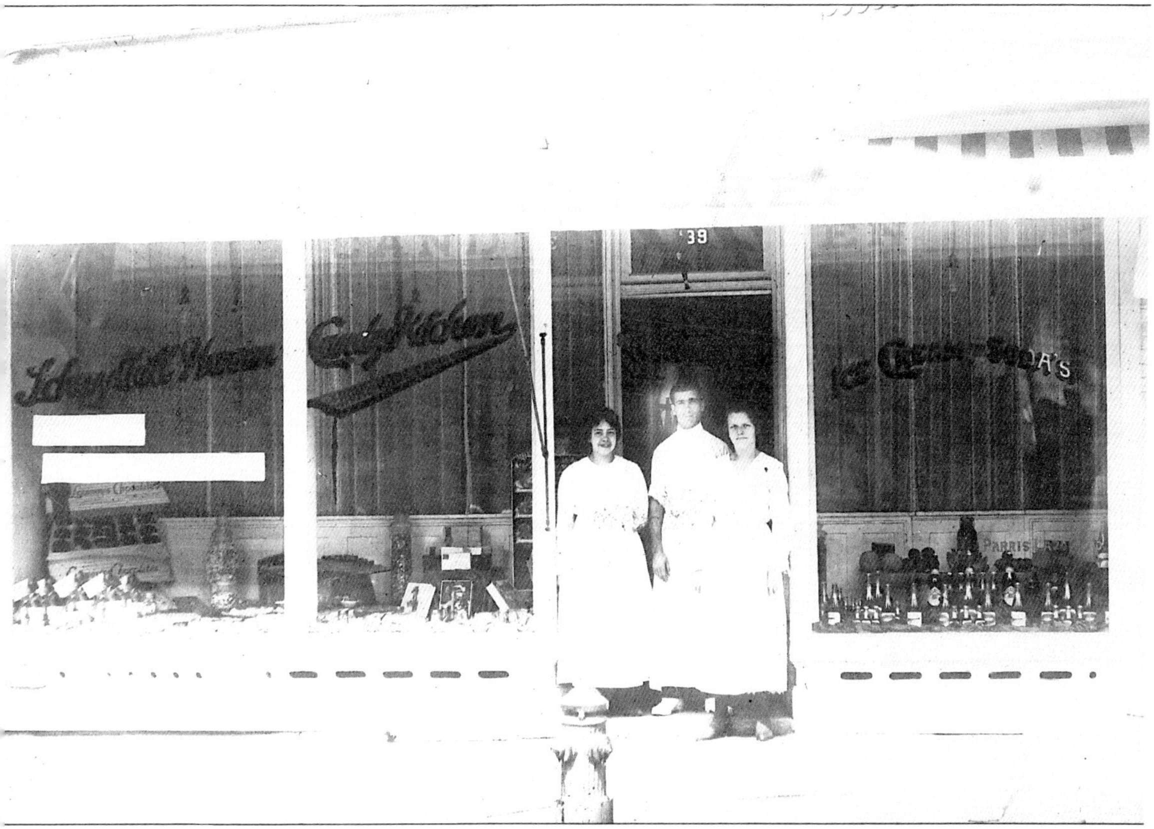

Opening Day at the Candy Kitchen in Schuylkill Haven, c. 1921. Located on Main Street, this candy store, owned by Parris Lazos, also offered ice cream and fountain sodas.

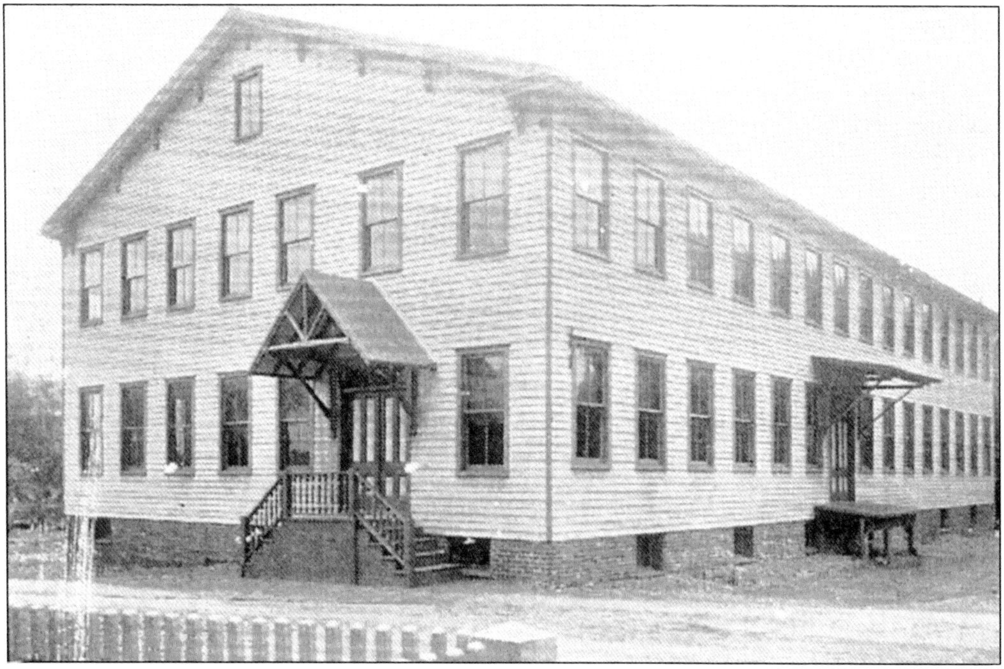

Meck and Company, manufacturer of underwear. On August 27, 1906, this company organized on the northwest corner of Parkway and Main Street. The company was formerly known as Meck and Reber.

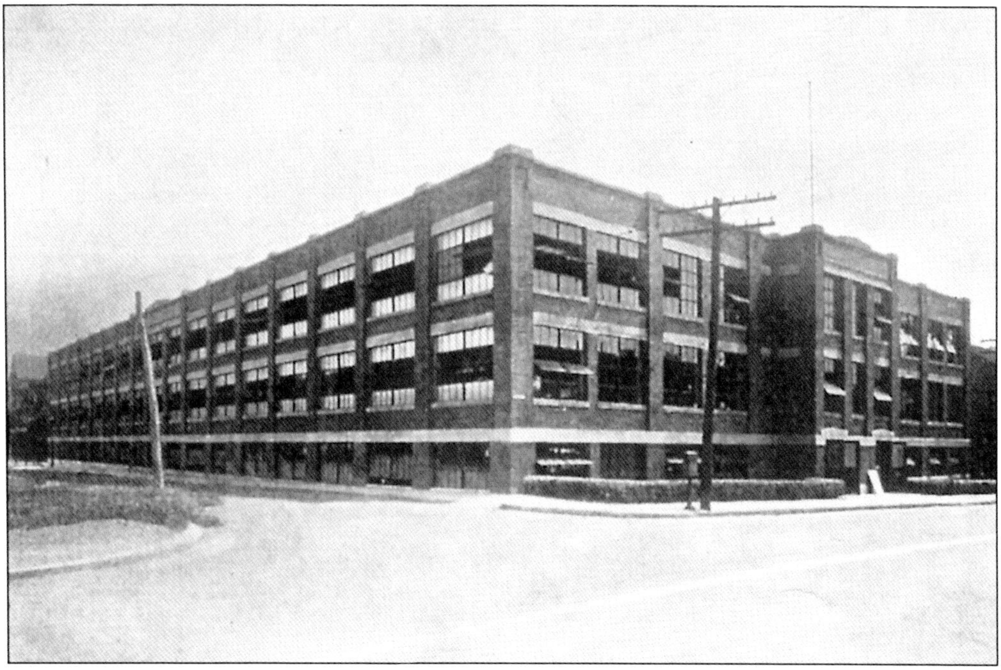

The Walkin Shoe Company in Schuylkill Haven. F.B. Keller and Harry Snayberger formed a partnership and built this three-story brick building for the purpose of manufacturing shoes. Harry Snayberger was a benefactor who generously supported many charitable causes, mainly education.

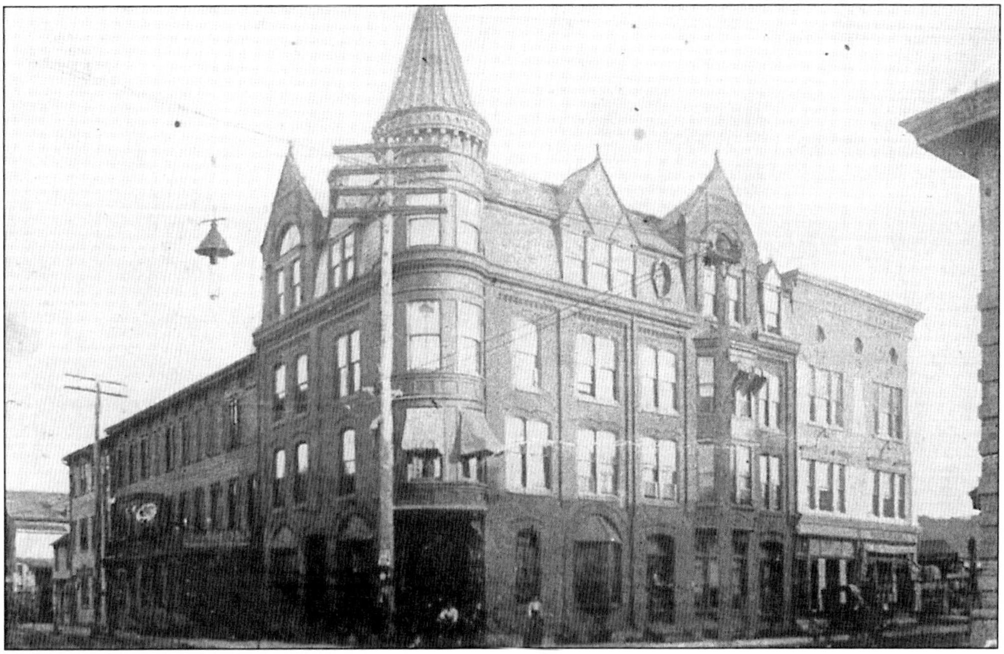

The Hotel Grand in Schuylkill Haven, *c.* 1911. This beautiful four-story hotel was built in 1895. After changing hands several times, the building was sold to the State Bank in September 1923. The structure, no longer in existence, was located on the southwest corner of Main and St. John Streets.

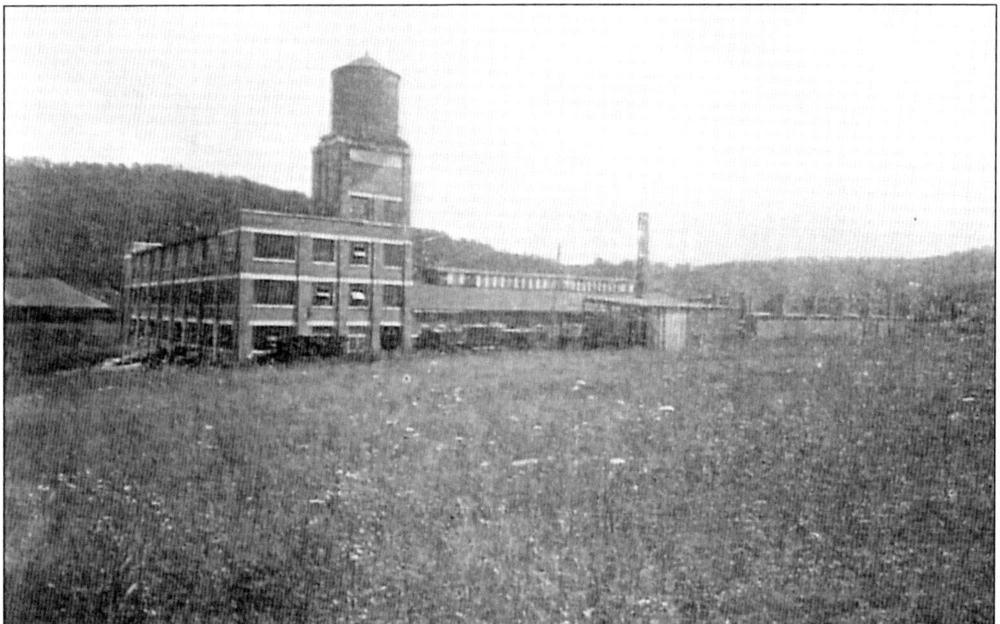

The Schuylkill Haven Casket Company, *c.* 1926. Originally the Schuylkill Haven Box and Lumber Company, established in 1915, this company reorganized in 1919 as the Schuylkill Haven Casket Company and is in operation today at its location on Liberty Street.

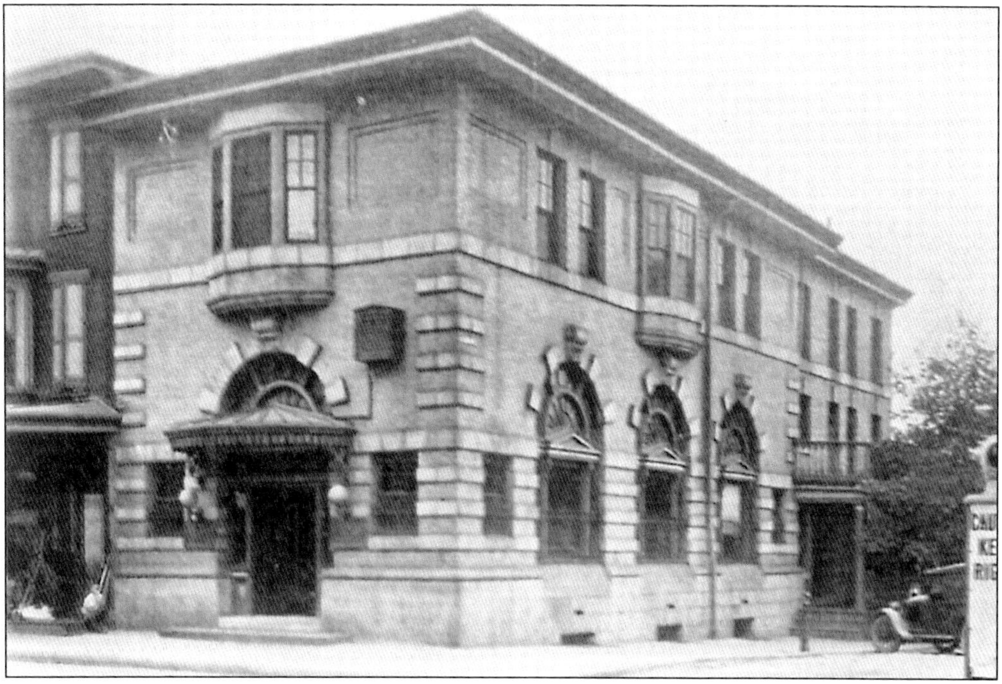

The First National Bank, Schuylkill Haven, *c.* 1920. The First National Bank of Schuylkill Haven was chartered on August 28, 1899. The building, which was built in 1904 and appears in this image, was the second location for the bank.

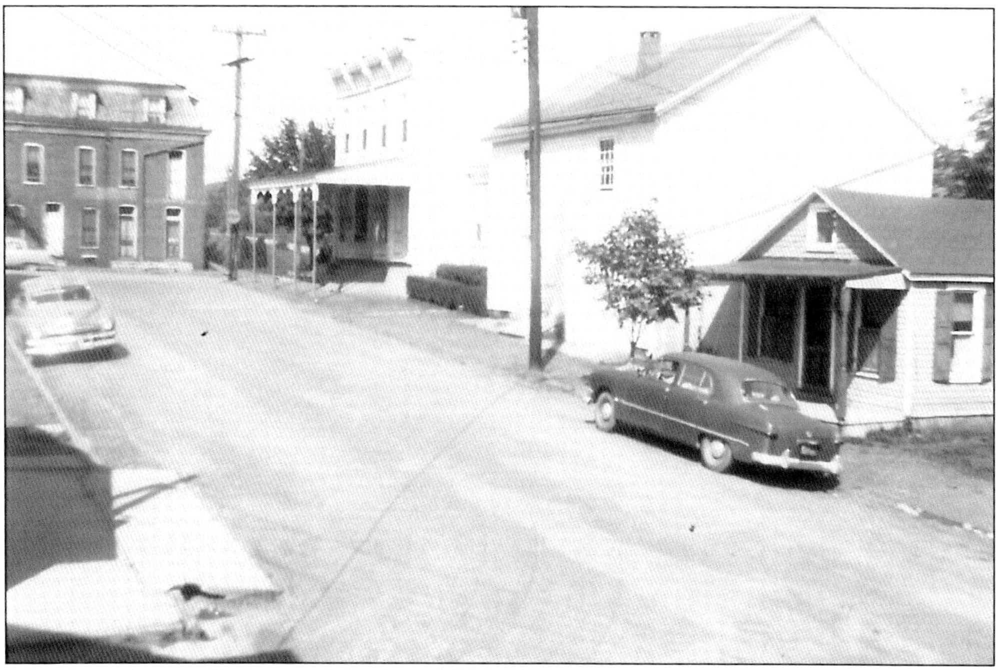

John Ramer's store (left center), built in 1874, sold groceries, dry goods, and shoes in Auburn. It was removed in 1956 and replaced by the Pennsylvania National Bank building. The tiny building on the right was Paul Klinger's Barber Shop.

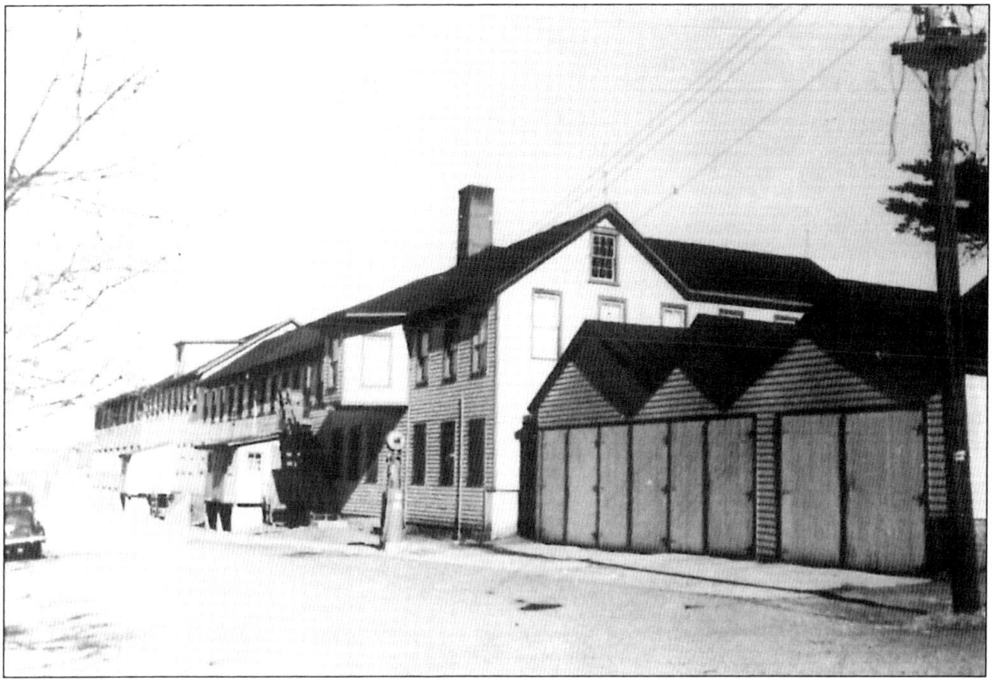

The Auburn Knitting Mill, *c.* 1940. Originally this was the site of the Auburn Broom Works and later a hosiery and underwear factory. Through the years, the mill produced a variety of garments, including sweaters and beachwear.

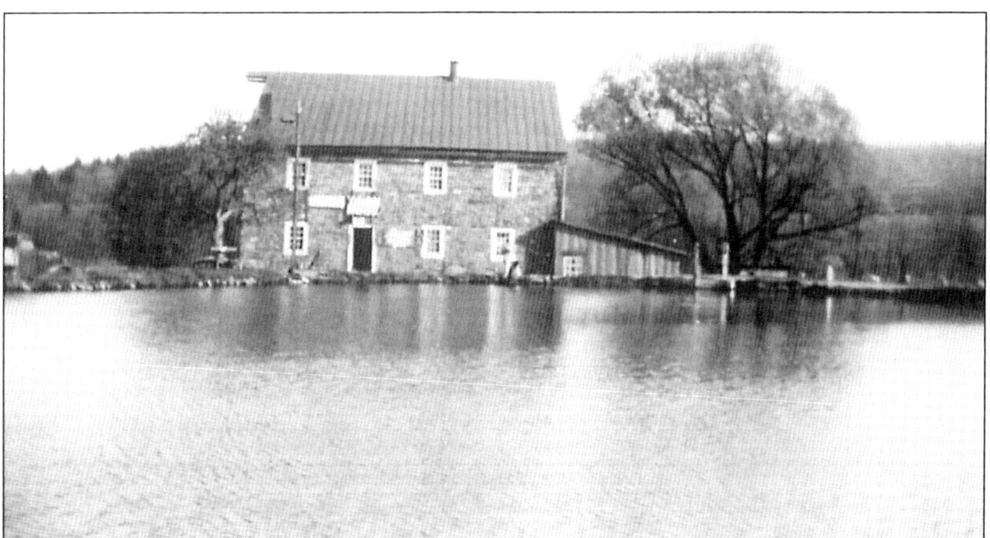

The Auburn Roller Mills. This feed mill is located west of the Auburn borough line and was built in 1821. Mills like this one were once common throughout southern Schuylkill County.

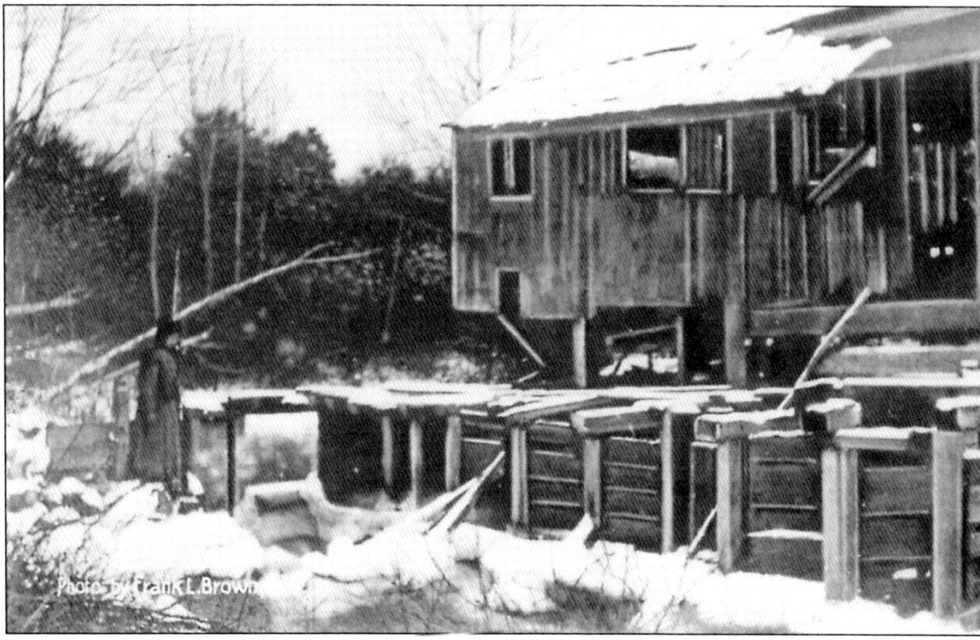

The old sawmill in Auburn, c. 1910.

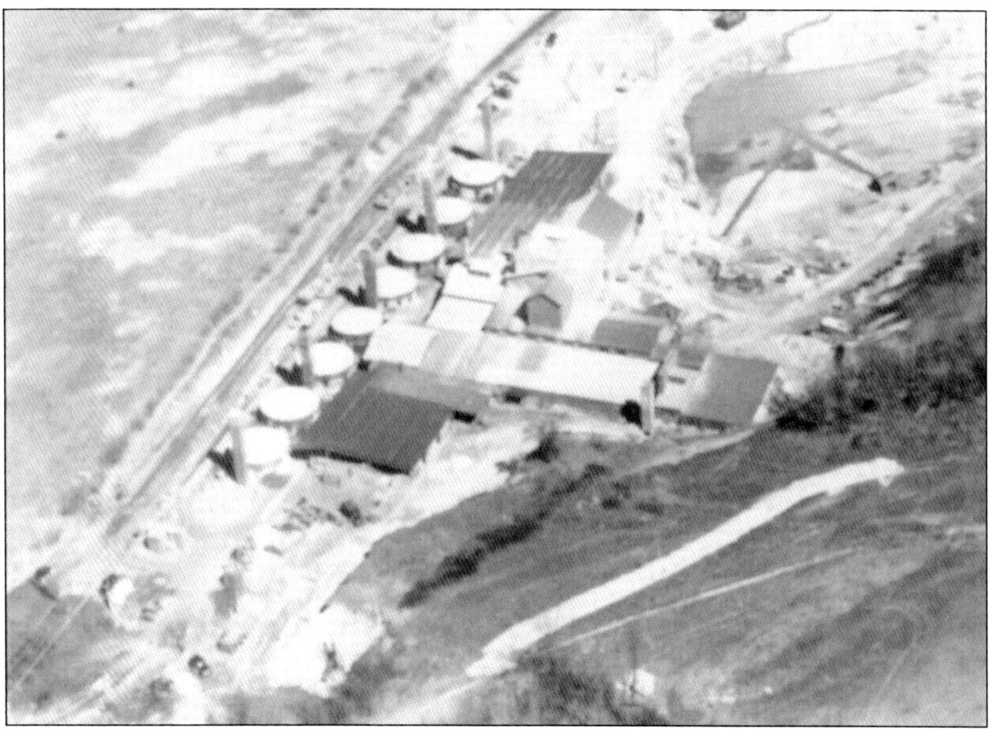

The Auburn Brick Company. This aerial view shows the Auburn Brick Company, which was organized in 1880. The first kilns were very small and bricks were made by hand.

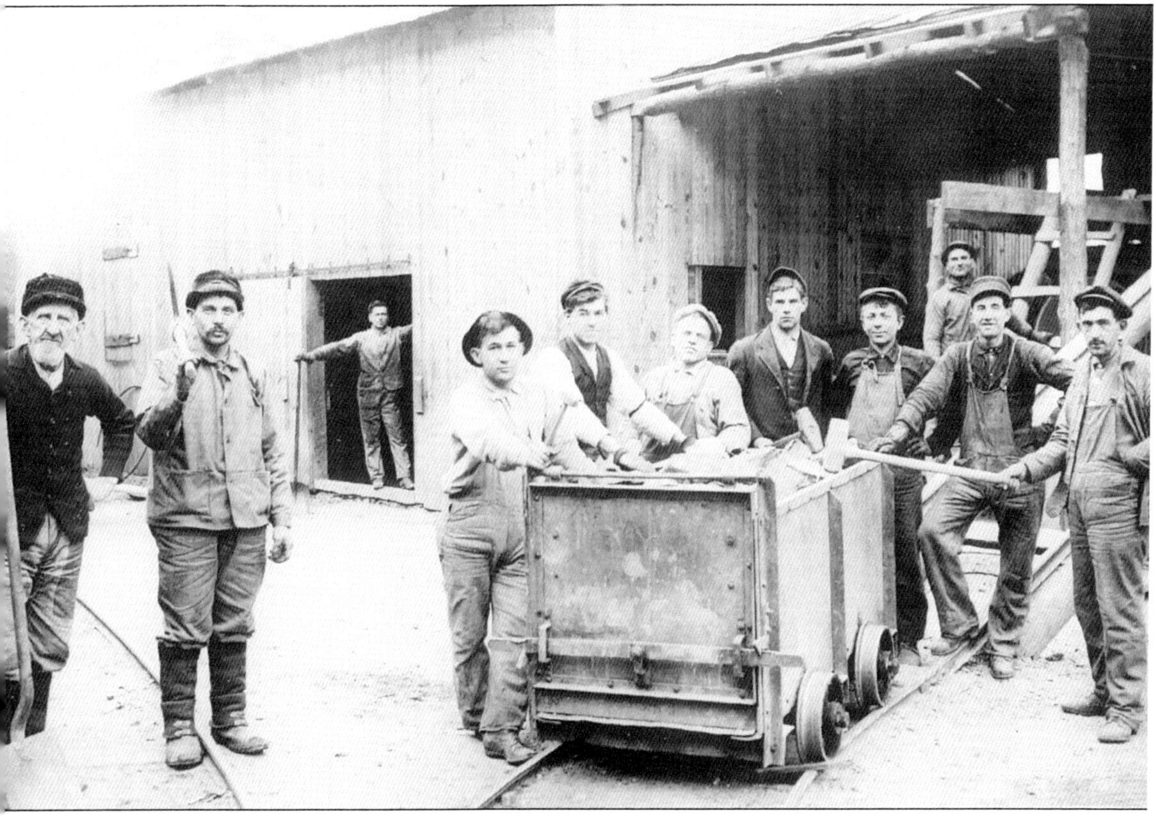

Mill workers at the Delaware Seamless Tube Company in Auburn. The mill, one of the first of its kind in the United States, worked three shifts around the clock making stainless steel tubing. The average wages in the early 1930s were 20¢ per hour.

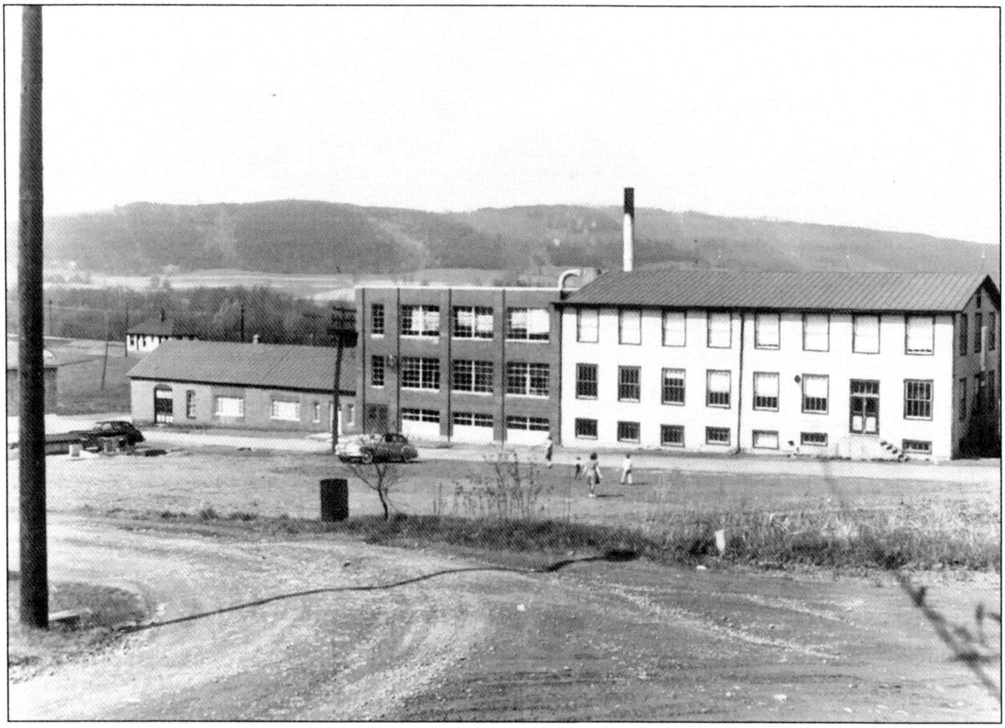

The Auburn Shoe Factory, built by the Auburn Board of Trade in 1914. This photograph shows the factory as it appeared in 1948.

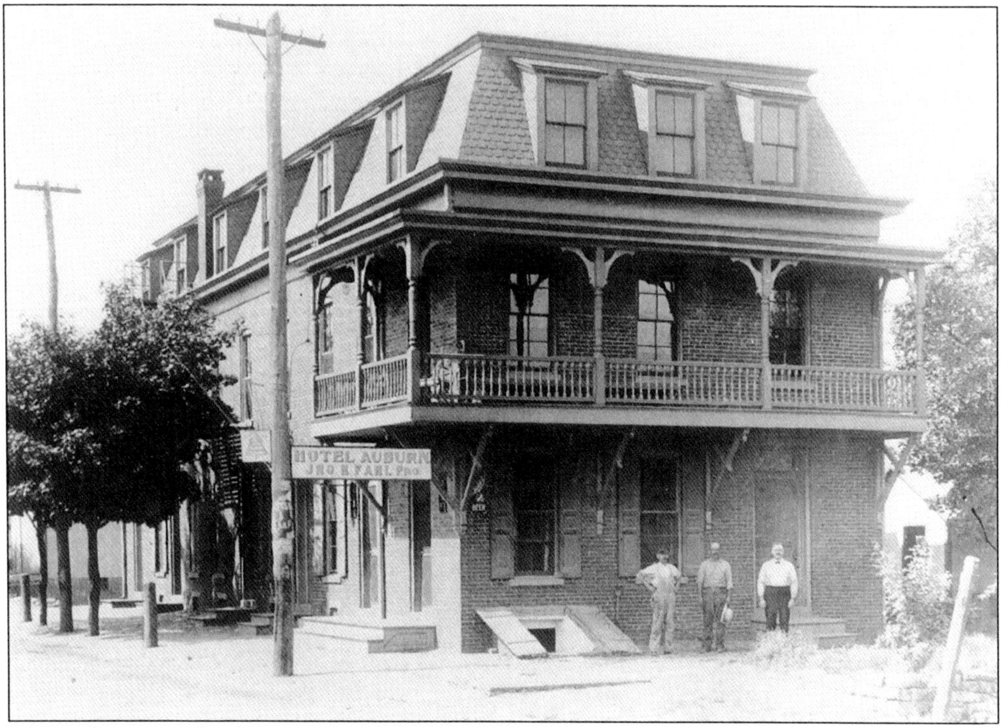

The Auburn Hotel. This image of the Auburn Hotel was taken around the late 1800s.

Five

Pathmakers and Times to Remember

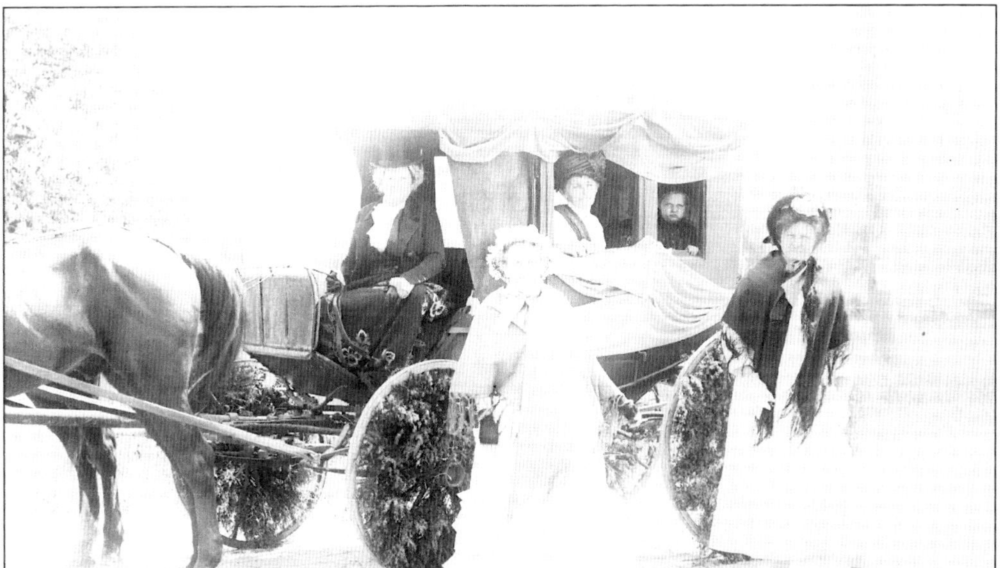

Participants in Orwigsburg's Centennial Celebration. Orwigsburg hosted a week-long series of events commemorating the borough's 100th birthday in 1913.

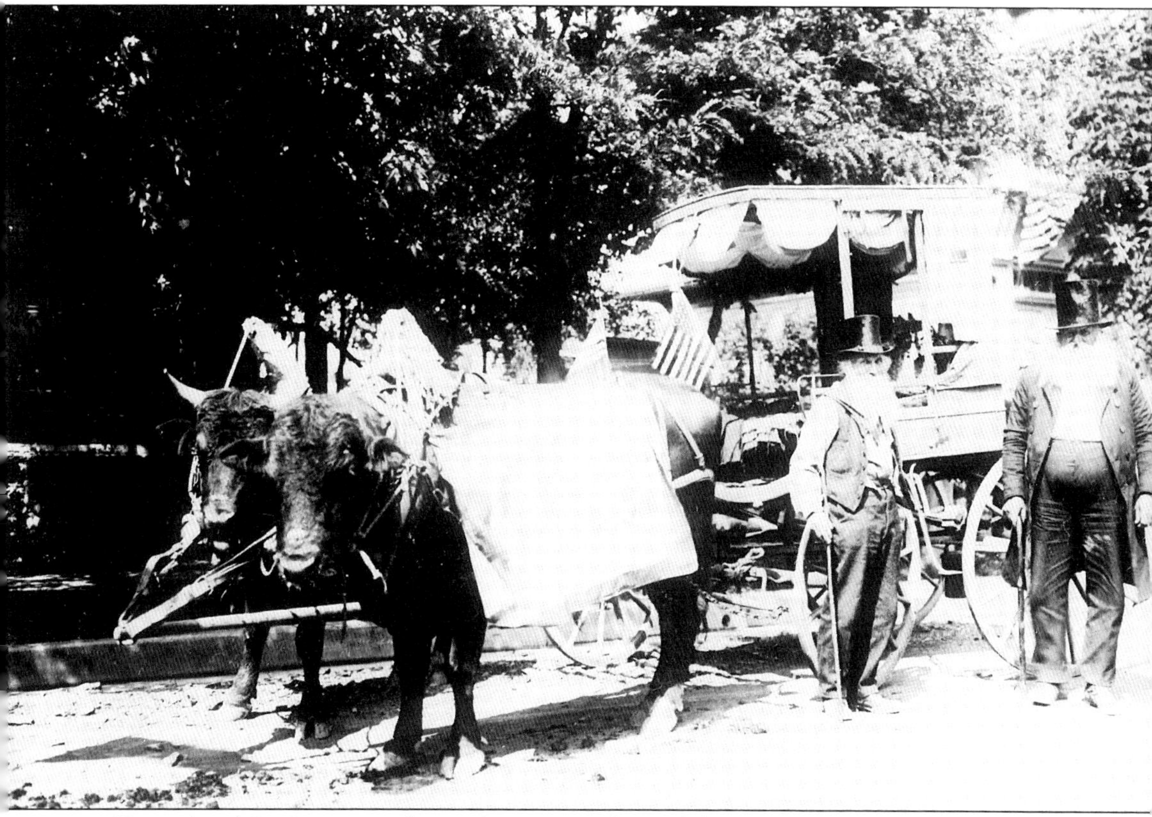

Kimmel and Son's entry in the 1913 Centennial Parade held in Orwigsburg.

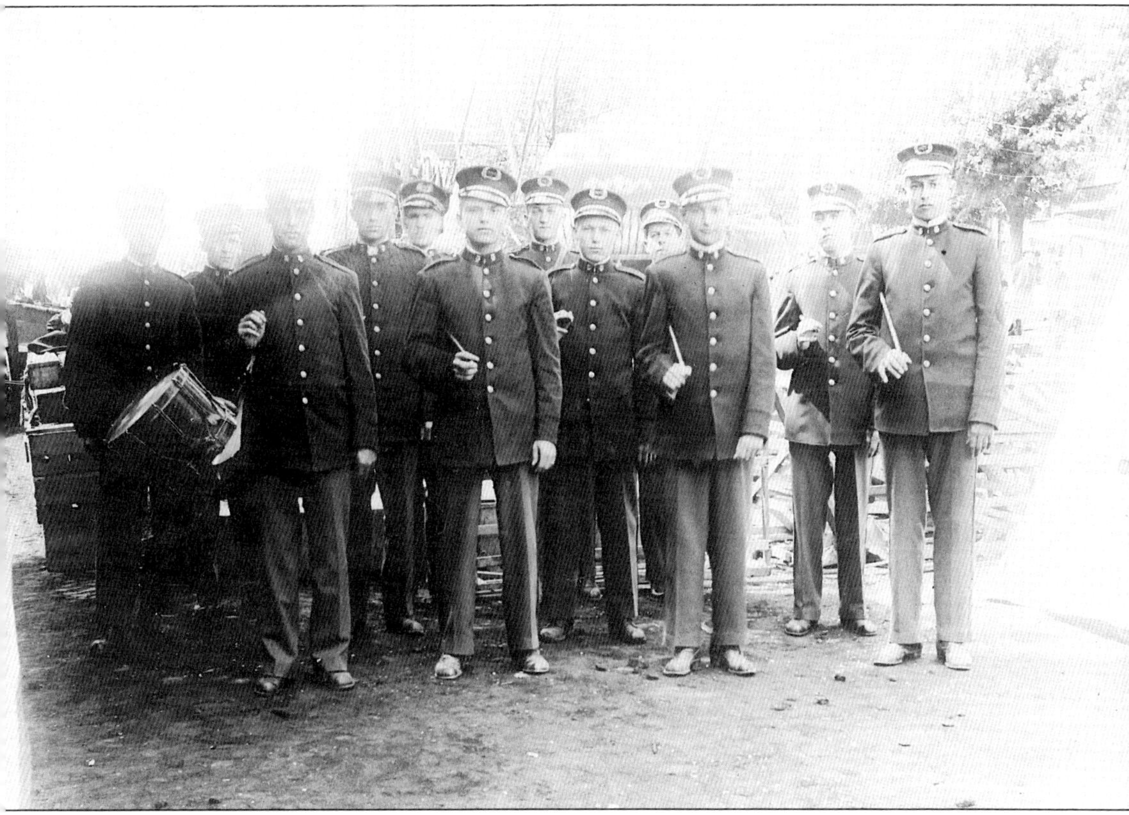

An Orwigsburg band preparing for the 1913 Centennial Parade down Market Street. The old Schuylkill County Court House can also be seen in the background of this image. The members are, from left to right, John Weaver, Guy Seigfried, Burd Bachman, Rich Miller, John Music, Ralph Moyer, John Moyer, William "Whitey" Moyer, Norman Seigfried, Russell Lindenmuth, Salem Weaver, and George Moyer.

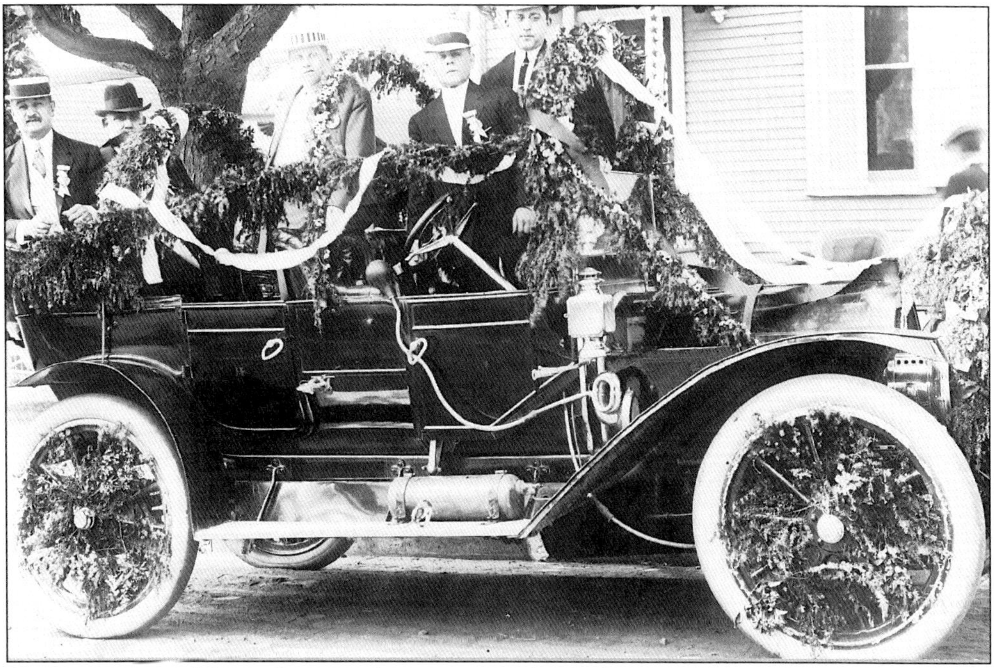

An eager group of Orwigsburg revelers preparing for the big centennial parade in Orwigsburg, c. 1913.

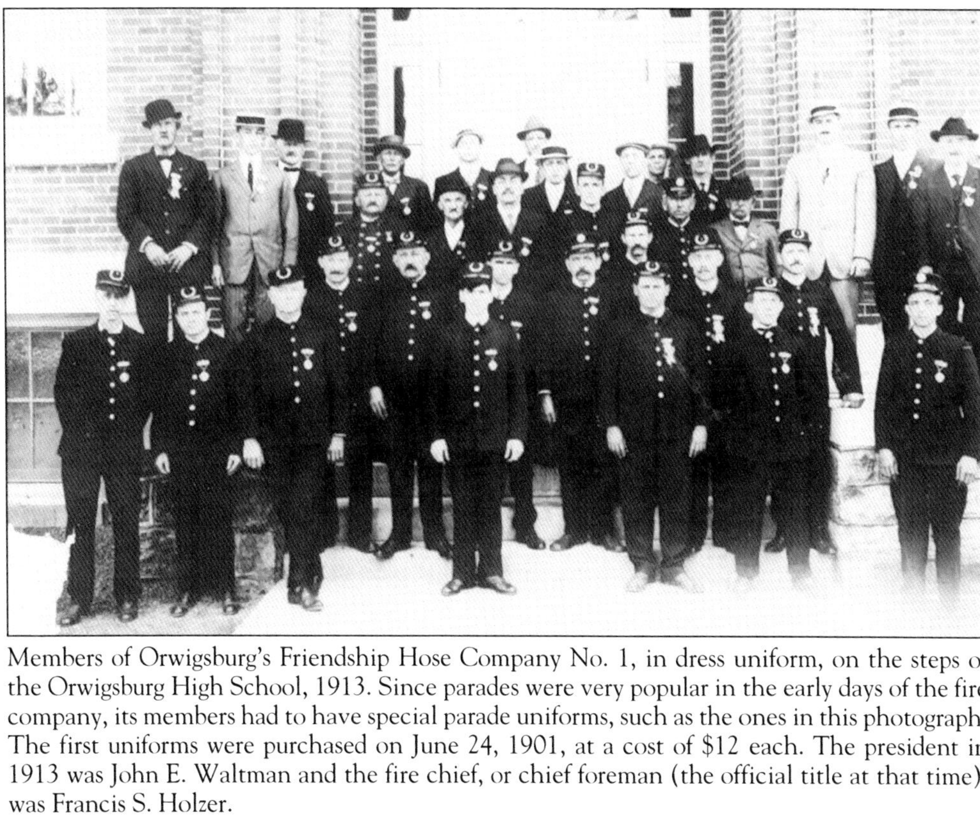

Members of Orwigsburg's Friendship Hose Company No. 1, in dress uniform, on the steps of the Orwigsburg High School, 1913. Since parades were very popular in the early days of the fire company, its members had to have special parade uniforms, such as the ones in this photograph. The first uniforms were purchased on June 24, 1901, at a cost of $12 each. The president in 1913 was John E. Waltman and the fire chief, or chief foreman (the official title at that time), was Francis S. Holzer.

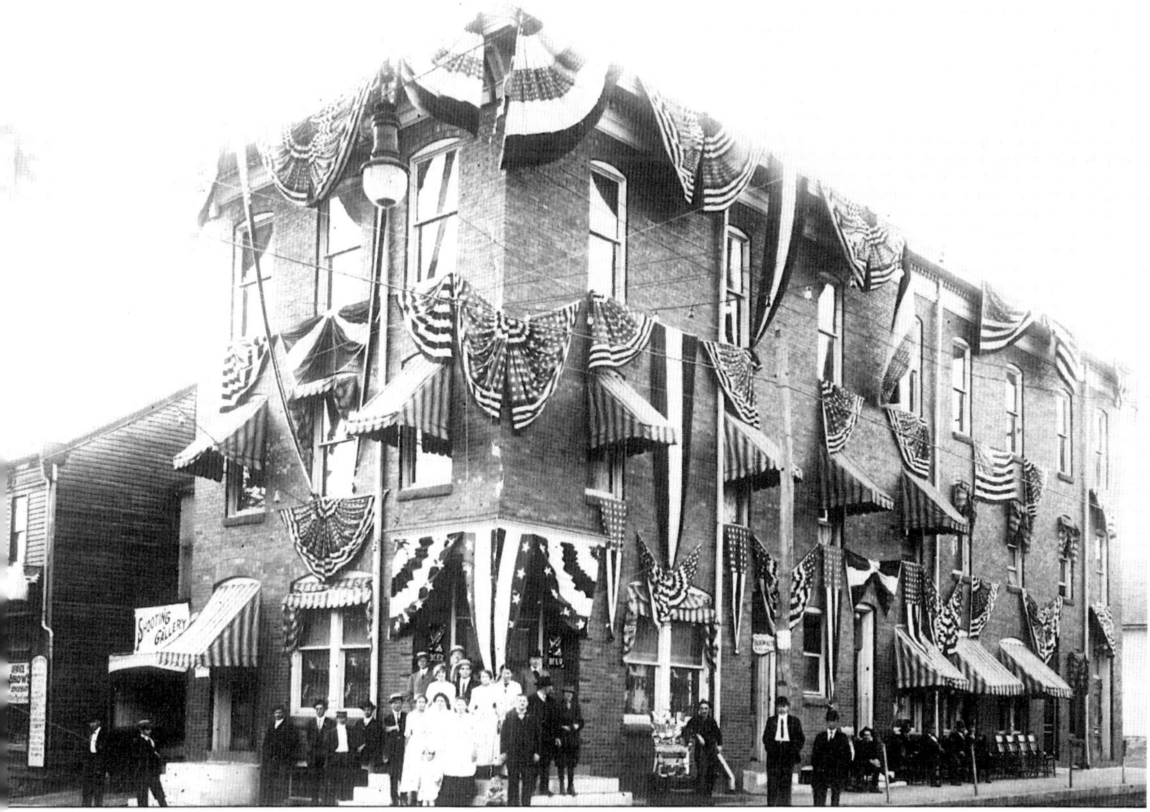

The Harlem Hotel, *c.* 1913. The Harlem Hotel, owned by John Knarr at the time this image was taken, shows the extent to which folks in Orwigsburg went for a celebration as big as the centennial.

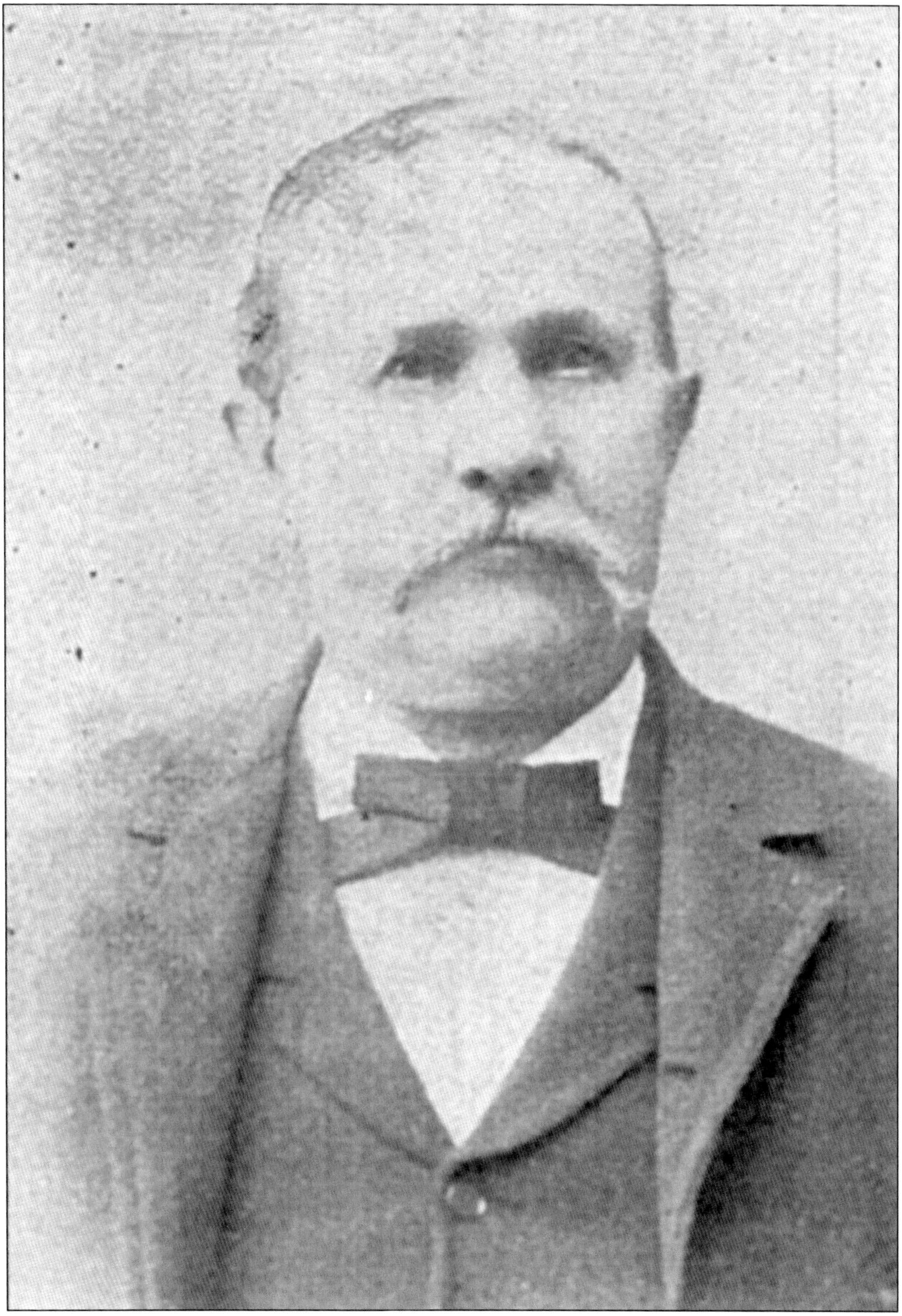

Thomas Hoy. An influential citizen of Orwigsburg during the mid-1800s, Hoy is credited with establishing the first shoe factory in Orwigsburg. The factory, which Hoy started in 1873, was housed in the former Schuylkill County Court House, once located on East Market Street.

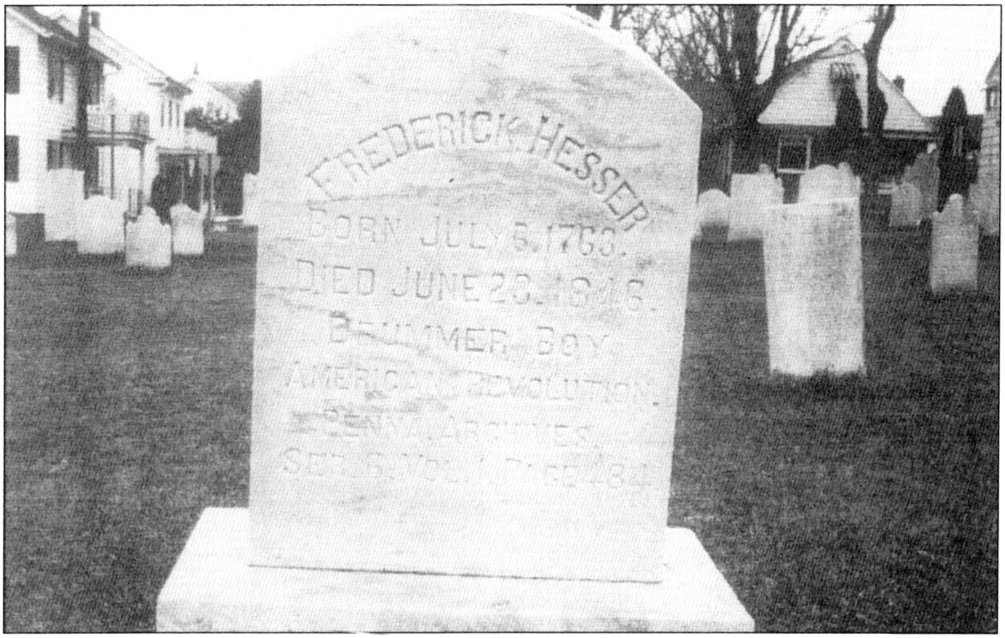

The grave of Frederick Hesser of Orwigsburg. At age 13, Frederick and his brother John, who was 15, joined the army during the Revolutionary War. Both boys took part in Washington's crossing of the Delaware on December 25, 1776. Frederick served as a drummer boy with General Washington's Continental Army until the age of 14. He became a resident of Orwigsburg in 1814 and became Schuylkill County's sheriff for a four-year term. Later, Frederick served as the town's court crier, using his drum to call court sessions.

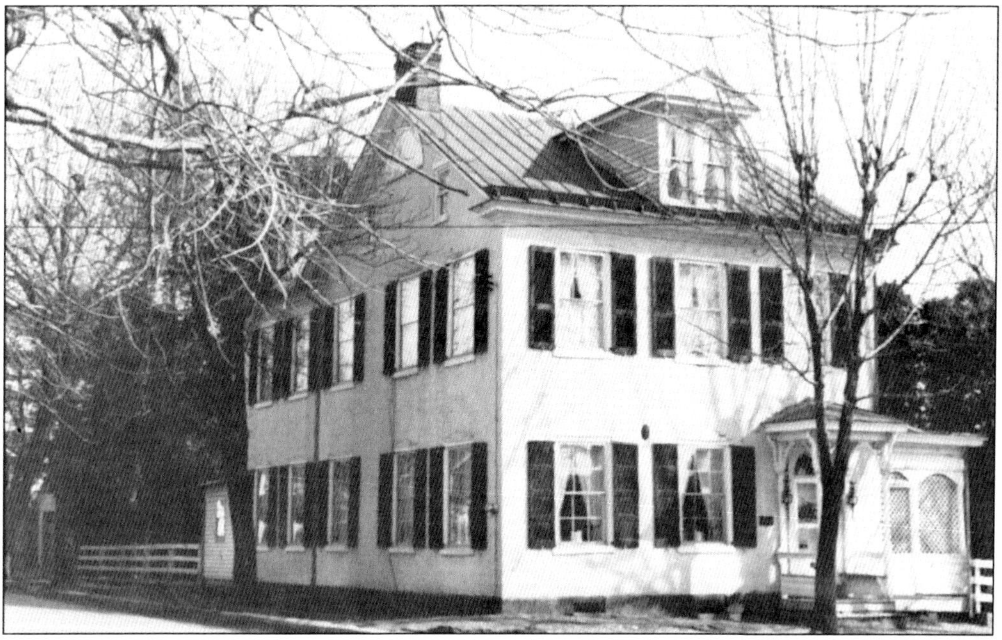

Historic property on South Warren Street, Orwigsburg. The first canal boat to be launched on the Schuylkill River was built on this site by William Wildermuth in 1830. The property is a private residence today.

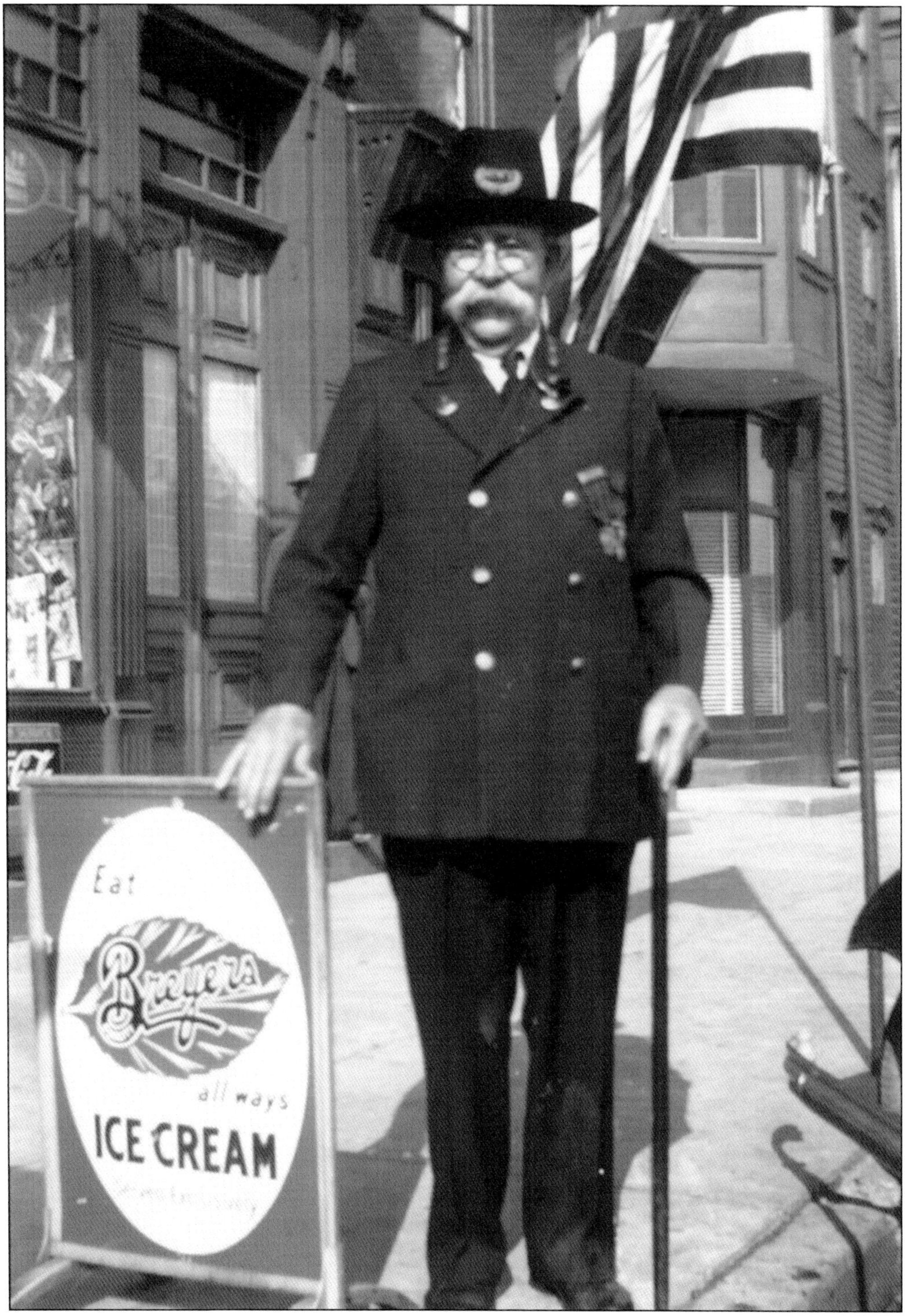

Captain Henry Smith, posing on East Market Street in Orwigsburg. Captain Smith, a native of Orwigsburg, was one of the last "Indian Fighters" from Schuylkill County who participated in the Indian campaigns throughout the Dakotas in the late 1800s.

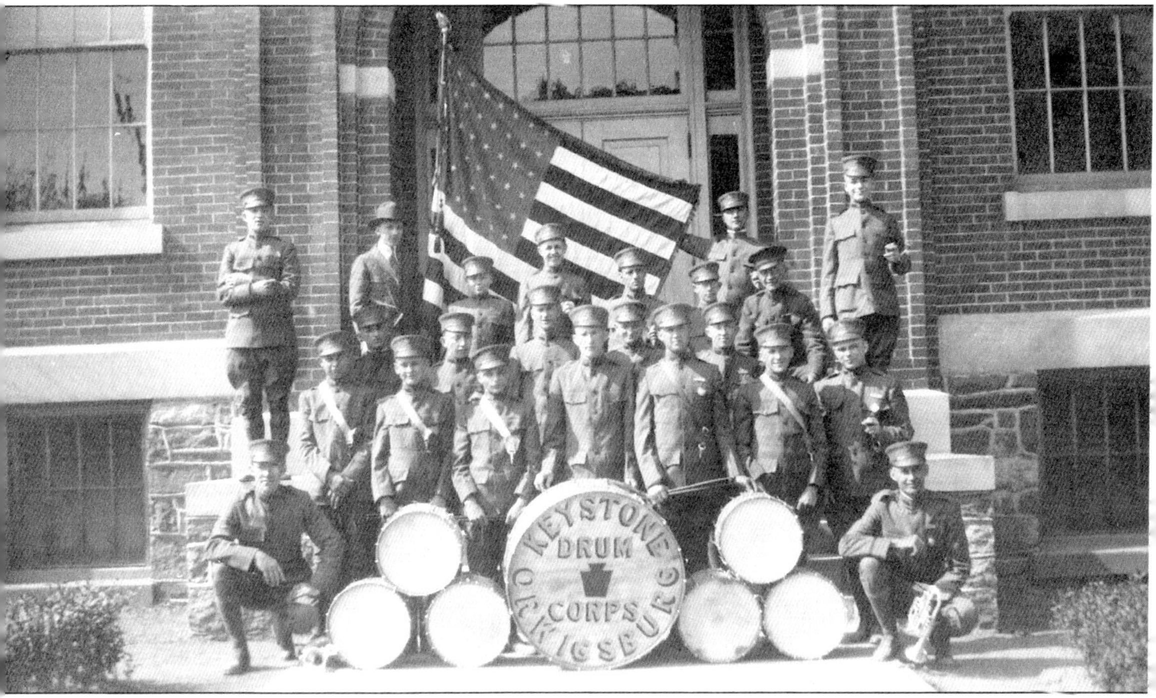

The Keystone Drum Corps of Orwigsburg. This is one of many community bands that originated in Orwigsburg. The photograph was taken on the steps of the Orwigsburg High School, located on Mifflin Street.

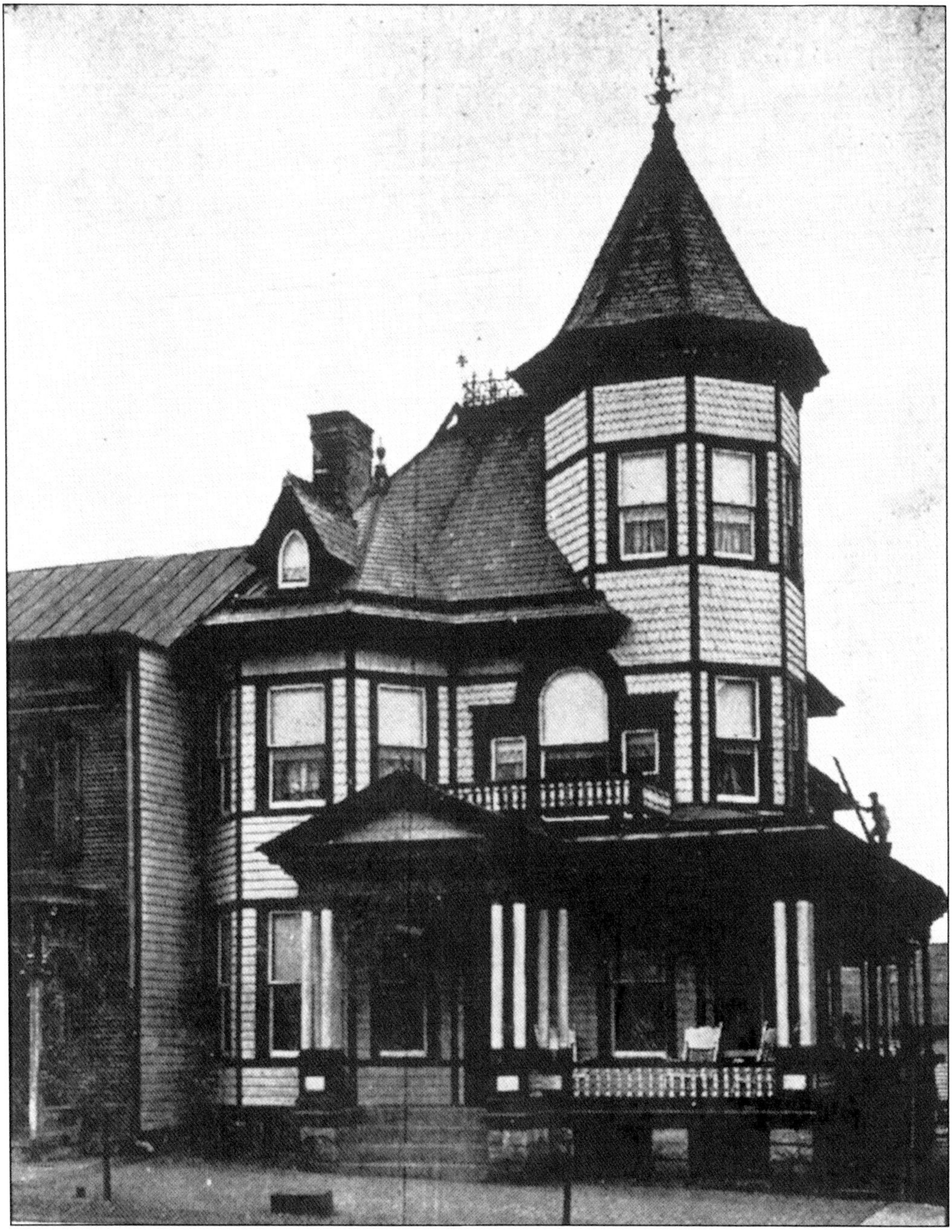

The home of E. Ray Linder, *c.* 1913. He was the owner of Linder's clothing and shoe store, which was located on Centre Square in Orwigsburg.

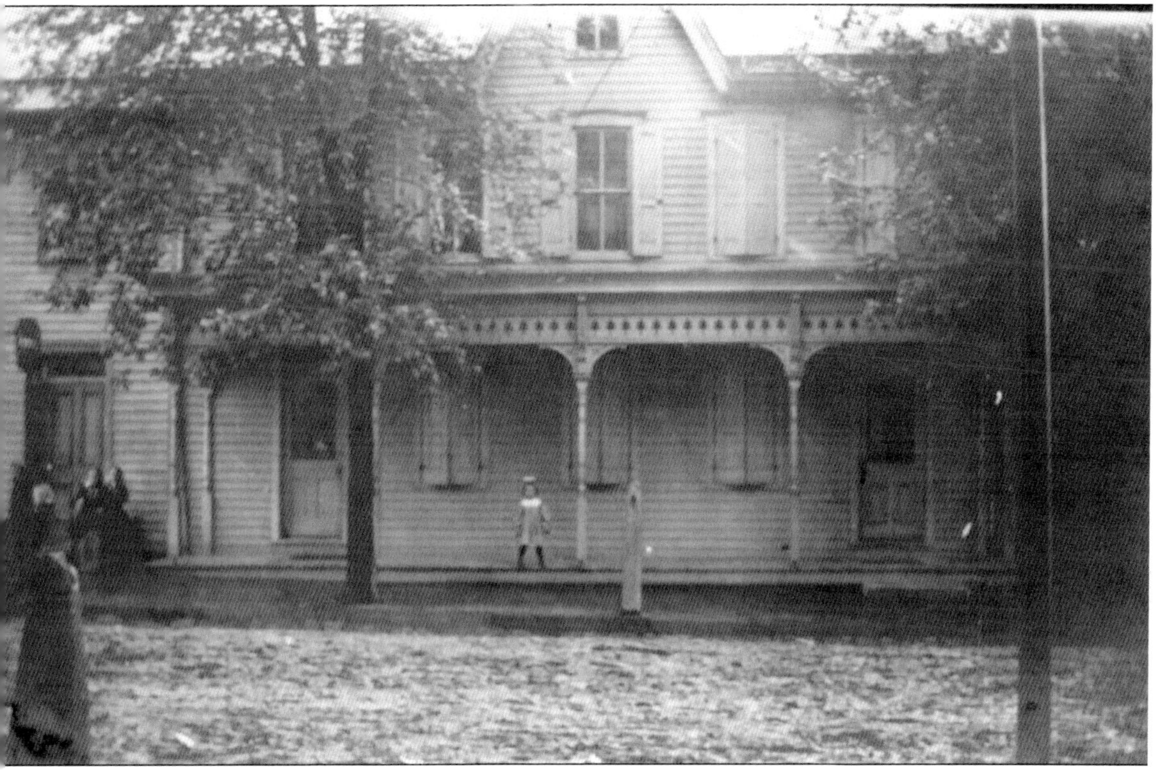

The home of Rutherford Lebengood. This interesting Victorian structure was attached on both sides to other homes, as was typical in Orwigsburg and other Schuylkill County communities at that time. The property later became the homestead of Samuel Deibert.

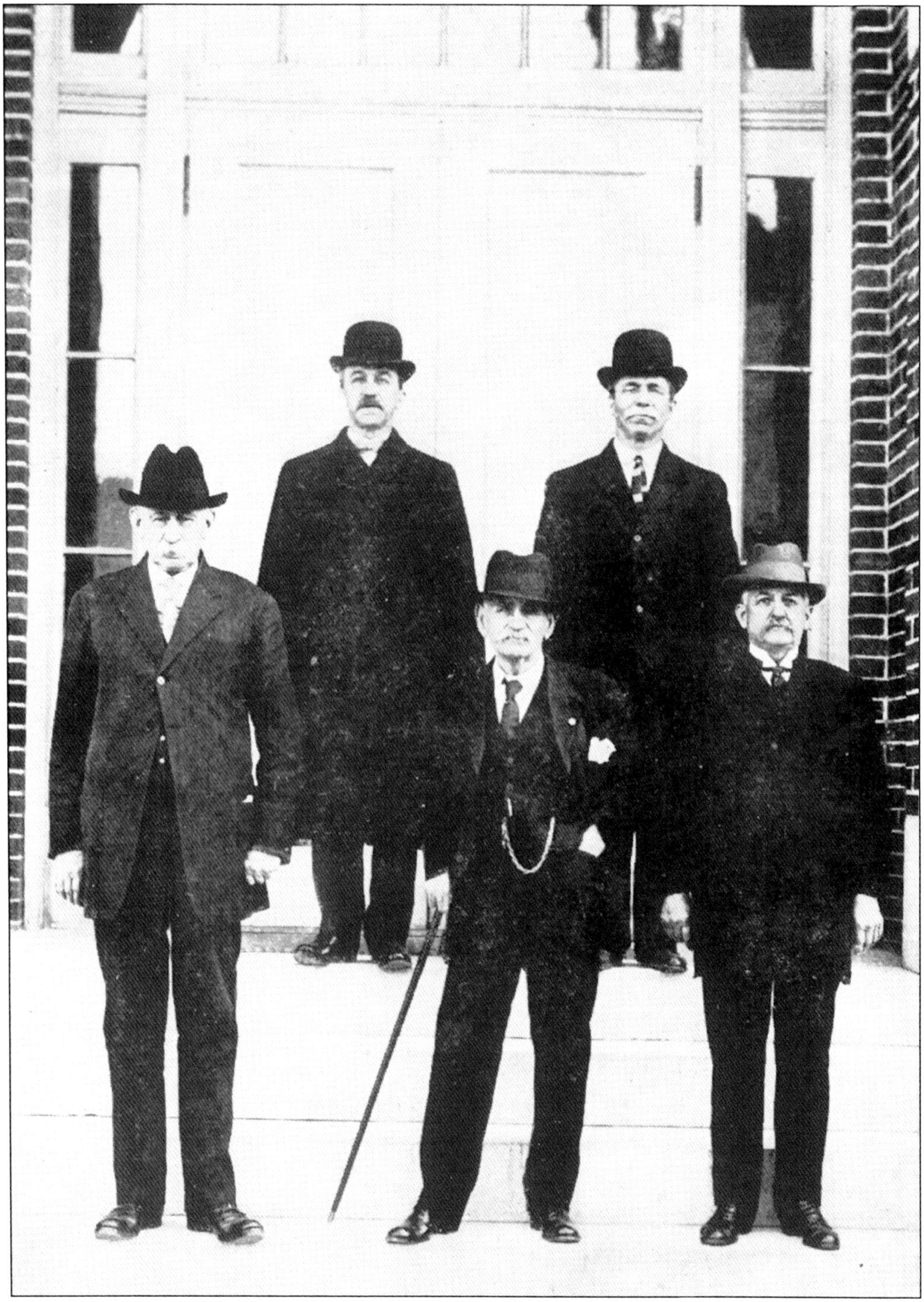

One of the centennial planning committees in Orwigsburg, 1913. In addition to politics, John T. Shoener (first row, third from the left) operated a shoe-manufacturing company and ran a successful farming business.

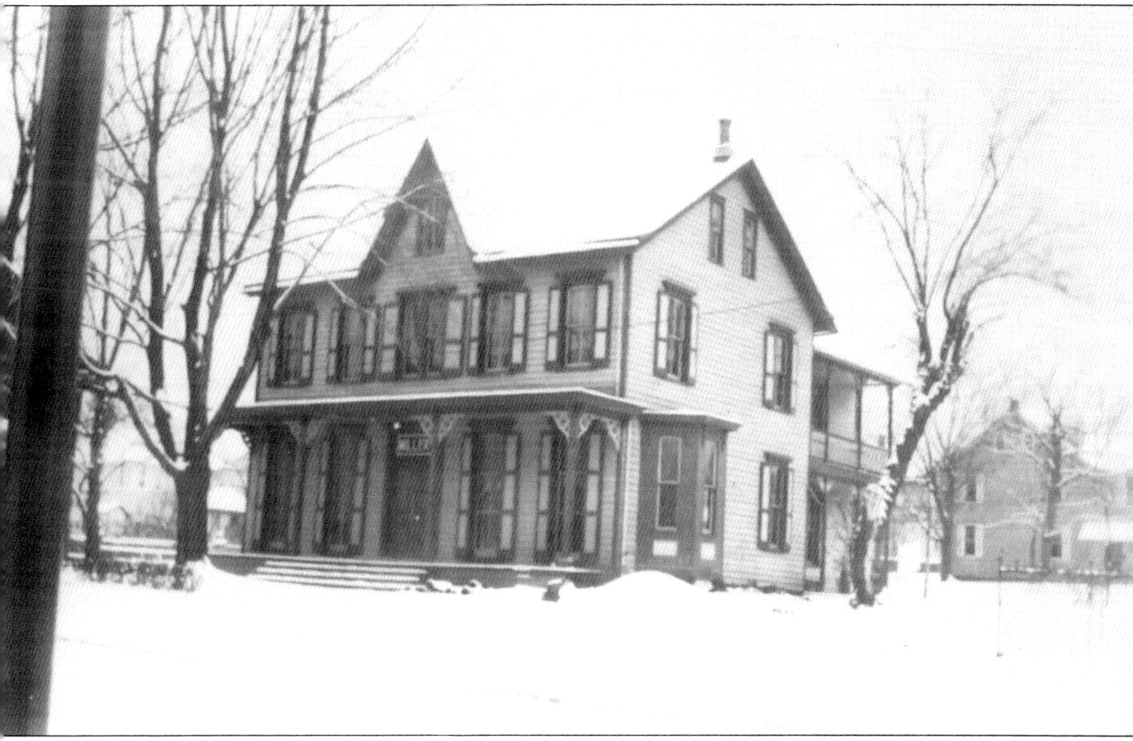

The home of John T. Shoener, located at 401 East Market Street in Orwigsburg. John T. Shoener served as a state representative of the fourth legislative district. He was responsible for the establishment of the Miners' Hospital at Fountain Springs in 1879, and for this reason he remained a political power throughout Schuylkill County. In the mid-1900s, a portion of this home was also utilized as a police barracks.

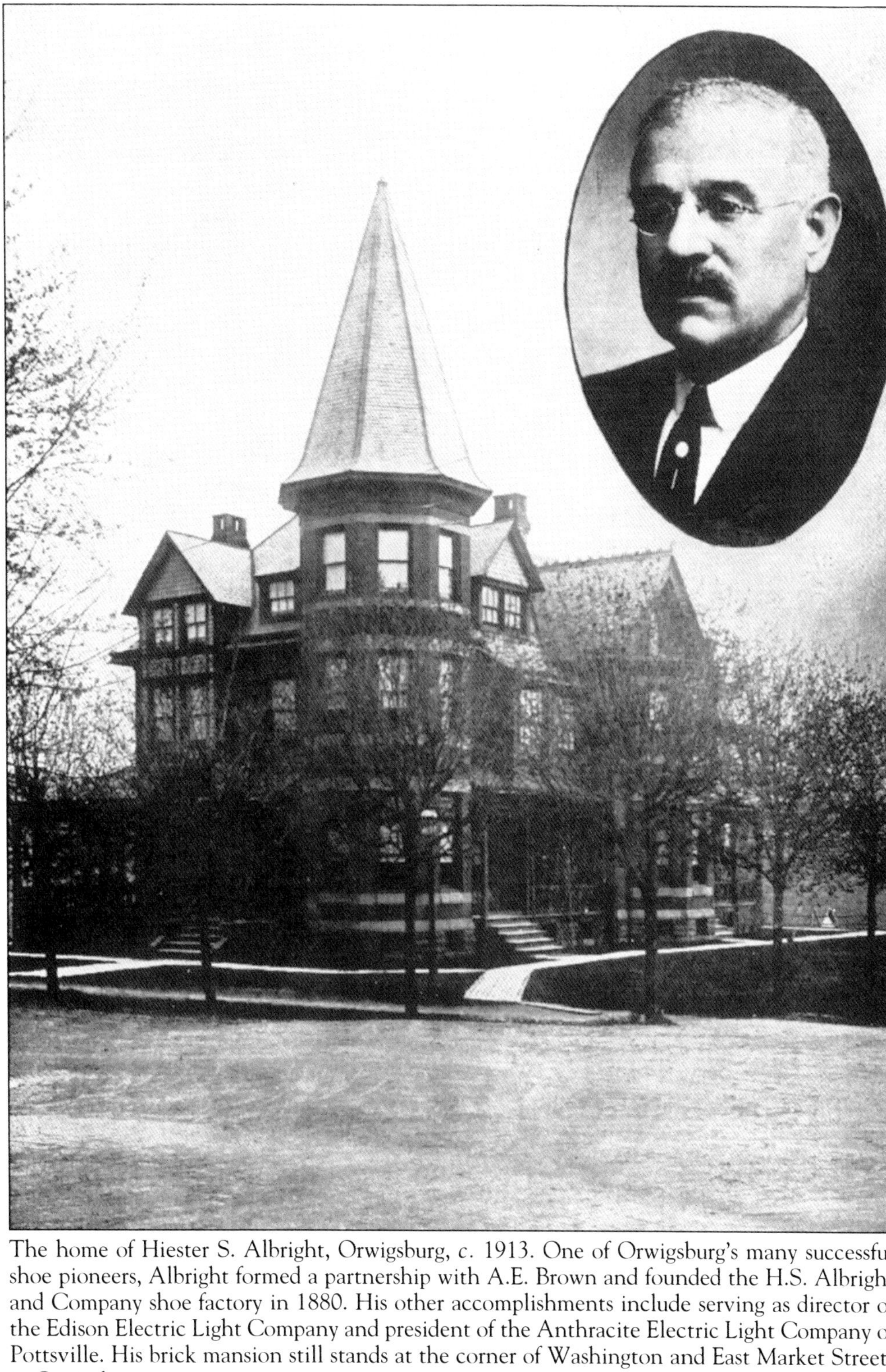

The home of Hiester S. Albright, Orwigsburg, *c.* 1913. One of Orwigsburg's many successful shoe pioneers, Albright formed a partnership with A.E. Brown and founded the H.S. Albright and Company shoe factory in 1880. His other accomplishments include serving as director of the Edison Electric Light Company and president of the Anthracite Electric Light Company of Pottsville. His brick mansion still stands at the corner of Washington and East Market Streets in Orwigsburg.

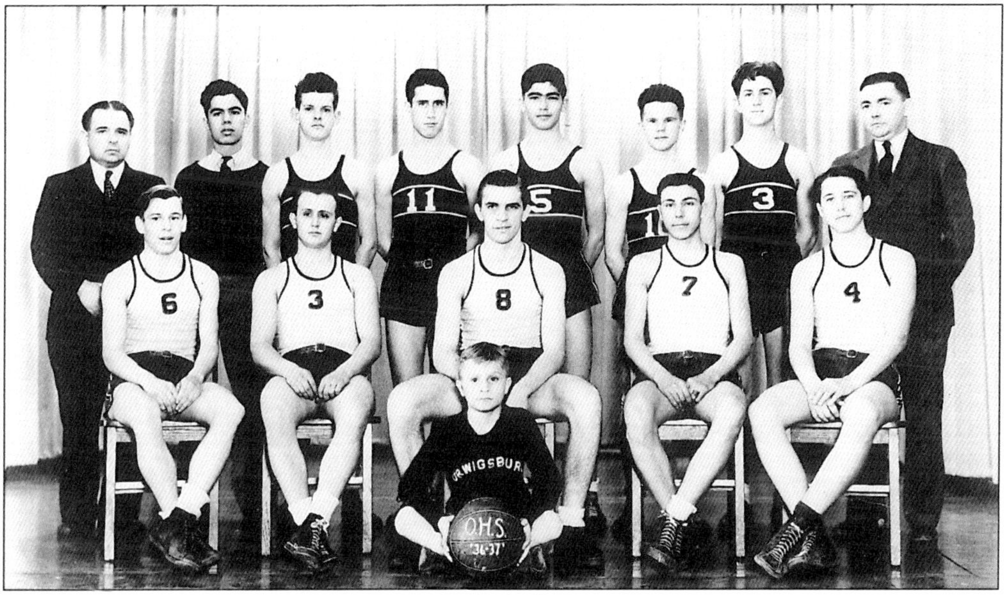

The Orwigsburg High School 1936–37 basketball team. Basketball proved to be a popular sport for students who attended Orwigsburg High School. The 1936–37 team members in this photograph are as follows: (front row) G. Fisher, B. Gerhard, C. Diefenderfer, H. Wagner, and R. Zulick; (back row) P. Heim, H. Eisenhuth, B. Fridirici, A. Dixon, J. Eisenhuth, T. Houtz, L. Shoener, and Dr. Darkes. The team mascot was L. Diefenderfer.

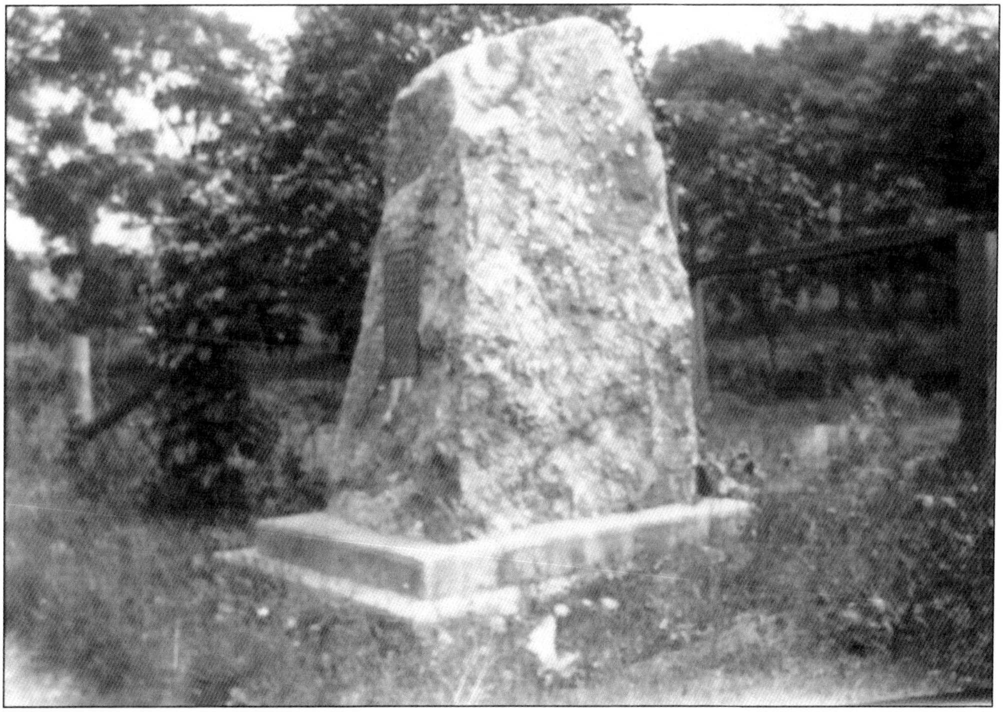

The Fort Lebanon monument located near Auburn. In 1756, Captain Jacob Morgan built a fort where 53 soldiers were stationed to patrol and protect the area from Native American tribes. The monument was erected in 1913 by the Daughters of the American Revolution.

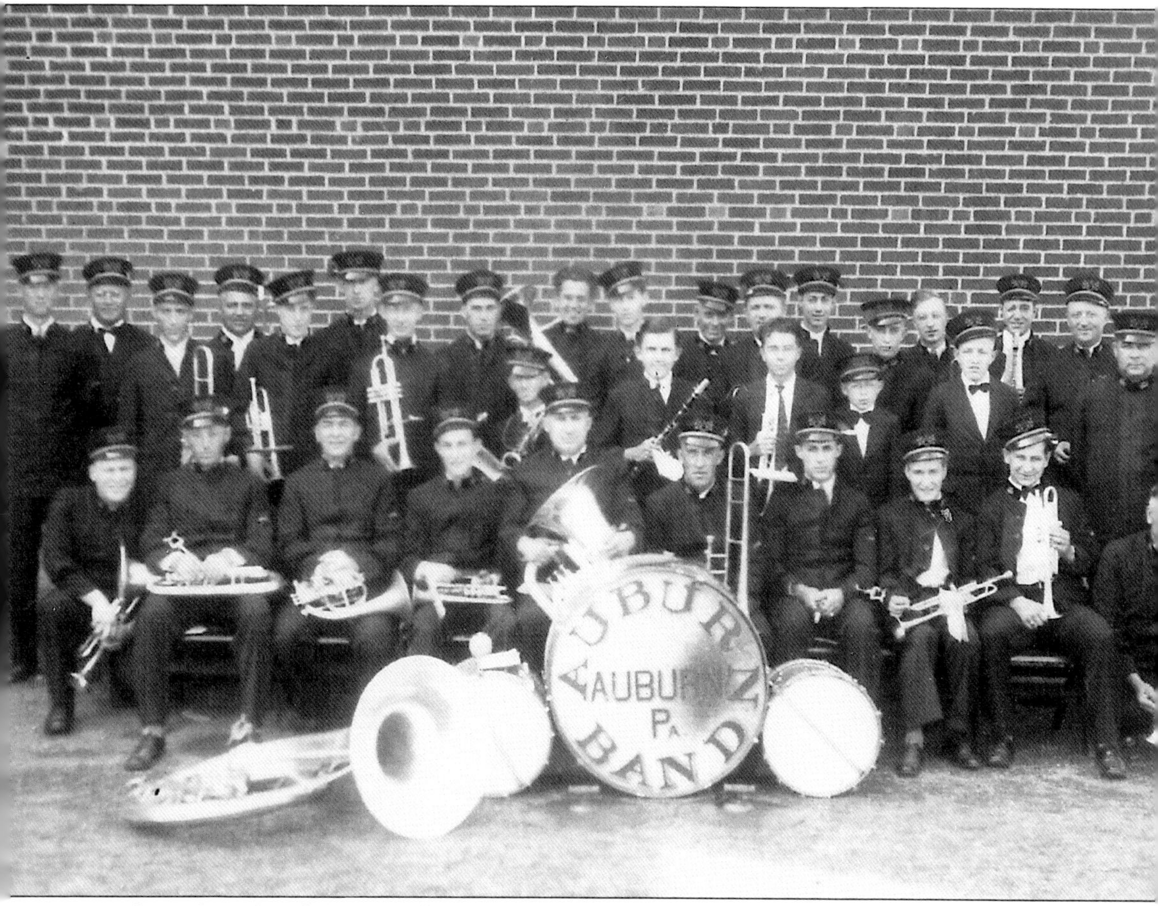

The Auburn Band. Organized in October of 1907 by Irvin Dewald, the original band was made up of about 20 members ranging in age from 11 to 16.

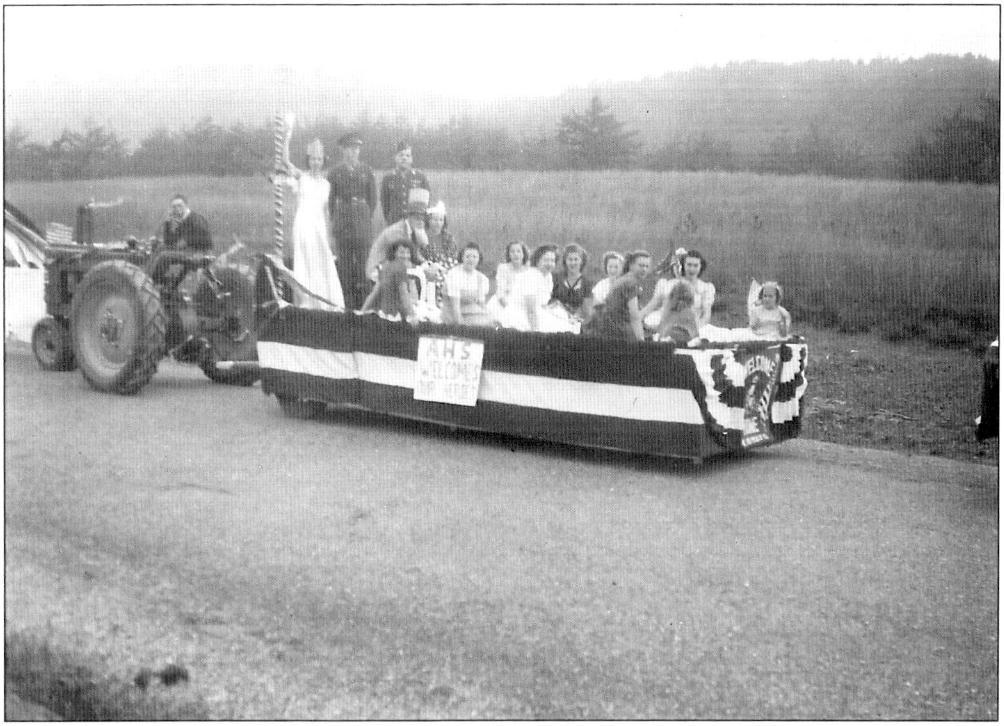

Patriotic students from Auburn. Intense patriotism has always permeated the communities of Schuylkill County. This image, taken in October of 1946, shows a group of Auburn High School students honoring their local World War II soldiers who had recently returned.

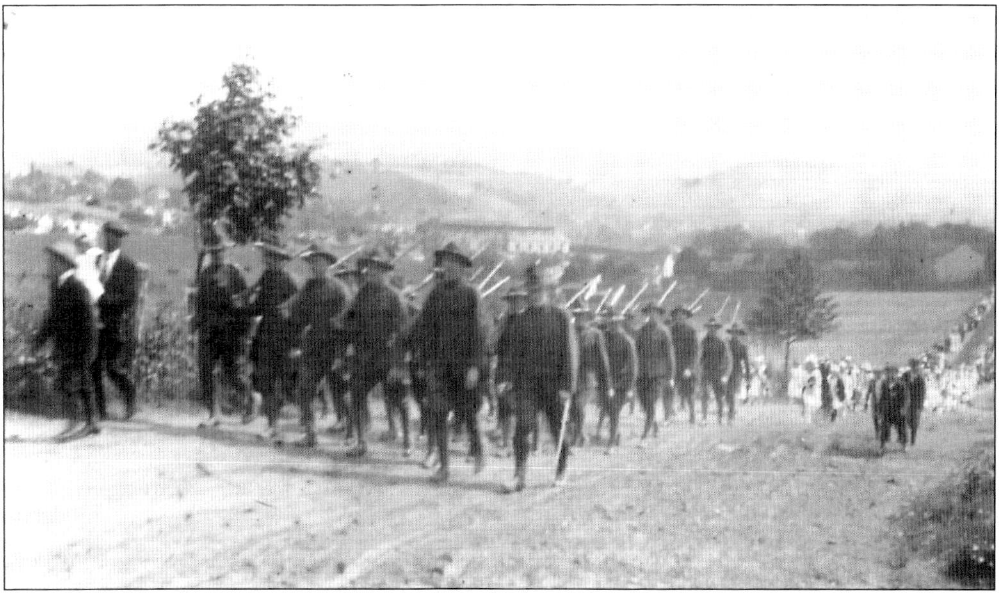

A Memorial Day parade in Cressona, c. 1920. Patriotic celebrations were always very popular and well attended in most Schuylkill County communities. This photograph shows World War I veterans leading the parade up Cemetery Hill.

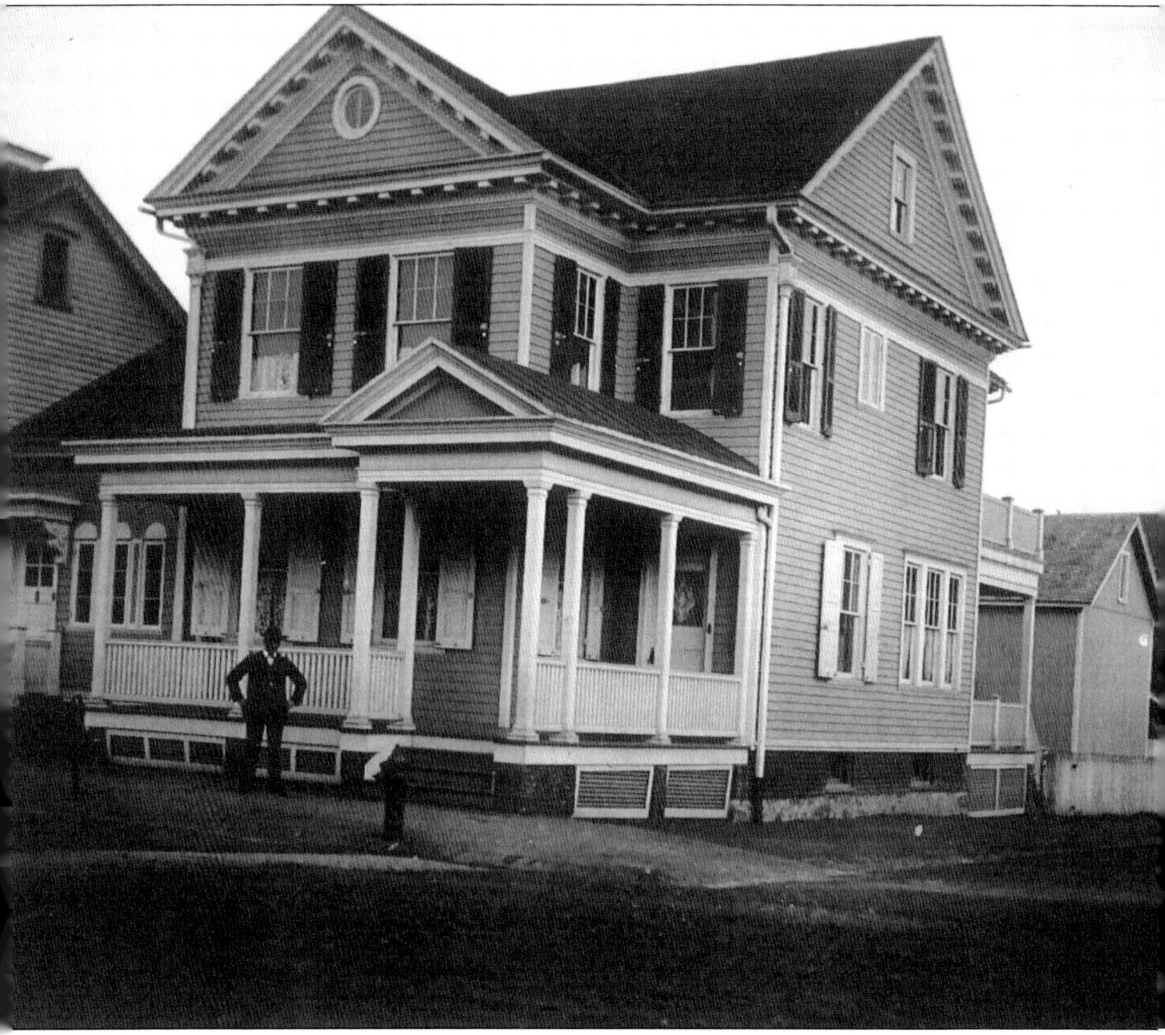

The home and office of Dr. Lewis Robinhold in Auburn. A typical office visit with Dr. Robinhold cost 50¢ at the time he practiced. Dr. Robinhold's son Guy also became a doctor and practiced medicine at the Fountain Springs Hospital in Ashland. In 1933 Guy was appointed chief surgeon of the hospital.

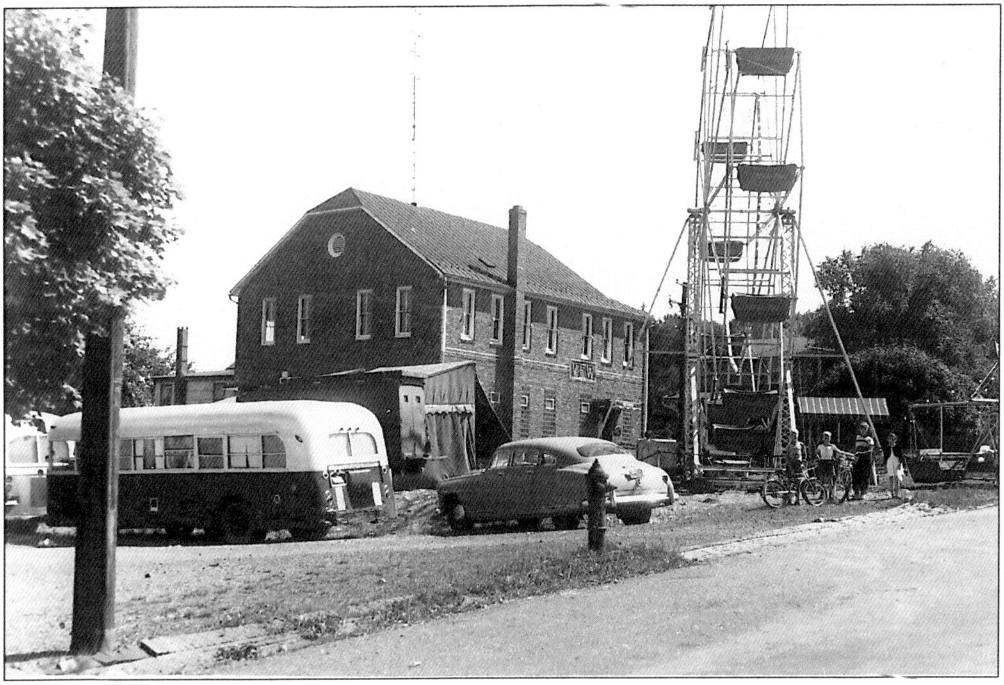

The V.F.W. building in Auburn, *c.* 1940. Circuses, carnivals, and block parties were a favorite form of entertainment for many people throughout the history of Schuylkill County.

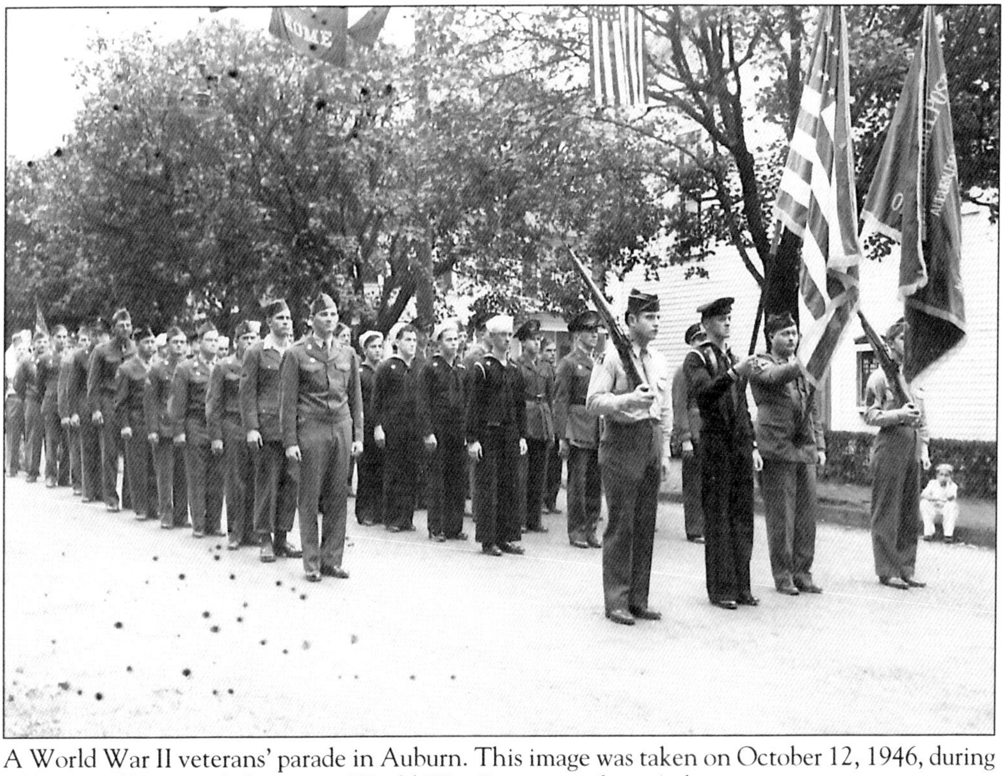

A World War II veterans' parade in Auburn. This image was taken on October 12, 1946, during a Veterans Day parade honoring World War II veterans from Auburn.

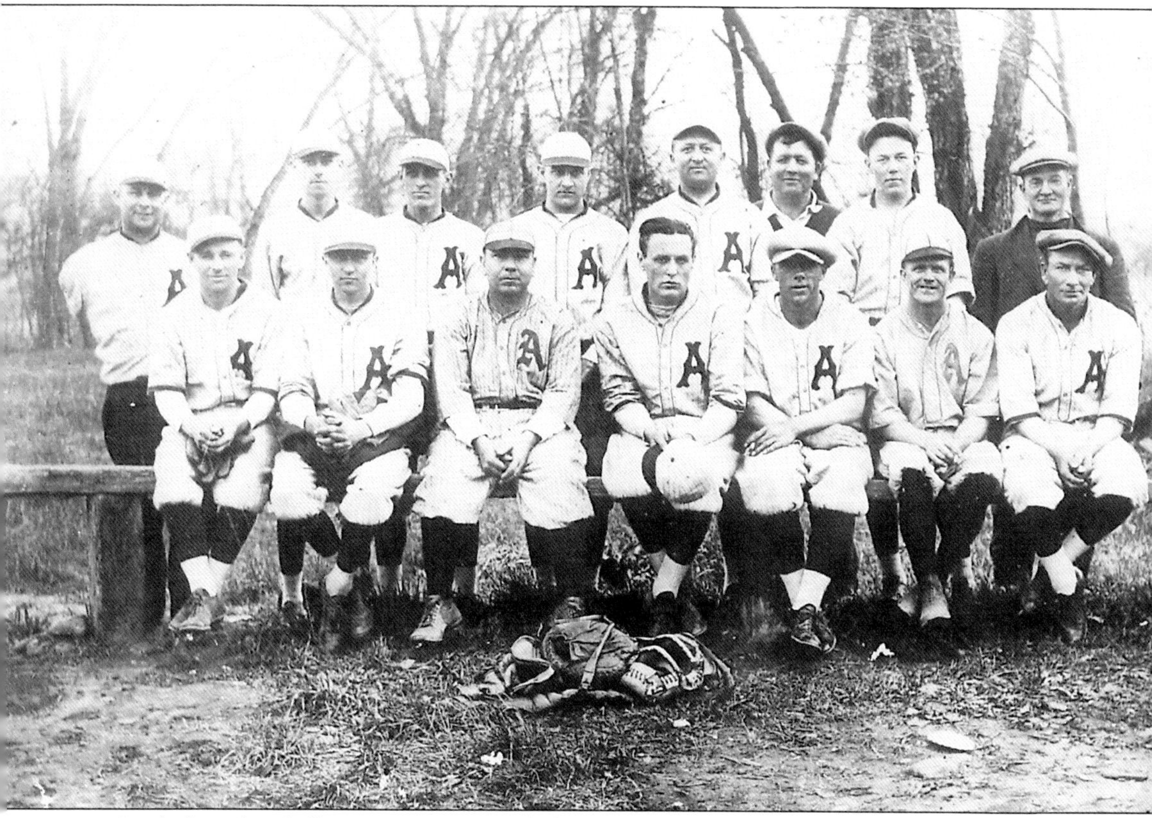

An Auburn baseball team, c. 1924. Baseball was the prominent sport in Auburn for many years. The first team was organized in 1872 and named the "Free and Easy Baseball Club." Pictured in this 1924 team photograph are, from left to right, the following: (front row) Mark Borkey, Butch Borkey, unidentified, Harry Koerper, Joe Herring, Charles Mellon, and ? Long; (back row) Scrappy Staller, ? Seitzinger, Raymond Staller, ? Wenrich, Fred Borkey, unidentified, Guy Steffy, and Larry Long.

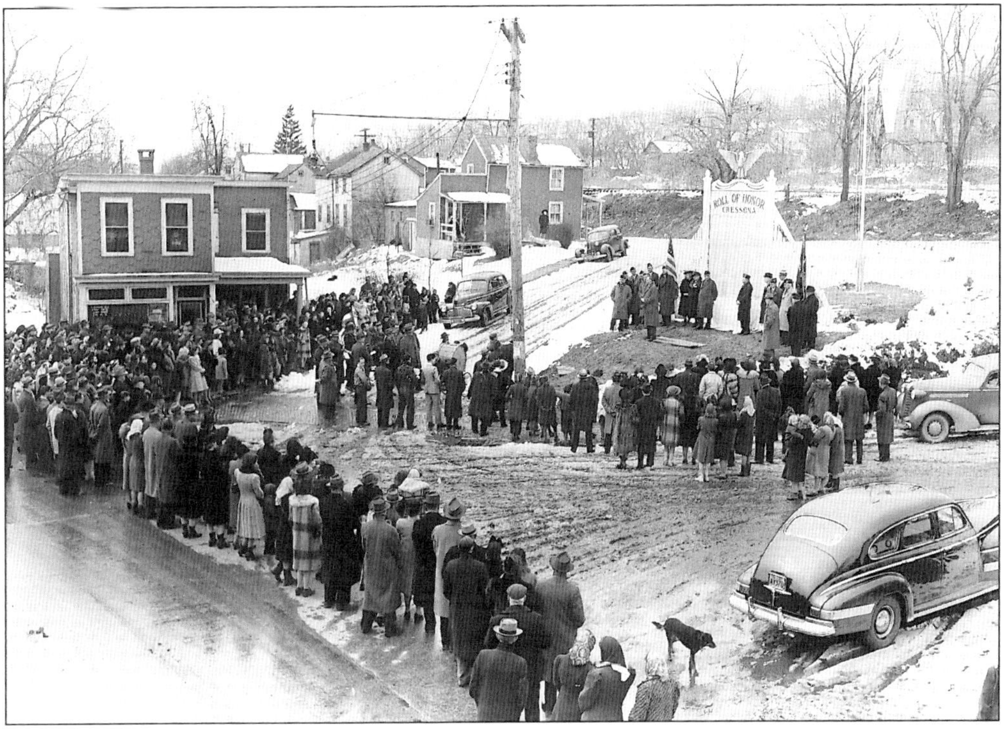

The dedication of the "Role of Honor" in Cressona. World War II veterans and those who didn't return were respectfully honored at a special ceremony at Cressona's American Legion Plaza. The present home of the American Legion can be seen in the left foreground.

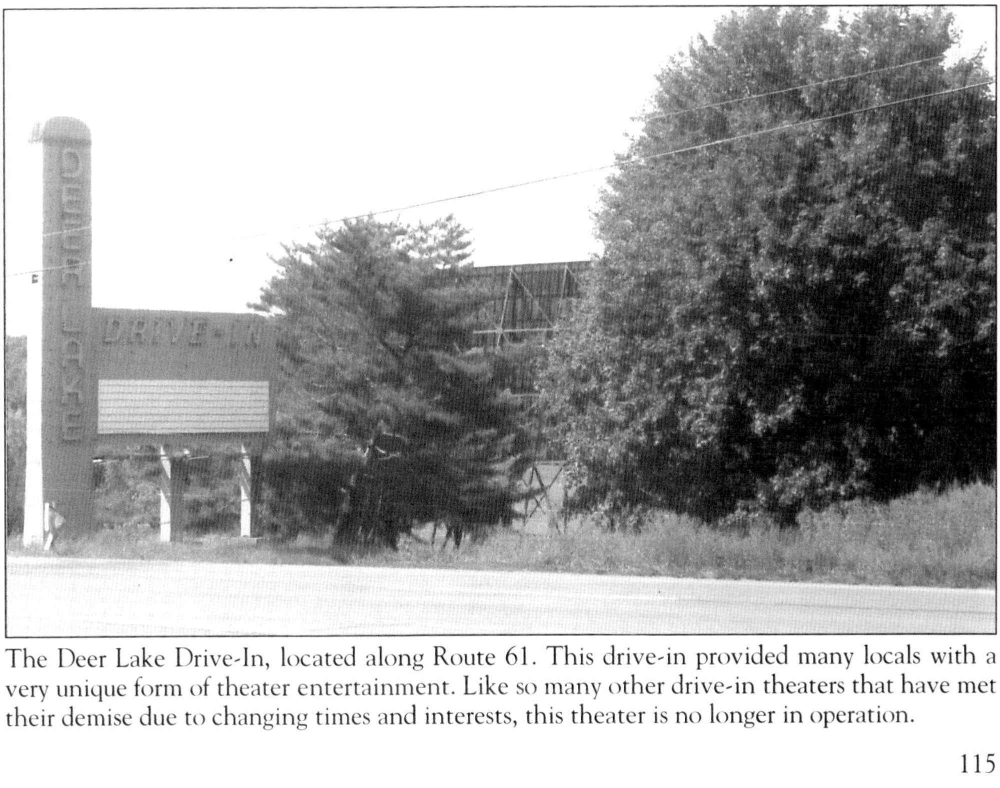

The Deer Lake Drive-In, located along Route 61. This drive-in provided many locals with a very unique form of theater entertainment. Like so many other drive-in theaters that have met their demise due to changing times and interests, this theater is no longer in operation.

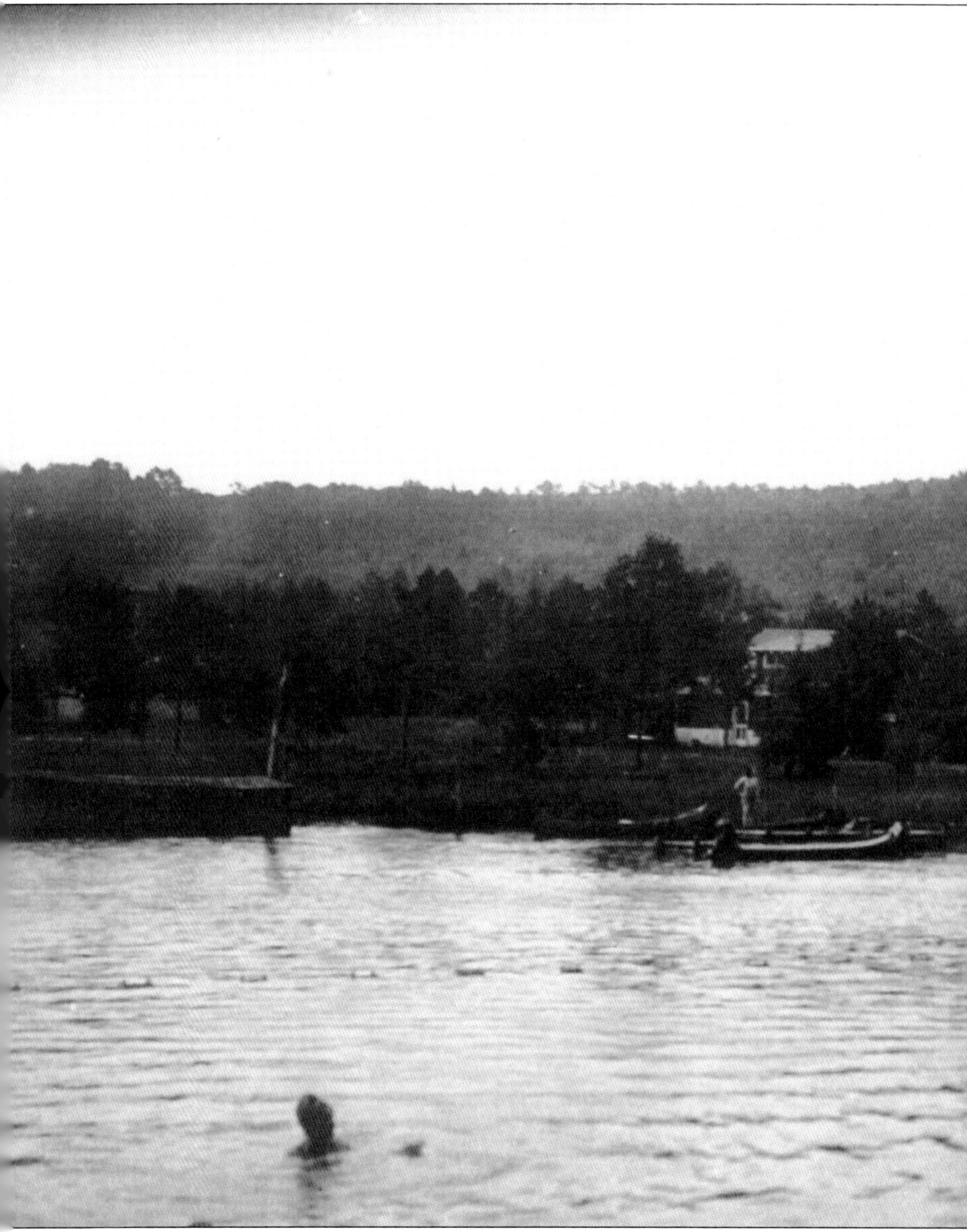

The giant water slide in Deer Lake Park. The slide entertained many visitors of this popular resort and recreational spot. A large number of residents of Schuylkill County owned summer

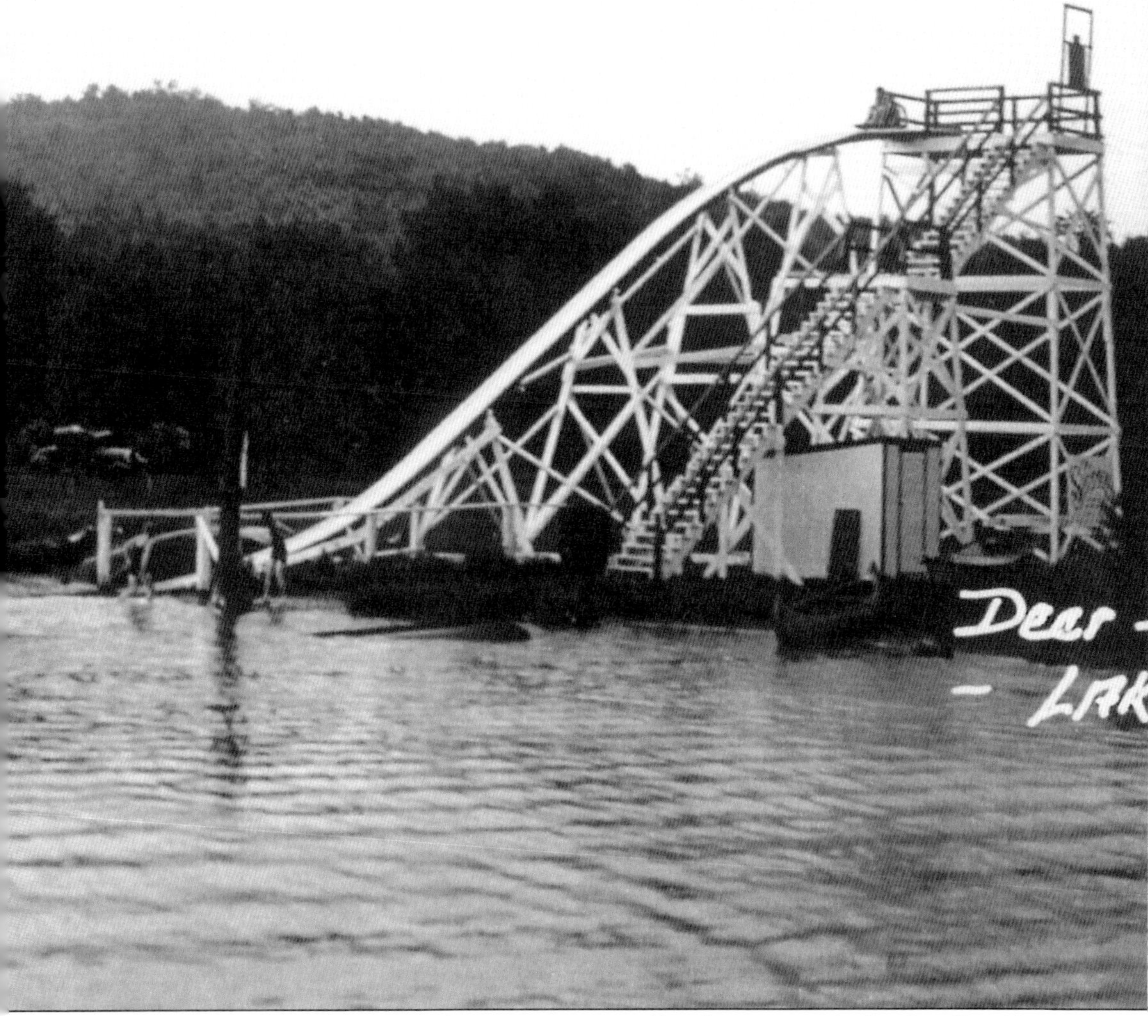

homes along Deer Lake and enjoyed the recreation, as well as the peace and solitude, offered by a cottage nestled in the secluded woodlands.

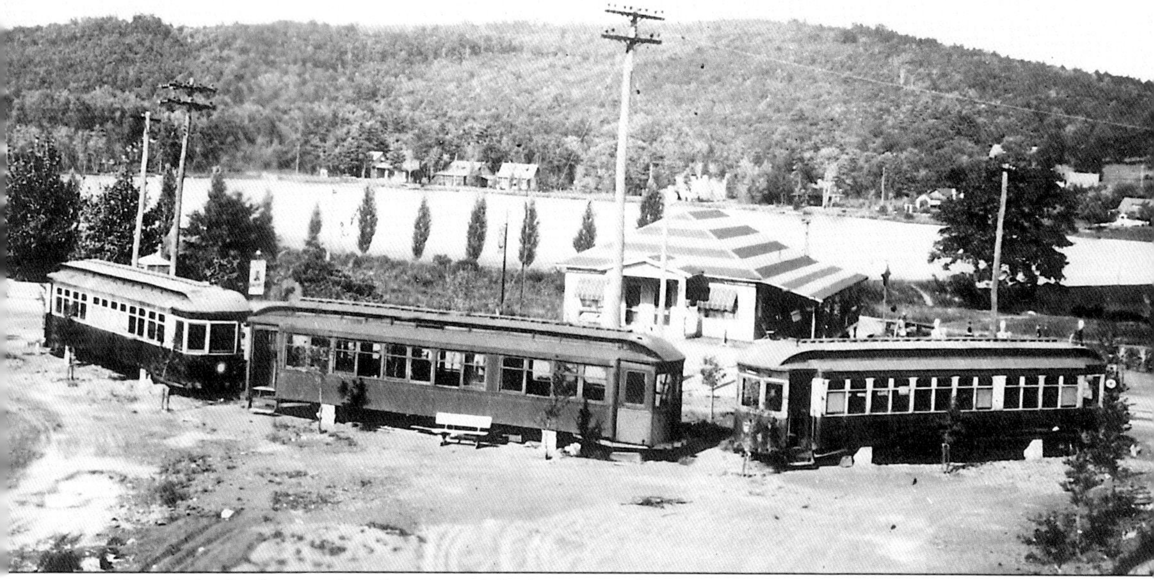

Deer Lake Park in its heyday. In 1925, the Pottsville Construction Company began excavation of the lake pictured here. A two-handled scoop pulled by horses was used for the job.

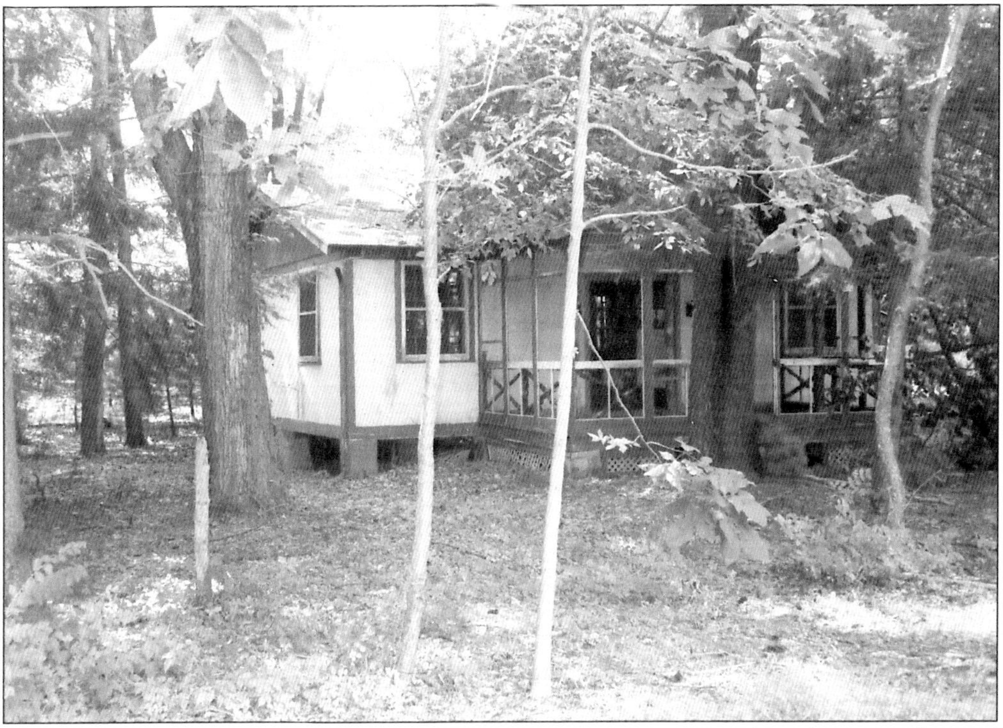

An original "summer cottage" in Deer Lake. To promote Deer Lake, Eben Kingsbury of Harrisburg was hired. A small bungalow, similar to the one pictured, was "chanced off" as a promotional activity to generate interest in the Deer Lake resort area.

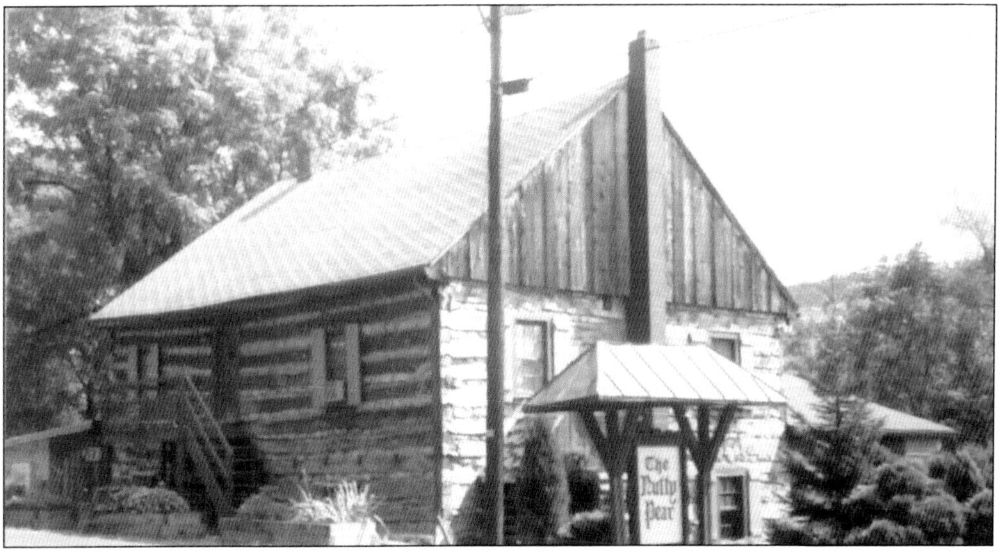

A historic tavern. First known as the Cowshed and later as the 1792 House, this tavern, located along the Adamsdale Road between Adamsdale and Schuylkill Haven, still exists today as a restaurant. The property was originally owned by relatives of pioneer Daniel Boone.

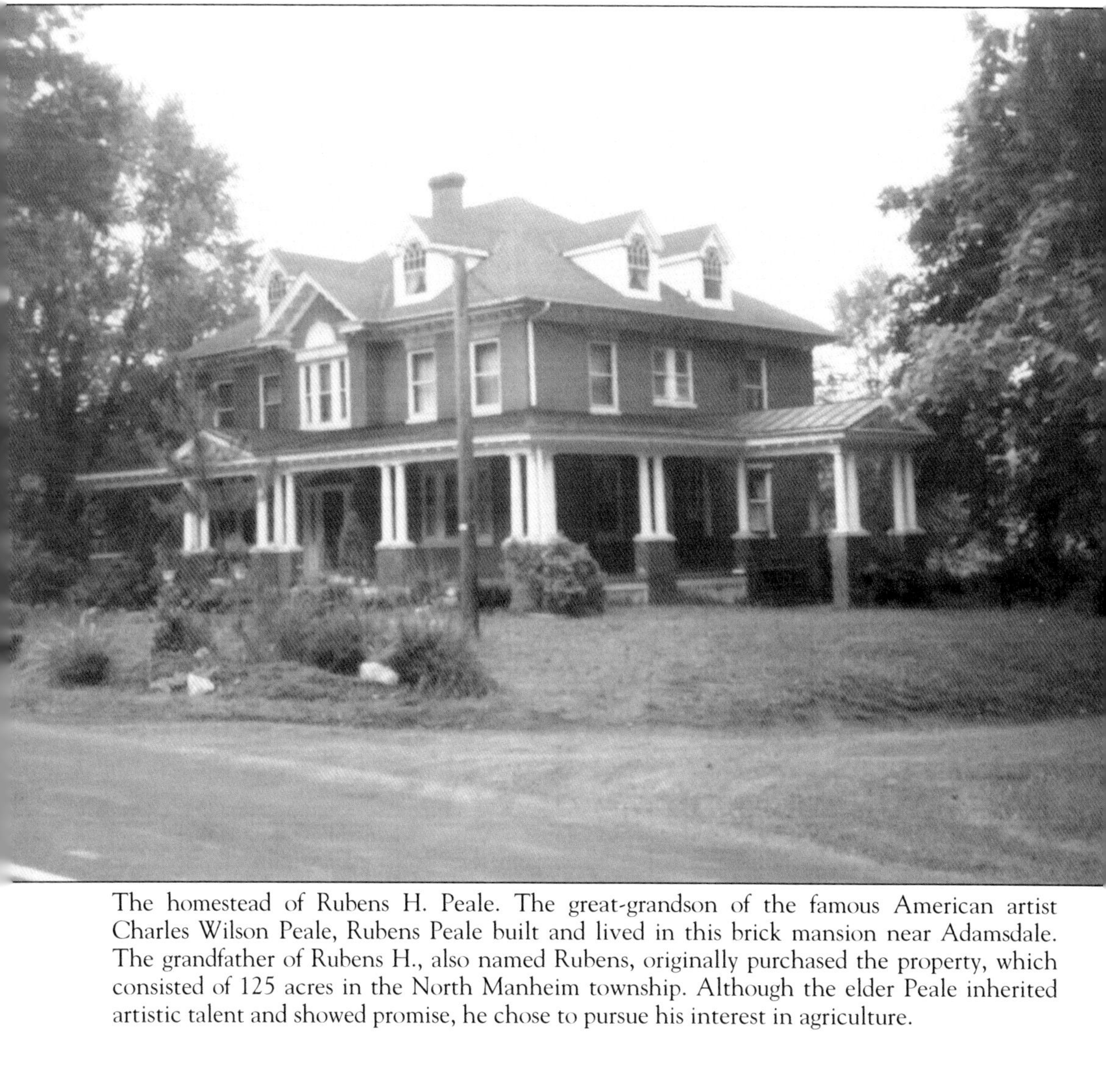

The homestead of Rubens H. Peale. The great-grandson of the famous American artist Charles Wilson Peale, Rubens Peale built and lived in this brick mansion near Adamsdale. The grandfather of Rubens H., also named Rubens, originally purchased the property, which consisted of 125 acres in the North Manheim township. Although the elder Peale inherited artistic talent and showed promise, he chose to pursue his interest in agriculture.

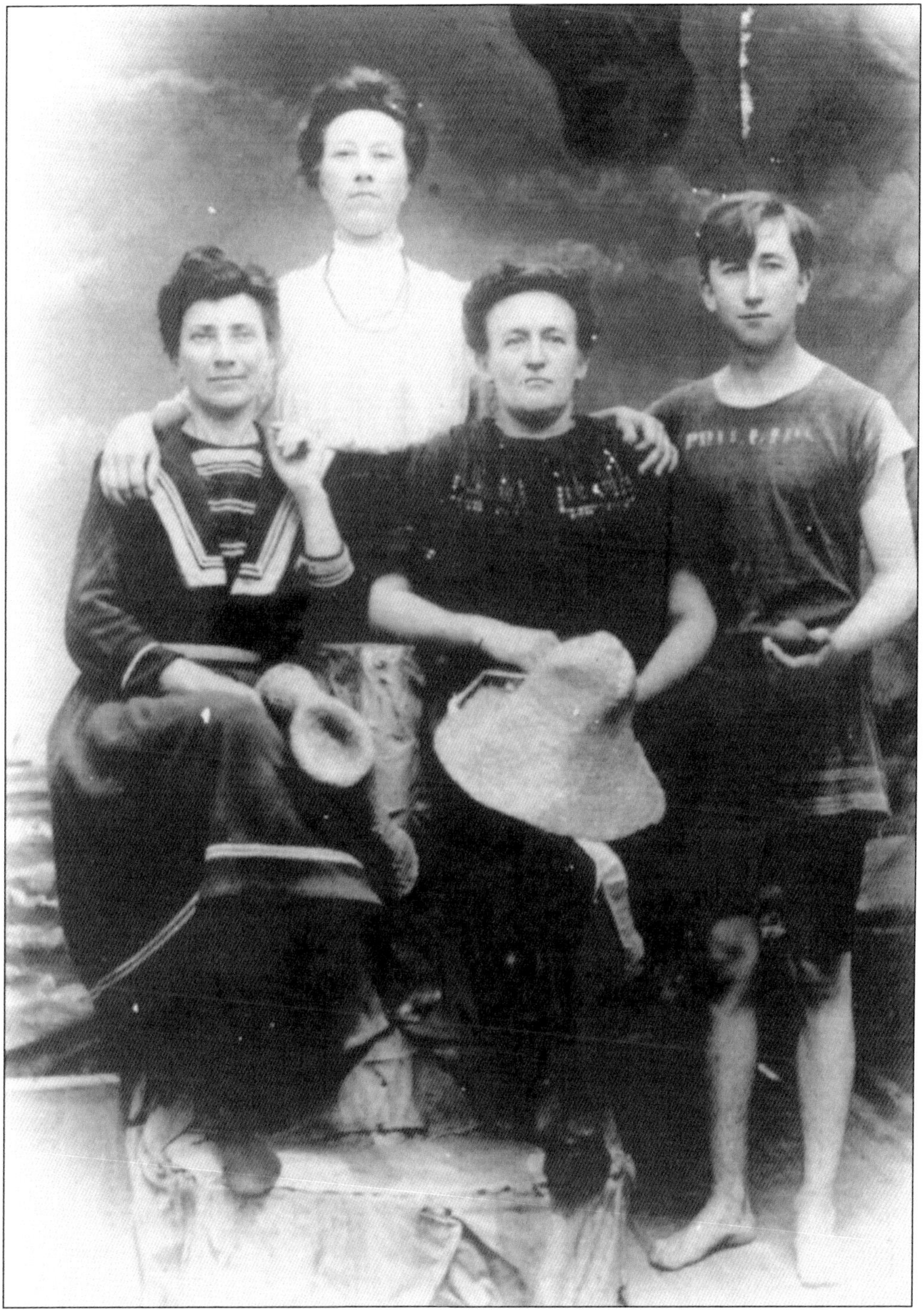

A family from Schuylkill Haven posing for a photograph while vacationing at the New Jersey shore. The photograph, taken in the early 1900s, gives us an idea of how dramatically beachwear has changed through the years. The young boy in this image was Warren Bowen of Schuylkill Haven.

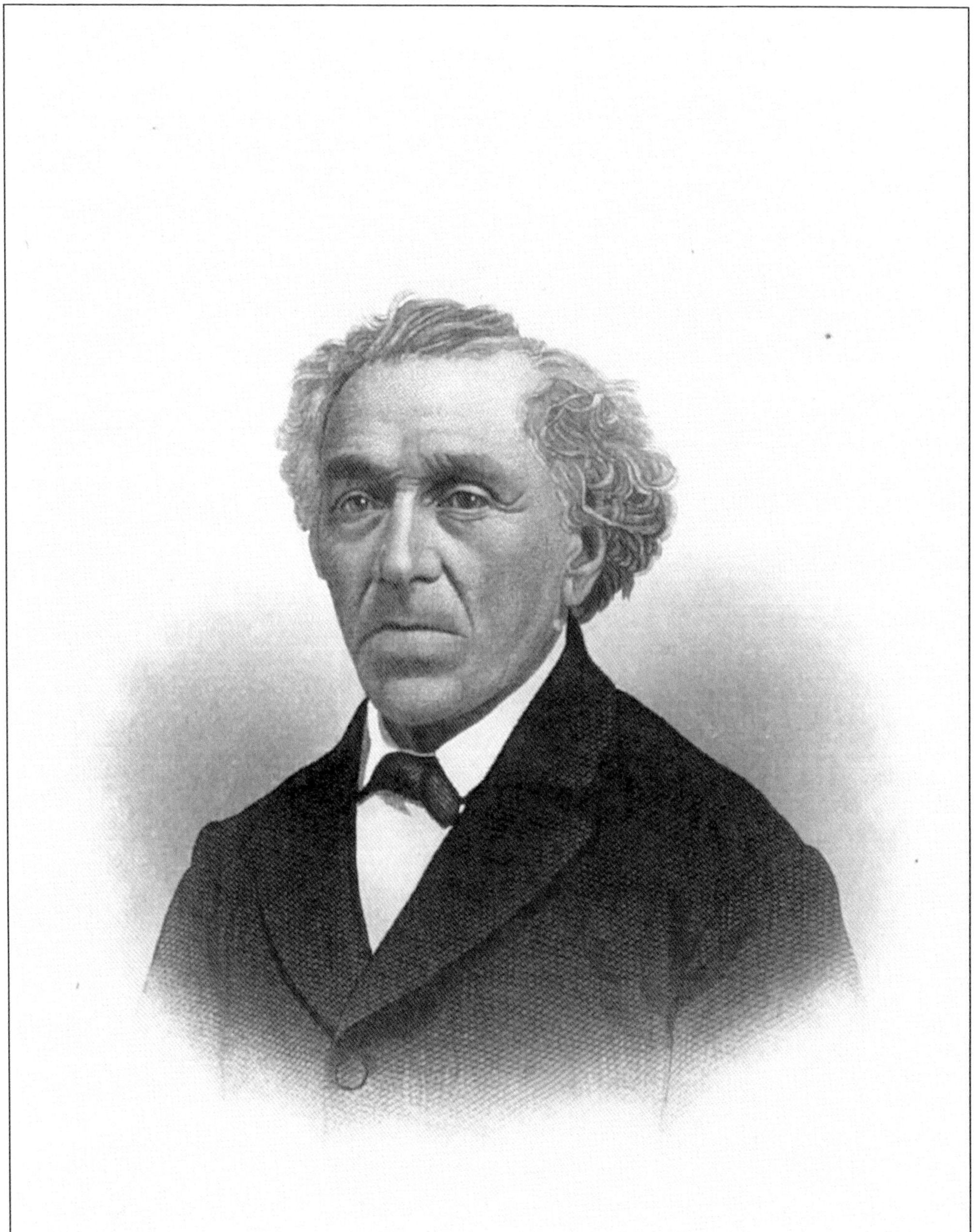

Gideon Bast of Schuylkill Haven. He was one of Schuylkill County's most prominent and successful merchants and coal operators during the 1800s.

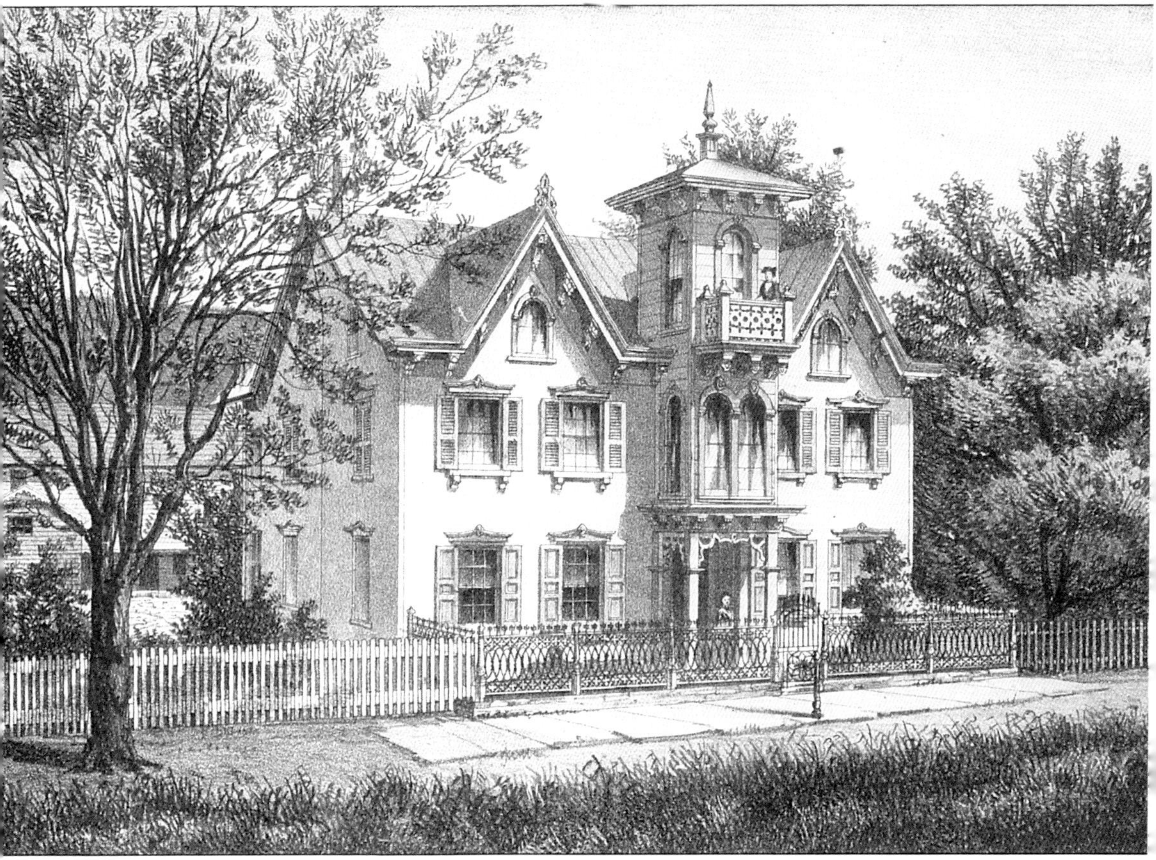

The homestead of Gideon Bast in Schuylkill Haven. This *c.* 1880 sketch shows the Gideon Bast estate, which was built in 1845. Gideon Bast was a great philanthropist who contributed considerably to the construction of Jerusalem Church, built in 1878 near the Bast property.

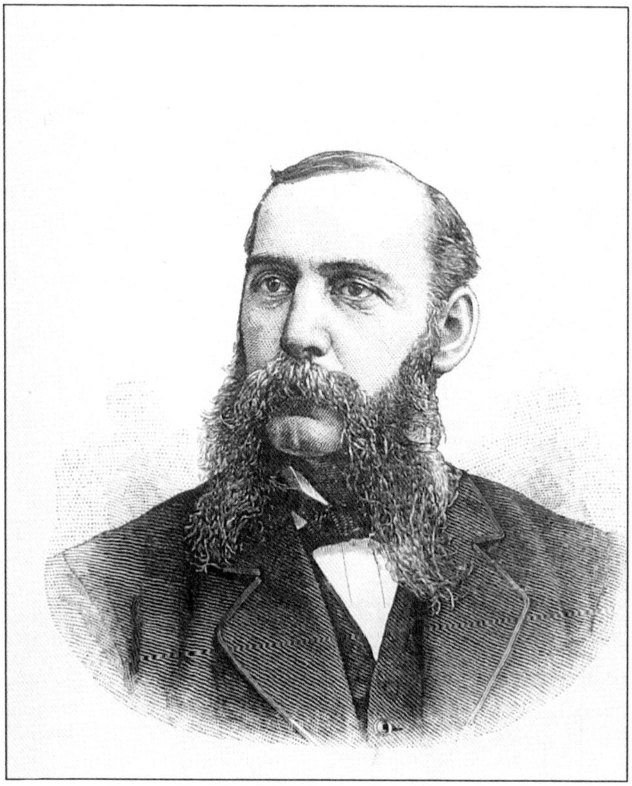

George W. Weiss. He served as the principal of the Schuylkill Haven High School from 1877 until 1881. In May of 1881, he was elected to the prominent position of superintendent of schools for Schuylkill County. George W. Weiss dedicated his entire life to education and to its progress throughout Schuylkill County.

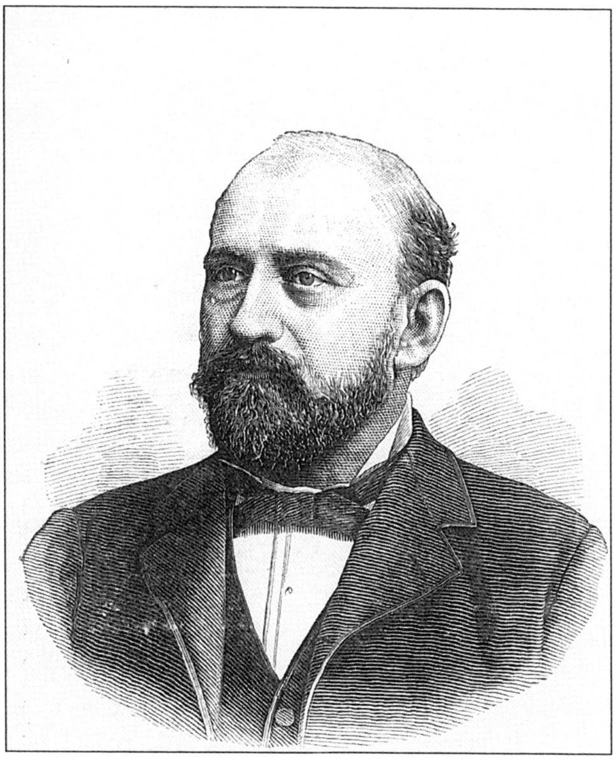

Samuel A. Losch, a resident of Schuylkill Haven during the 1800s. He served as a member of the Pennsylvania State Legislature from 1874 until 1876. Due to his outstanding military record with the 50th Regiment, Company C, during the Civil War, Losch was offered numerous government positions and emerged as a leader of the Republican Party in Schuylkill County. In 1880, Losch was chosen to be a delegate to the national convention of the Republican Party and was one of 306 delegates who voted for Ulysses S. Grant.

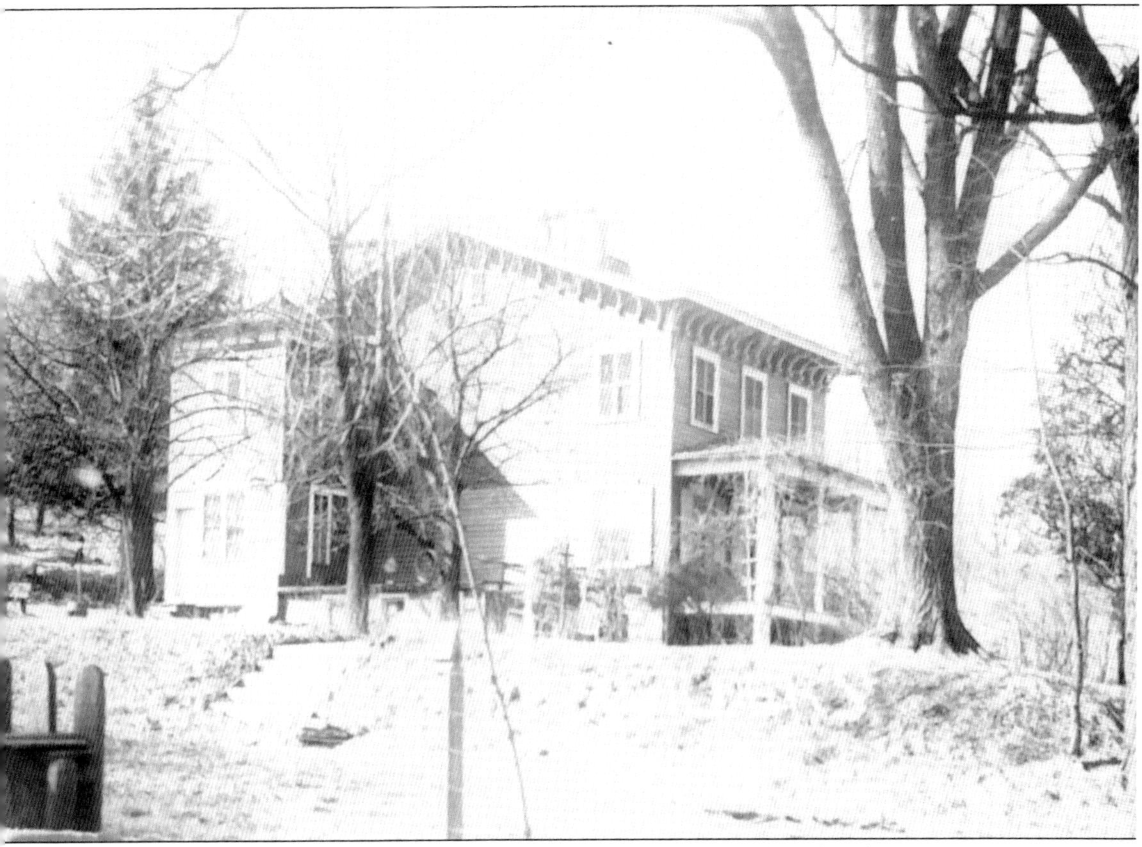

The Cressona home of Rufus Wilder, superintendent of the Mine Hill Railroad. Born in 1817, Wilder was a self-taught engineer and is credited with redesigning the Gordon Plane, using his invention called the electro-magneto bell system. A street at the foot of this plane was named for him. Wilder applied his experience with the Gordon Plane in the construction of the Mahanoy Plane, built in 1861. Rufus Wilder also designed the first armored car, built by the Baldwin Locomotive Works during the Civil War. In retirement, Wilder turned his attention toward the community and worked diligently in the field of education. His mansion in Cressona still stands today on Wilder Street, appropriately named after him.

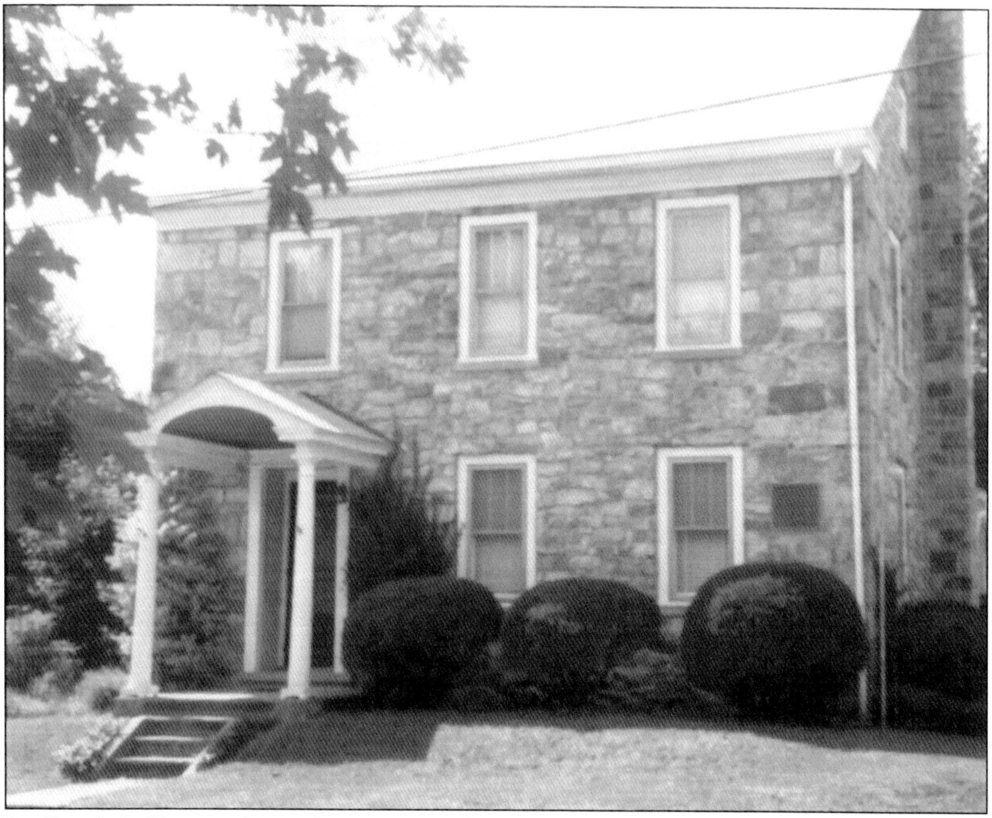

Reiffsnyder's Tavern, located in McKeansburg. Until the first courthouse was erected in Orwigsburg, court was held at this tavern, owned by Abraham Reiffsnyder. Judge Robert Porter presided over the opening session, which was held on December 17, 1811.

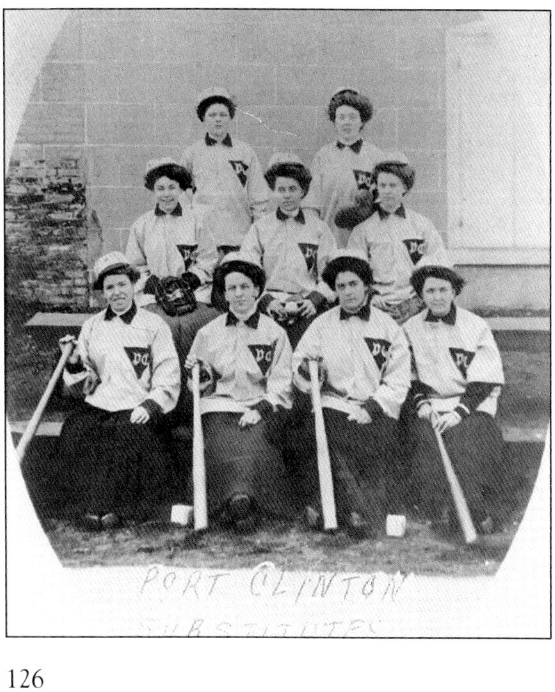

The Port Clinton Substitutes, c. 1909. Women's softball teams were very popular throughout Schuylkill County in the early 1900s.

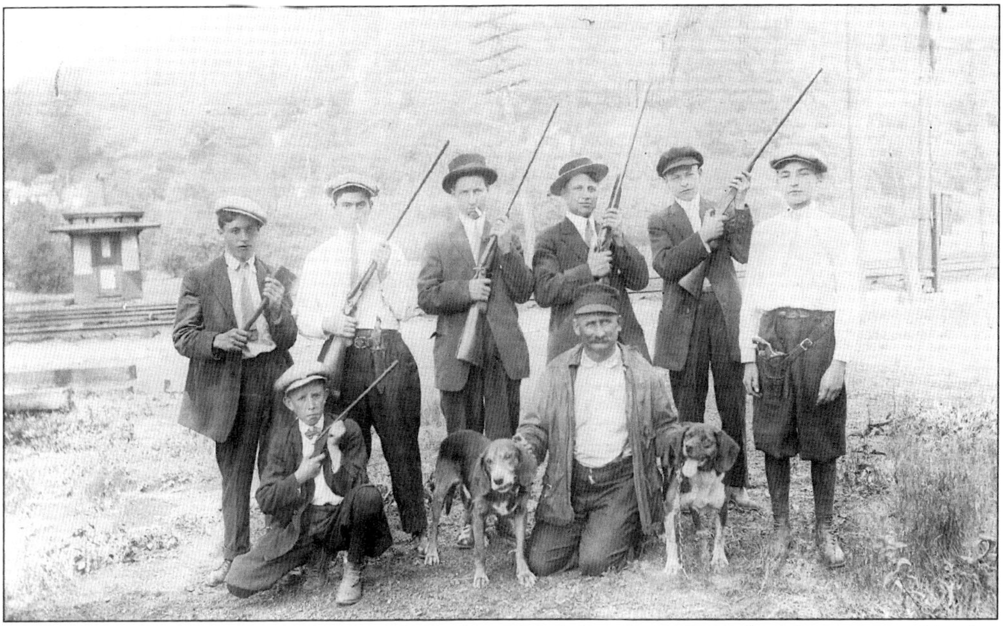

A formidable group of hunters poses for a photograph between the railroad station and bridge near Port Clinton. The members of this group are, from left to right, as follows: (front) William Henry and "Nailer" Heckman, with hounds; (rear) unidentified, Harry Kauffman, unidentified, Ralph Knoblauch, Chuck Freeze, and Jer Freeze.

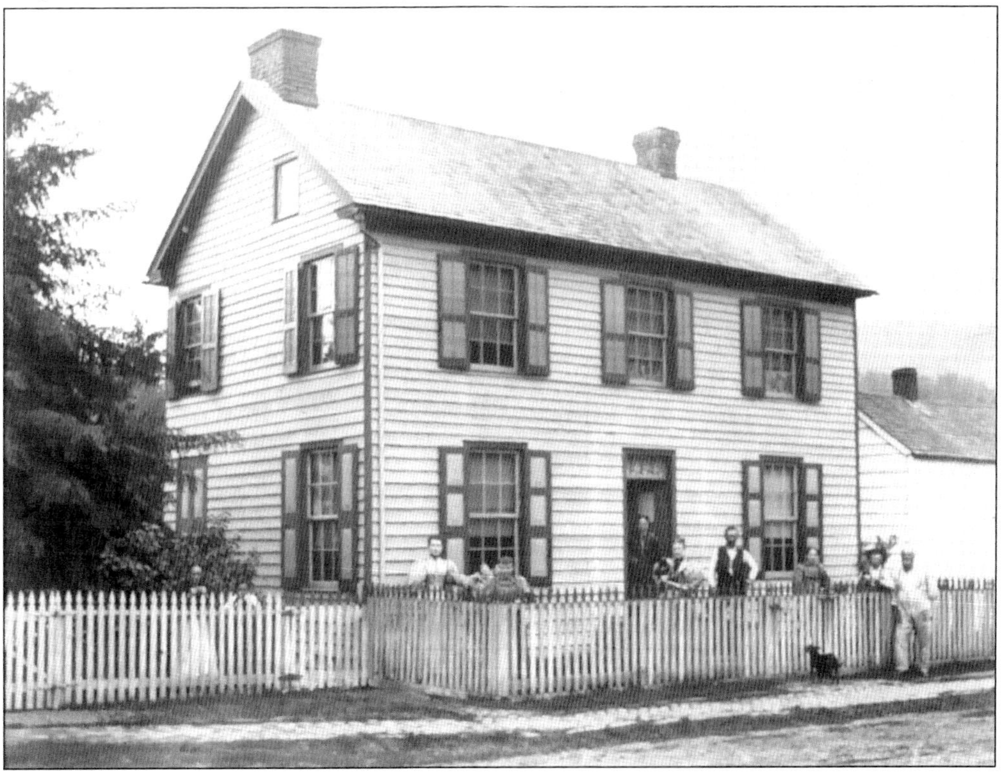

An early home in Port Clinton, situated along the Centre Turnpike.

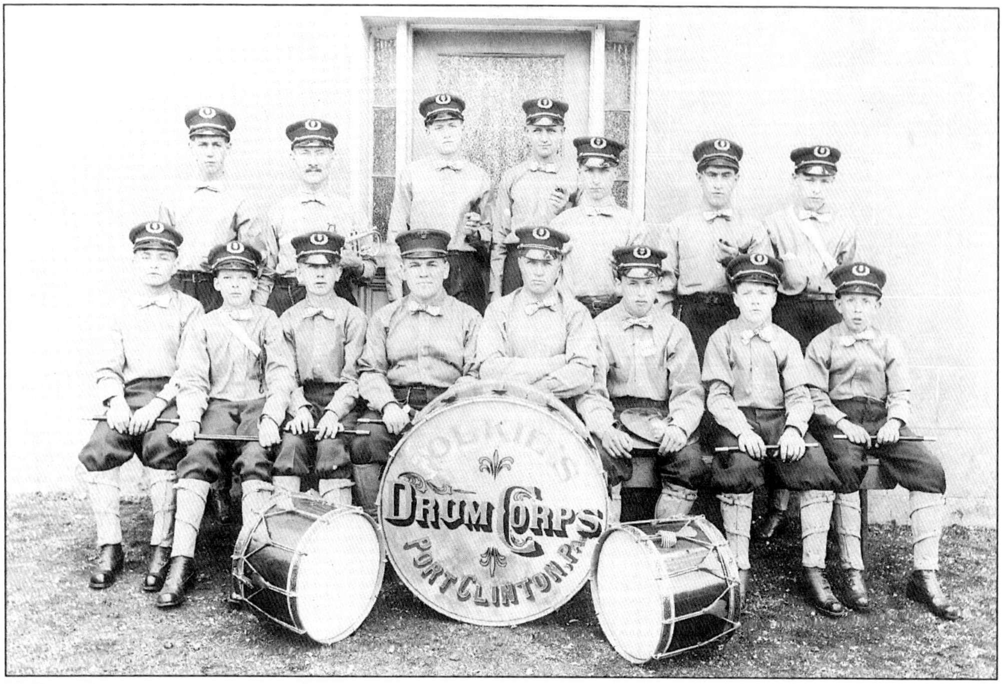

Folkies Drum Corps, Port Clinton. Drum and bugle corps and marching bands served as both a form of entertainment and a social outlet for folks throughout the county. Note how young some of the members appear to be.

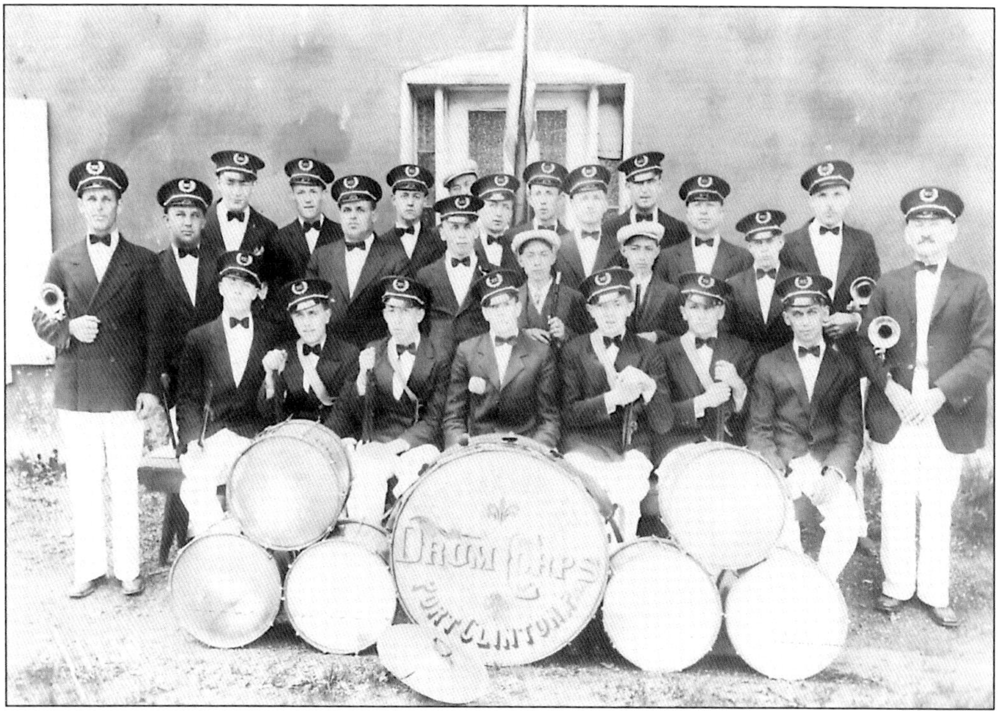

A later photograph of Folkies Drum Corps, c. 1930. This photograph shows a marked change in the band uniforms as well as an increase in membership.